FIRE FROM HEAVEN

PATH TO
THE ERA OF PEACE

By Maureen Flynn
Co-Author Of The Thunder Of Justice

FIRE FROM HEAVEN

Declarations

Since the abolition of Canons 1399 and 2318 of the former Code of Canon Law by Pope Paul VI in AAS 58 (1966), p. 1186, publications about new apparitions, revelations, prophecies, miracles, etc., have been allowed to be distributed and read by the faithful without the express permission of the Church, providing that they contain nothing that contravenes faith and morals. This means no imprimatur is necessary. However it is welcome!

In Chapter II, No. 12 of the Second Vatican Council's *Lumen Gentium*, we read:
"The Holy Spirit... distributes special gifts among the faithful of every rank... Such gifts of grace, whether they are of special enlightenment or whether they are spread more simply and generally, must be accepted with gratefulness and consolation, as they are specially suited to, and useful for, the needs of the Church...Judgment as to their genuineness and their correct use lies with those who lead the Church and those whose special task is not indeed to extinguish the spirit but to examine everything and keep that which is good." (confer 1 Thess. 5: 19-21)
"That private revelations occur in all times is evident as appears from the testimony of the Sacred Scripture and tradition. To stamp these testimonies as untruths gives scandal and bears witness to impiety."

Cardinal Bona

Published by ST. DOMINIC MEDIA
P.O. BOX 345, Herndon, Virginia 20172-0345
Phone 703-327-2277 / Fax 703-327-2888

www.sign.org

Library of Congress Catalog Card Number:
ISBN:

Cover Design by: Carolyn Robel

A2

Table Of Contents

Foreword

Many hands will be directed to pick up this book to take from it whatever it might offer for the satisfaction, enlightenment, fulfillment and/or growth of the one who directs them. If one's mere curiosity is the motivational force behind these hands, the would-be reader should go no further, should close the book and give it away. The material contained therein has not been compiled, and is not being presented to satisfy anyone's curiosity. It is being offered by the author who is sustained by a quality far more noble than that, that of sharpening the awareness of the reader to future events, and preparing him/her to cope with God's gradual unveiling of His plans for all mankind.

The present generation is submerged in a sea of confusion, doubt and futility. It has not found that which totally satisfies the cravings of the human soul. It is anxiously searching for that which it does not know or experience. It only knows that what it is experiencing is discomfort, and that this discomfort won't go away. It does not realize that it is looking for answers and solutions from sources which fail to offer anything better than what had already been tried and found wanting. If the people of this age, or at least, if its leaders, would risk a plunge into that which is beyond

A4

the human, and beyond all that which has already been ventured into, then maybe, just maybe, it would discover what it is truly looking for, something that would be forthcoming, not from man, but from God.

They, who live by faith, that is, by truths that come to mind and heart from the Triune God, live, not in darkness, but in divine light. They walk, not with faltering steps, but with a spirit of confidence and conviction. It is exactly this that brings on the peace and joy that the human heart is yearning for.

In addition to the ordinary problems of this generation, there is the added one of having to face the fact that it has a unique hurdle of being and living in what are known as the "End Times". This has reference to the inhabitants of this world who now find themselves in a period of time which is designed by God as the introduction to a brand-new age, the Era of Peace. This information, unfortunately, is known only by a relatively small percentage of people, to that segment, tipped off by the Virgin, to watch the skies for unusual signs and wonders. The Trinity has, in its final desperation to save mankind, directed and empowered the Mother of all children, to prepare them for what the future holds.

The Holy Spirit, the Spouse of Mary, has offered to mankind long ago through the Sacred Scriptures, a vision of what God has yet in store for the world. One can look into Zacharias, Daniel, Matthew, Luke, and Revelations, to get a sneak peak into what is just about

A5

ready to befall this unsuspecting generation. In addition, many prophecies have surfaced, prophecies within the realm of private revelation, are being presented particularly to those of us now living, to make its transition into the Era of Peace clothed with a dignity which befits the sons and daughters of the Most High God. Concerning these, the Holy Spirit offers the directive, "Do not despise prophecies. Test everything, retain what is good." (I Thess. 5:20 - 21)

One interested, will soon discover that there are more prophecies than any ordinary person can handle. We are invited to receive the words of the true prophet with joy. We are nonetheless, cautioned that discernment must be our detector of that which is true and that which is false. Jesus, Himself, had warned and continues to warn of false prophets, of wolves dressed in sheep's clothing. The prophets and prophecies presented in this book have been time tested and checked thoroughly making use of that instrument which Jesus offers, "by their fruits you will know them".

This book will be of great service to the faithful who are searching and wondering what to read, what to believe. The author, with discernment, has brought together prophecies from many different avenues for the reader's convenience and assurance. All that is being submitted is for the purpose of assisting the reader to prepare spiritually for what lies ahead. It should not and need not lead the reader into fear. Rather, it is to take into consideration the words of the Lord Who very often

A6

emphatically gave and still gives the counsel, "Be not afraid". This same advice is being advanced by our Holy Father, Pope John Paul II, whose entire reign has been highlighted by not only this single statement, but also in all of His talks, in his own exemplary life.

In conclusion, what, dear reader, should be your preparation in taking up this study? Read only when you are rested, and when prompted to do so by either Mother Mary or the Holy Spirit. Do not take it up in a whim of speculation. It is serious material and must be treated with a degree of reverence and awe. We are told from above that prayer and penances on the part of the faithful have already mitigated and shortened the days of God's cleansing of the earth in readiness for the Era of Peace. It is to be noticed that even before the final chastisement, the loving Father is going to offer a final gift of mercy, the Warning. Prayer and penance keep the gift of faith lively and helpful. So, when you read, read slowly, meditatively, and with a spirit of heavenly excitement.

Fr. Stephen Valenta, OFM Conv.
St. Francis Friary
Staten Island, New York

FIRE FROM HEAVEN

INTRODUCTION

This Current Marian Age And Satan's 100 Years

The sequence of events in these End of the Times. It is not the end of the world.

Without mitigation by Heaven the sequence of events currently expected is:

•Increasing chastisements, persecution- ongoing as this is written
•Apostasy-ongoing as this is written – Great Apostasy: Rome loses the Faith
•The Warning, Illumination of Conscience, Second Pentecost – fire from heaven
•Exile and/or Death of Pope John Paul II, either before or after the Warning
•The Antipope – False Prophet, The Antichrist in person and in the false church, the greatest persecution
•The Great Chastisement – nuclear war, asteroid or comet - fire falls from Heaven and 2/3 of humanity perishes

A9

FIRE FROM HEAVEN

•The Three Days of Darkness – casting of the False Prophet and the Antichrist and all his followers into the abyss
•The Triumph of the Sacred Heart of Jesus and the Immaculate Heart of Mary with the end of the evil age of Satan:

> The Era of Peace
> Return of Jesus in glory
> The Eucharistic Reign of Jesus
> Unity of the Church with one fold, one shepherd
> The Fulfillment of the Lord's Prayer – The Divine Will done on Earth as in Heaven

There is hope.

If humanity freely responds to the Warning by penance, penance, penance as proclaimed by the angel with the flaming sword in the third part of the secret of Fatima, God's wrath may be appeased and He may <u>totally mitigate</u> the Great Chastisement and Three Days of Darkness. Our Blessed Mother has been appearing frequently all over the world to bring us back to God the Father, her Divine Son and her Spouse the Holy Spirit.

With humanity's proper response to Heaven's intervention by means of the great act of God's mercy, the Warning, also called the Illumination, God may allow us to enter directly into the Era of Peace with the Triumph of the Two Hearts, The Sacred Heart of Jesus and the Immaculate Heart of Mary without the necessity of the cleansing of humanity by the Great

Chastisement. If we respond the remainder of the vision of the third secret of Fatima will be of events in the past up to the present; otherwise these events are in our immediate future.

Cardinal Ratzinger characterized the vision of the third part of the secret of Fatima as a prophetic vision of the 20th century in which the world is seen under "the threat of judgment" unless there is a conversion of hearts to Christ.

As revealed in the October 13, 1884 vision of Pope Leo XIII and to a message to Mirjana of Medjugorje prior to December 26, 1982, God at Satan's request allowed Satan during the twentieth century to tempt the Church and mankind.

God did not abandon us to Satan, but sent Mary, His Mother and our Mother to warn us and teach us so that we, by our own free wills, will accept God and reject Satan. During the twentieth century there has been an explosion of Marian apparitions, all calling us to conversion and penance, and informing us of the weapons we need to use to overcome Satan and his cohort of evil spirits.

Mankind has not responded to these heavenly warnings and instructions. Because of this, to awaken us, God has allowed mankind to experience a number of chastisements while increasingly calling us to convert, repent and return to Him.

All

FIRE FROM HEAVEN

We have experienced rumors of wars, two World Wars, fratricidal wars, earthquakes, volcanic eruptions, plagues, persecutions, holocausts, and a turning away from God to atheistic Marxism as Russia spread her errors, and to paganism with a rise in the occult New Age. We are now living a lifestyle worse than in Sodom and Gomorrah. We are living in an era worse than at the time of Noah.

Mary is the new Ark of the Covenant. We are to seek refuge in her Immaculate Heart.

The present Marian Era began at Rue de Bac, in Paris France in 1830. This was followed by a revelation of a detailed prophetic outline of future history of France, The Church, the Pope and the world by a weeping Mother Mary at **La Salette, France in 1846**.

This present Marian era was a response by Heaven to the attack on the Church and society by the philosophers of the Enlightenment and the Freemasons and their illuminized Grand Orient Lodges.

The Illuminati were founded by Adam Weishaupt on May 1, 1776 to overthrow existing nations, kill the crowned heads of Europe and destroy the Catholic Church.

Its plans were discovered by accident and the Illuminati suppressed. The organization went underground in the Masonic lodges it had infiltrated and taken over throughout Europe. The Illuminati operated deep within the power structures of the Grand Orient Lodges and affiliated Secret Societies.

After Weishaupt's death in 1830 the Alta Vendita or highest lodge of the Italian Carbonari exercised the supreme government of all the secret societies of the world, ruling the blackest Freemasonry of France, Germany and England. In 1834 Giuseppe Mazzini took over control of illuminized Freemasonry.

It was during this time that the illuminized Freemasons developed and initiated their blueprint of how to take over the Catholic Church from within, a plan that they acknowledged might take generations to accomplish. This plan was given in the Permanent Instructions of the Alta Vendita.

The League of Just Men, an Illuminati group, financed Karl Marx, who with Friedrich Engels co-authored the Communist Manifesto. Giuseppe Mazzini supported Marx in this. From this endeavor there developed the next attempt to produce an atheistic, communist state, this time in Russia. In 1905 this attempt failed, but in October 1917 it succeeded. Lenin, the head of this new communist state wrote: "Atheism is a natural and inseparable portion of Marxism, of the theory and practice of scientific socialism. Our propaganda necessarily includes propaganda for atheism."

Heaven intervened with a series of apparitions and

A13

messages given to three young children at Fatima, Portugal in 1917. The first two parts of the three part secret of July 13, 1917 were released by the Church and published in Lucy's Memoirs. The Church failed to do what Our Blessed Mother requested in the messages at Fatima. As a result Russia spread her errors throughout the world.

The members of the Catholic Church who knew about Fatima had expected that the third part of the Secret of Fatima, called the Third Secret of Fatima, would be released in 1960, but it was not.

Heaven during this current Marian Era gave visions and messages through other visionaries and locutionists as well.

Marie-Julie Jahenny, the Breton stigmatist, born 1850, died 1941, received messages about France related to the Apparition and Message of La Sallete and in addition about the Three Days of Darkness. She received messages and visions well into the twentieth century.

In Amsterdam, Holland [Netherlands], from March 25, 1945 to May 31, 1959 Our Lady appeared as The Lady of All Nations and gave visions and messages of admonition, prophecy and warning to Ida Peerdeman about mankind, the Church, and the promulgation by

A14

the Pope of the Final Marian Dogma: Mary is
Coredemptrix, Mediatrix, and Advocate. When this
Dogma has been proclaimed the Lady of All Nations will
give true Peace to the world, a new era will start for
mankind.

These apparitions were followed by Eucharistic
experiences, visions and images in symbolic language.
Permission had been given for public devotion on May
31, 1996. Ida died June 17, 1996.

Pope John XXIII on January 25, 1959 announced
Vatican Council II, the twenty-first ecumenical
council, to seek the renewal of the Church and
modernize its forms and institutions. Pope John
XXIII hoped to foster unity among Christians.
Vatican II's opening session was on October 11, 1962. In
1965 the Council closed under Pope Paul VI's leadership.

The suppressed spirit of **Modernism**, condemned by
Pope St Pius X as the **Synthesis of All Heresies**,
resurfaced at Vatican II in the so-called spirit of Vatican
II. Modernism, he stated, is founded upon the false
modern philosophical systems which attack the
Church, the divinity of Christ, Church dogmas,
discipline, authority and the papacy. He stated that
modernism leads to pantheism and atheism.

A resurgent Modernism, the so-called spirit of
Vatican II, has produced a distortion of this pastoral
council, leading to confusion of the faithful, lack of

discipline, division, persecution, promotion of doctrinal errors, and a growing confrontation directed against the Magisterium that threatens the very foundation of the Church.

The papacy has been under severe attack through the media. Lately the attack against the Popes has reached back to **Pope Pius IX** who defined the Marian Dogma of The Immaculate Conception on December 8, 1854, published *The Syllabus of Errors* December 8, 1864, and called Vatican Council I, the twentieth ecumenical council, which defined papal infallibility.

The Vatican I definition of papal infallibility is: "We teach and define it to be a dogma divinely revealed that the Roman Pontiff, when he speaks *ex cathedra*, that is, when acting in his office of pastor and teacher of all Christians, by his supreme Apostolic authority, he defines a doctrine concerning faith or morals to be held by the whole Church, through the divine assistance promised him in Blessed Peter, he enjoys that infallibility with which the divine Redeemer willed his Church to be endowed in defining doctrine concerning faith and morals; and therefore such definitions of the said Roman Pontiff are irreformable of themselves, and not from the consent of the Church."

The Vatican I Council began on December 8, 1869 and ended in permanent suspension in July 1870 when Garibaldi's troops entered Rome during the Italian Revolution.

Pope Pius XII who defined the Marian Dogma of the Assumption of Mary into Heaven has been under recent, sustained severe attack by some in the media, although many others have come to his defense in his role in the Holocaust.

Our current Pope John Paul II has been under severe, relentless attack by many theologians, cardinals, bishops, priests religious and liberal and ultraconservative members of the Catholic Church. He has suffered a great deal from these attacks and from his current physical frailties of age.

At Garabandal Spain, 1961-1965, Our Lady and St. Michael appeared to four young children. They were given messages about the Eucharist, the Church, Cardinal against Cardinal, Bishop against Bishop and Priest against Priest. They had visions and received messages about the Warning, The Miracle and the Permanent Sign. Through them we were also warned that if mankind didn't respond there would be a great chastisement. This great chastisement was conditional, depending upon our response to the Warning, The Miracle and the Permanent Sign.

At Akita, Japan in 1973 Our Lady gave us messages which spelled out in more detail, than in the released first two parts of the secret of Fatima, what awaited mankind and the Church if we didn't pray, repent and better ourselves. Cardinal Ratzinger had been quoted as saying that this was the Third Secret of Fatima.

FIRE FROM HEAVEN

The Marian Movement of Priests originated at Fatima in May 8, 1972 in an inspiration given to Father Don Stefano Gobbi while he was praying in the little Chapel of the Apparitions in Fatima for some priests who, besides having personally given up their own vocations, were attempting to form themselves into associations in rebellion against the Church's authority.

An interior force urged him to have confidence in the Immaculate Heart of Mary. Our Lady, making use of him as a poor and humble instrument, would gather all those priests who would accept her invitation to consecrate themselves to her Immaculate Heart, to be strongly united to the Pope and to the Church united with him, and to bring the faithful into the secure refuge of her motherly Heart.

On July 7, 1973 Father Gobbi began receiving public messages from Our Lady concerning her plan to defeat her Adversary Satan, save her children and the Church and asking for prayers to protect the Pope of her secret, Pope John Paul II. Cenacles, family cenacles, children's cenacles, the daily recitation of the Holy Rosary, frequent confession and reception of Holy Communion, are instruments in her plan to bring about the Triumph of her Immaculate Heart which had been promised at Fatima. Father Gobbi's public messages ended December 31, 1997.

These public messages, which Our Lady gave in great, coherent detail, described the attacks of Satan and his

A18

cohorts, the Red Dragon of Marxist atheism, the Black Beast like a leopard –Freemasonry, Ecclesiastical Masonry, the beast with two horns like a lamb, the infiltration by the Freemasons into the interior of the Church setting up their stronghold in the very place where the Vicar of Christ, the Pope lives and works, the great apostasy, the Illumination of souls, the second Pentecost, the Antichrist, the man of iniquity penetrating into its interior and sitting in the very temple of God and perpetrating the horrible sacrilege predicted by Daniel, the abolishment of the daily Sacrifice, the great chastisement, the ultimate Triumph of her Immaculate Heart related to the Jubilee of the year 2000, the New Era of Peace, the return of Jesus in Glory, the Eucharistic Reign of Jesus, the Divine Will being done on earth as in Heaven, and the renewed splendor of the Church, with one flock, one shepherd.

At Medjugorje, Yugoslavia, on June 24, 1981 Our Lady began appearing to two children, Mirjana Dragicevic and Ivanka Ivankovic, and on June 25, 1981 to four other children Vicka, Ivan, Maria Pavlovic and Jacov Colo. giving messages for us to pray, fast, convert, repent. She appears to them as Queen of Peace. These apparitions are still ongoing and each visionary has been given 9 or 10 secrets. Those with 9 secrets are still awaiting their 10th secret.

In the United States Janie Garza, a stigmatist from Austin, Texas on February 15, 1989 began to receive

A19

visions and messages from Our Lady, St. Joseph, from Jesus, from the Archangels and from St. Philomena. She has received many messages about the family and the Illumination, chastisements and our country.

Joanne Kriva, a mid-western housewife, during the period from September 10, 1990 through August 23, 1998 received many locutions from the Lord Our God about our need for conversion and repentance. The messages are about abortion, this country, the secrets of the Book of Revelation, the chastisements, the Church, the Apostasy, the Pope, the Antichrist, Freemasonry, the New World Order and the New Era of Peace.

Sadie Jaramillo, California, began on August 1, 1992 to receive visions and messages about this country, the Warning, the Church, Pope John Paul II, the Final Marian Dogma, a schism, the Antipope, and the Antichrist.

Denise Curtin and Joseph DellaPuca, Connecticut, in January 1996 began to receive messages from our Heavenly Mother for the purification and the era of peace. In the year 2000 they are receiving messages for the world.

Christina Gallagher of Ireland since 1988 has received visions and messages about chastisements, earthquakes, fire falling from heaven, and the Antichrist.

Maria Esperanza of Venezuela at age five had a vision of St Therese who threw her a rose which she gave to her mother. On March 25, 1976 Our Blessed Mother began appearing at Betania, Venezuela as "Mother of Reconciliation of All People. Maria has the stigmata, the aroma of roses, and at times the Eucharist miraculously appears on her tongue. Maria has received a message about the great day of light, [the Warning] along with many other apocalyptic messages.

Luz Amparo Cuevas, a stigmatist from Escorial, Spain, since June 14, 1981 has received a vision of Our Lord on the Cross and visions and many messages from Our Lady about the chastisements and the three days of darkness.

Jim Singer born in Zagreb, Croatia in 1952 [Yugoslavia] and now living in Ontario, Canada received 100 messages from Our Lord from May 1989 to September 1989. The events in Croatia were foretold to him. He had also been told about the Beast and its relation to the G-7 and Russia. Satan, in Jim's messages has been called the Shining Darkness.

Joseph Terelya from the Ukraine and now living in Canada has received visions and messages from Our Blessed Mother. The visions began while he was imprisoned by Russia. These visions and messages from Our Blessed Mother and from some saints have been about Russia, Yeltsin, the United Nations, false ecumenism, a potential World War III.

The messages these visionaries and locutionists and

many others have received from Heaven stress prayer, especially the Holy Mass as the perfect prayer, and the Holy Rosary, and the call for fasting, conversion, repentance, penance and return to God. These are the measures we are to use to appease God and thus heal the apostasy and mitigate chastisements and even prevent the great chastisement.

It is in light of these repeatedly presented, urgent messages from heaven that Fatima should be interpreted, but hasn't been in the official release by the Church on June 26, 2000. Any interpretation without reference to these messages fails to do justice to the interpretation of the message of Fatima.

In a Vatican press conference on June 26 Cardinal Ratzinger said: "There does not exist an official definition or official interpretation of this vision on the part of the Church."

We will therefore present the official Vatican release and the Vatican's unofficial interpretation, and critique them in Chapter 1. In the remaining chapters of this book we will present in detail what Heaven has so urgently said about what is happening and what could happen to the Church and to humanity and what could have and can be done to prevent or mitigate what had been foretold in La Salette and in Fatima. This will give us a deeper and greater understanding of the great impact Fatima was meant to have had upon the course of Church history and humanity's return to God the Father as we cross the threshold of hope into the third millennium on the way to the Era of Peace during which the Divine Will will be done on Earth as in Heaven.

FIRE FROM HEAVEN

Chapter 1

The Secret of Fatima

The Vatican Release Of The Three Parts Of The Secret Of Fatima

THE "SECRET" OF FATIMA
FIRST AND SECOND PART OF THE "SECRET"
ACCORDING TO THE VERSION
PRESENTED BY SISTER LUCIA
IN THE "THIRD MEMOIR" OF 31 AUGUST 1941
FOR THE BISHOP OF LEIRIA-FATIMA

(translation) [6]
... This will entail my speaking about the secret, and thus answering the first question.

What is the secret? It seems to me that I can reveal it, since I already have permission from Heaven to do so. God's representatives on earth have authorized me to do this several times and in various letters, one of which, I believe, is in your keeping. This letter is from Father José

Fire From Heaven

Bernardo Gonçalves, and in it he advises me to write to the Holy Father, suggesting, among other things, that I should reveal the secret. I did say something about it. But in order not to make my letter too long, since I was told to keep it short, I confined myself to the essentials, leaving it to God to provide another more favourable opportunity.

In my second account I have already described in detail the doubt which tormented me from 13 June until 13 July, and how it disappeared completely during the Apparition on that day.

Well, the secret is made up of three distinct parts, two of which I am now going to reveal.

The first part is the vision of hell.

Our Lady showed us a great sea of fire which seemed to be under the earth. Plunged in this fire were demons and souls in human form, like transparent burning embers, all blackened or burnished bronze, floating about in the conflagration, now raised into the air by the flames that issued from within themselves together with great clouds of smoke, now falling back on every side like sparks in a huge fire, without weight or equilibrium, and amid shrieks and groans of pain and despair, which horrified us and made us tremble with fear. The demons could be distinguished by their terrifying and repulsive likeness to frightful and unknown animals, all black and transparent. This vision lasted but an instant. How can we ever be grateful enough to our kind heavenly Mother, who had already prepared us by promising, in the first Apparition, to take us to heaven. Otherwise, I think we would have died of fear and terror.

We then looked up at Our Lady, who said to us so kindly and so sadly:

"You have seen hell where the souls of poor sinners go. To save them, God wishes to establish in the world de- votion to my Immaculate Heart. If what I say to you is done, many souls will be saved and there will be peace. The war is going to end: but if people do not cease offending God, a worse one will break out during the Pontificate of Pius XI. When you see a night illumined by an unknown light, know that this is the great sign given you by God that he is about to punish the world for its crimes, by means of war, famine, and persecutions of the Church and of the Holy Father. To prevent this, I shall come to ask for the consecration of Russia to my Immaculate Heart, and the Communion of reparation on the First Saturdays. If my requests are heeded, Russia will be converted, and there will be peace; if not, she will spread her errors throughout the world, causing wars and persecutions of the Church. The good will be martyred; the Holy Father will have much to suffer; various nations will be annihilated. In the end, my Immaculate Heart will triumph. The Holy Father will consecrate Russia to me, and she shall be converted, and a period of peace will be granted to the world".[7]

Fire From Heaven

THIRD PART OF THE "SECRET"

"J.M.J.
The third part of the secret revealed at the Cova da Iria-
Fatima, on 13 July 1917.

I write in obedience to you, my God, who command me
to do so through his Excellency the Bishop of Leiria and
through your Most Holy Mother and mine.

After the two parts which I have already explained, at
the left of Our Lady and a little above, we saw an Angel
with a flaming sword in his left hand; flashing, it gave
out flames that looked as though they would set the
world on fire; but they died out in contact with the
splendour that Our Lady radiated towards him from her
right hand: pointing to the earth with his right hand, the
Angel cried out in a loud voice: 'Penance, Penance, Penance!'. And we saw in an immense light that is God:
'something similar to how people appear in a mirror
when they pass in front of it' a Bishop dressed in White
'we had the impression that it was the Holy Father'.
Other Bishops, Priests, men and women Religious going
up a steep mountain, at the top of which there was a big
Cross of rough-hewn trunks as of a cork-tree with the
bark; before reaching there the Holy Father passed
through a big city half in ruins and half trembling with
halting step, afflicted with pain and sorrow, he prayed
for the souls of the corpses he met on his way; having
reached the top of the mountain, on his knees at the foot
of the big Cross he was killed by a group of soldiers who
fired bullets and arrows at him, and in the same way

4

there died one after another the other Bishops, Priests, men and women Religious, and various lay people of different ranks and positions. Beneath the two arms of the Cross there were two Angels each with a crystal aspersorium in his hand, in which they gathered up the blood of the Martyrs and with it sprinkled the souls that were making their way to God.

Tuy-3-1-1944".

The June 26, 2000 Vatican release included "An attempt to interpret the 'secret' of Fatima" by Cardinal Ratzinger.

The first and second parts of the "secret" of Fatima have already been so amply discussed in the relative literature that there is no need to deal with them again here. I would just like to recall briefly the most significant point. For one terrible moment, the children were given a vision of hell. They saw the fall of "the souls of poor sinners". And now they are told why they have been exposed to this moment: "in order to save souls"—to show the way to salvation. The words of the First Letter of Peter come to mind: "As the outcome of your faith you obtain the salvation of your souls" (1:9). To reach this goal, the way indicated —surprisingly for people from the Anglo-Saxon and German cultural world—is devotion to the Immaculate Heart of Mary. A brief comment may suffice to explain this. In biblical language, the "heart" indicates the centre of human life, the point where reason, will, temperament and sensitivity converge, where the person finds his unity and his interior orientation.

According to Matthew 5:8, the "immaculate heart" is a heart which, with God's grace, has come to perfect interior unity and therefore "sees God". To be "devoted" to the Immaculate Heart of Mary means therefore to embrace this attitude of heart, which makes the *fiat*—"your will be done"—the defining centre of one's whole life. It might be objected that we should not place a human being between ourselves and Christ. But then we remember that Paul did not hesitate to say to his communities: "imitate me" (*1 Cor* 4:16; *Phil* 3:17; *1 Th* 1:6; *2 Th* 3:7, 9). In the Apostle they could see concretely what it meant to follow Christ. But from whom might we better learn in every age than from the Mother of the Lord?

Thus we come finally to the third part of the "secret" of Fatima which for the first time is being published in its entirety. As is clear from the documentation presented here, the interpretation offered by Cardinal Sodano in his statement of 13 May was first put personally to Sister Lucia. Sister Lucia responded by pointing out that she had received the vision but not its interpretation. The interpretation, she said, belonged not to the visionary but to the Church. After reading the text, however, she said that this interpretation corresponded to what she had experienced and that on her part she thought the interpretation correct. In what follows, therefore, we can only attempt to provide a deeper foundation for this interpretation, on the basis of the criteria already considered.

"To save souls" has emerged as the key word of the first and second parts of the "secret", and the key word of this third part is the threefold cry: "Penance, Penance, Penance!" The beginning of the Gospel comes to mind: "Repent and believe the Good News" (Mk 1:15). To understand the signs of the times means to accept the urgency of penance – of conversion – of faith. This is the correct response to this moment of history, characterized by the grave perils outlined in the images that follow. Allow me to add here a personal recollection: in a conversation with me Sister Lucia said that it appeared ever more clearly to her that the purpose of all the apparitions was to help people to grow more and more in faith, hope and love —everything else was intended to lead to this.

Let us now examine more closely the single images. The angel with the flaming sword on the left of the Mother of God recalls similar images in the Book of Revelation. This represents the threat of judgement which looms over the world. Today the prospect that the world might be reduced to ashes by a sea of fire no longer seems pure fantasy: man himself, with his inventions, has forged the flaming sword. The vision then shows the power which stands opposed to the force of destruction—the splendour of the Mother of God and, stemming from this in a certain way, the summons to penance. In this way, the importance of human freedom is underlined: the future is not in fact unchangeably set, and the image which the children saw is in no way a film preview of a future in which nothing can be changed. Indeed, the whole point of the vision is to bring freedom onto the scene and to steer freedom in a positive direction. The purpose of the vision is not to show a film of an irrevocably fixed future. Its meaning is exactly the opposite: it is meant to mobilize the forces of change in the right direction. Therefore we must totally discount fatalistic explanations of the "secret", such as, for example, the claim that the would-be assassin of 13 May 1981 was merely an instrument of the divine plan guided by Providence and could not therefore have acted freely, or other similar ideas in circulation. Rather, the vision speaks of dangers and how we might be saved from them.

The next phrases of the text show very clearly once again the symbolic character of the vision: God remains immeasurable, and is the light which surpasses every vision of ours. Human persons appear as in a mirror. We must always keep in mind the limits in the vision itself, which here are indicated visually. The future appears only "in a mirror dimly" (*1 Cor* 13:12). Let us now consider the individual images which follow in the text of the "secret". The place of the action is described in three symbols: a steep mountain, a great city reduced to ruins and finally a large rough-hewn cross. The mountain and city symbolize the arena of human history: history as an arduous ascent to the summit, history as the arena of human creativity and social harmony, but at the same time a place of destruction, where man actually destroys the fruits of his own work. The city can be the place of communion and progress, but also of danger and the most extreme menace. On the mountain stands the cross—the goal and guide of history. The cross transforms destruction into salvation; it stands as a sign of history's misery but also as a promise for history.

At this point human persons appear: the Bishop dressed in white ("we had the impression that it was the Holy Father"), other Bishops, priests, men and women Religious, and men and women of different ranks and social positions. The Pope seems to precede the others, trembling and suffering because of all the horrors around him. Not only do the houses of the city lie half in ruins, but he makes his way among the corpses of the dead. The Church's path is thus described as a *Via Crucis*, as a journey through a time of violence, destruction and persecution. The history of an entire century can be seen represented in this image. Just as the places of the earth are synthetically described in the two images of the mountain and the city, and are directed towards the cross, so too time is presented in a compressed way. In the vision we can recognize the last century as a century of martyrs, a century of suffering and persecution for the Church, a century of World Wars and the many local wars which filled the last fifty years and have inflicted unprecedented forms of cruelty. In the "mirror" of this vision we see passing before us the witnesses of the faith decade by decade. Here it would be appropriate to mention a phrase from the letter which Sister Lucia wrote to the Holy Father on 12 May 1982: "The third part of the 'secret' refers to Our Lady's words: 'If not, [Russia] will spread her errors throughout the world, causing wars and persecutions of the Church. The good will be martyred; the Holy Father will have much to suffer; various nations will be annihilated'".

In the *Via Crucis* of an entire century, the figure of the Pope has a special role. In his arduous ascent of the mountain we can undoubtedly see a convergence of different Popes. Beginning from Pius X up to the present Pope, they all shared the sufferings of the century and strove to go forward through all the anguish along the path which leads to the Cross. In the vision, the Pope too is killed along with the martyrs. When, after the attempted assassination on 13 May 1981, the Holy Father had the text of the third part of the "secret" brought to him, was it not inevitable that he should see in it his own fate? He had been very close to death, and he himself explained his survival in the following words: "... it was a mother's hand that guided the bullet's path and in his throes the Pope halted at the threshold of death" (13 May 1994). That here "a mother's hand" had deflected the fateful bullet only shows once more that there is no immutable destiny, that faith and prayer are forces which can influence history and that in the end prayer is more powerful than bullets and faith more powerful than armies.

The concluding part of the "secret" uses images which Lucia may have seen in devotional books and which draw their inspiration from long-standing intuitions of faith. It is a consoling vision, which seeks to open a history of blood and tears to the healing power of God. Beneath the arms of the cross angels gather up the blood of the martyrs, and with it they give life to the souls making their way to God. Here, the blood of Christ and the blood of the martyrs are considered as one: the blood of the martyrs runs down from the arms of the cross. The martyrs die in communion with the Passion of Christ, and their death becomes one with his. For the sake of the body of Christ, they complete what is still lacking in his afflictions (cf. *Col* 1:24). Their life has itself become a Eucharist, part of the mystery of the grain of wheat which in dying yields abundant fruit. The blood of the martyrs is the seed of Christians, said Tertullian. As from Christ's death, from his wounded side, the Church was born, so the death of the witnesses is fruitful for the future life of the Church. Therefore, the vision of the third part of the "secret", so distressing at first, concludes with an image of hope: no suffering is in vain, and it is a suffering Church, a Church of martyrs, which becomes a sign-post for man in his search for God. The loving arms of God welcome not only those who suffer like Lazarus, who found great solace there and mysteriously represents Christ, who wished to become for us the poor Lazarus. There is something more: from the suffering of the witnesses there comes a purifying and renewing power, because their suffering is the actualization of the suffering of Christ himself and a communication in the here and now of its saving effect.

And so we come to the final question: What is the meaning of the "secret" of Fatima as a whole (in its three parts)? What does it say to us? First of all we must affirm with Cardinal Sodano: "... the events to which the third part of the 'secret' of Fatima refers now seem part of the past". Insofar as individual events are described, they belong to the past. Those who expected exciting apocalyptic revelations about the end of the world or the future course of history are bound to be disappointed. Fatima does not satisfy our curiosity in this way, just as Christian faith in general cannot be reduced to an object of mere curiosity. What remains was already evident when we began our reflections on the text of the "secret": the exhortation to prayer as the path of "salvation for souls" and, likewise, the summons to penance and conversion.

I would like finally to mention another key expression of the "secret" which has become justly famous: "my Immaculate Heart will triumph". What does this mean? The Heart open to God, purified by contemplation of God, is stronger than guns and weapons of every kind. The *fiat* of Mary, the word of her heart, has changed the history of the world, because it brought the Saviour into the world—because, thanks to her *Yes*, God could become man in our world and remains so for all time. The Evil One has power in this world, as we see and experience continually; he has power because our freedom continually lets itself be led away from God. But since God himself took a human heart and has thus steered human freedom towards what is good, the freedom to choose evil no longer has the last word. From that time forth, the word that prevails is this: "In the world you will have tribulation, but take heart; I have overcome the world" (*Jn* 16:33). The message of Fatima invites us to trust in this promise.

Joseph Card. Ratzinger
Prefect of the Congregation
for the Doctrine of the Faith

In June 2000, just after the release of The Third Secret of Fatima, Bishop Serafim de Sousa of Leiria-

Fatima , a good friend of Sister Lucia, gave an interview to the Spanish weekly newspaper "Alfa y
Omega," concerning the Third Secret of Fatima

Interview with Bishop Serafim de Sousa of Leiria-Fatima

Q. You were an eye-witness of the meeting of
Archbishop Tarcisio Bertone, secretary of the Congregation for the Doctrine of the Faith, with Sister Lucia, in
April of this year, when the official text of the theological commentary was presented to the visionary. Could
you describe the emotion you felt?

Bishop de Sousa: Indeed, I was present at that meeting,
but only as an intermediary. Rather than emotional, it
was a simple meeting; indeed Archbishop Bertone himself said he was very happy to see how Sister Lucia answered lucidly, relating, consciously and coherently,
everything that was said to her.

Q. You are one of the few persons in the world who
know Sister Lucia personally. What impresses you most
about her?

Bishop de Sousa: I would highlight her sincerity, she is
an enormously sincere and courageous woman; she does
nothing but repeat what she saw and heard, without
adding or subtracting anything. In addition, she is convinced that she is still on earth with a concrete mission:
although she would like to be with her cousins Jacinta

and Francisco, she is convinced that her long life (she is older than 90) is to witness the Fatima message to the world, seeing to it that Our Lady's requests are obeyed in the way intended.

Q. In your opinion, is there a reason why the "secret" was published during the Jubilee 2000?

Bishop de Sousa: I think the date itself is of little importance. I suppose the Pope intended to publish the secret after the attempt, although not immediately, as if awaiting confirmation that this part of the secret referred to him. Moreover, it must be kept in mind that this Jubilee is a very convenient occasion, as it is the year of reconciliation, also for the beatification of the little shepherds.

Q. What part of the secret would you underline?

Bishop de Sousa: There are many aspects, for instance, when "the bishop dressed in white" walks together with other bishops, priests, and laymen, as an important sign of the Church's universality, made up of unequal members who walk united. Moreover, soldiers must understand one another, more than as concrete persons, as the struggle of secular States against the Church. Another aspect is that Christians are martyred not only with bullets, but also with arrows, which represents persecutions in different cultures, including the Third World. On another count, I think the vision of the two angels is very important, a mysterious vision made in biblical language, which invites us always to remember the thousands of martyrs of this century.

Q. Do you think that, with the publication of the secret, in a certain sense the 20th century comes to a close?

Bishop de Souza: Rather than closes, I would say that a window of hope has opened in this century, the hope of the personal conversion of each one of us, so that humanity may finally find peace.

Q. From here on, what will change in Fatima and Portugal?

Bishop de Sousa: I think Fatima doesn't change: it continues to be that spiritual lung, that place of conversion. Of course, if it is true that both the beatification of Francisco and Jacinta, as well as the official publication of the "secret," confirm the validity of the message of Fatima.

Critique of This Vatican Release

In this attempted interpretation of the third part of the secret of Fatima the full document from Joseph Cardinal Ratzinger's office fails to take into account any of the apparitions and messages mentioned in the Introduction to this book and the numerous other apparitions, visions and messages from Heaven. Studying these in relation to the secret of Fatima would further aid us in better understanding and interpreting Fatima and its secret.

The Vatican release, after the sentence "The Holy Fa-

ther will consecrate Russia to me, and she will be converted, and a period of peace will be granted to the
world.", leaves off the already revealed statement
which can be found on page 167 of *Fatima in Lucia's Own
Words, Sister Lucia's Memoirs*. In *The Fourth Memoir*, on
page 167 we find the statement: "In Portugal, the
dogma of the Faith will always be preserved; etc... Do
not tell this to anybody. Francisco, yes, you may tell
him."

In the "Fourth Memoir" of December 8, 1941 Sister
Lucia writes: "I shall begin then my new task, and thus
fulfill the commands received from Your Excellency as
well as the desires of Dr Galamba. With the exception
of that part of the Secret which I am not permitted to
reveal at present, I shall say everything. I shall not
knowingly omit anything, though I suppose I may forget just a few small details of minor importance".

In the "Fourth Memoir" Sister Lucia adds: "In Portugal, the dogma of the faith will always be preserved,
etc. ...".

What is the etc.? Our Lady's message is not continued
in this official release of the third part of the secret.
Why did the Vatican not use the Fourth Memoir
rather than the Third?

This missing section of the third part of the secret is a
statement by Our Lady not a vision, since Francisco
could only see Our Lady, but could not hear her. If it
were the vision Francisco would have seen it and would

16

not need to be told.

The statement in the Vatican release is: " Sister Lucia was in full agreement with the Pope's claim that 'it was a mother's hand that guided the bullet's path and in his throes the Pope halted at the threshold of death' (Pope John Paul II, *Meditation from the Policlinico Gemelli to the Itaian Bishops*, 13 May 1994)." This is true, however, this statement does not mean that this was the event concerning Pope John Paul II that was seen in this vision.

The reference to this Holy Father in this released vision notes he was killed by a group of soldiers who fired bullets and arrows at him. Ali Agca who attempted to kill Pope John Paul II on May 13, 1981 and failed was not a soldier and definitely not soldiers.

The statement is made in the Church's attempted interpretation of the third part of the secret: "What does it say to us? First of all we must affirm with Cardinal Sodano: '... the events to which the third part of the 'secret' of Fatima refers now seem part of the past.' Insofar as individual events are described, they belong to the past."

It may seem to Cardinal Ratzinger and to Cardinal Sodano that this is a past event, but the vision as revealed by Sister Lucia is, as it is stated, of the suffering Pope, after climbing Calvary, being killed by a group of soldiers. This vision is not necessarily entirely symbolic, but rather than only being symbolic, it is probably also a true vision of the future events relating to this Pope, the Church, cardinals, bishops, priests, religious and laity.

Fire From Heaven

In a locution to Father Gobbi, message #594, May 8, 1997 at Fatima, Our Blessed Lady revealed this third secret <u>as both a prediction and a vision</u>. In this Vatican release which used Lucia's Third Memoir and not her Fourth Memoir <u>we have the vision, but not the completion of Our Lady's statement, the prediction.</u>

In message #594 given at Fatima to Fr. Gobbi on May 8, 1997 Our Blessed Mother said in section j: "*It is the message of Fatima which is being fulfilled* in your pledge of love, of prayer and of unity with the Pope and with the Church united to him. Here<u>, I have predicted and have shown in a vision</u> to the little children to whom I appeared, the sufferings, the oppositions, and the bloody trials of the Pope. These prophecies of mine are being fulfilled above all in this Pope of mine, John Paul the Second, who is the masterpiece formed in my Immaculate Heart...."

The released text in addition is not consistent with Pope John Paul II's statement at Fulda, Germany in November 1980.

In the locution given to Father Gobbi on September 8, 1985, Message #313, *The Hour of Public Witness*, Our Blessed Mother said: "Everything that my Pope has said in this place corresponds with the truth.

"You are close to the greatest chastisement, and I say to you: entrust yourselves to me, and remember that the weapon to use in these terrible moments is that of the holy rosary. Then you will form my cohort which I am leading, in these times, to its greatest victory."

This is a 1983 report of what Pope John Paul II said at Fulda, Germany. [From QUEEN Magazine, published by the Montfort Fathers – Bayshore, New York, September, 1983.]

The Pope was in Germany from November 15 –19, 1980.

John Paul II, Fulda, Germany and The Third Secret of Fatima

The German magazine, "Stimme des Glaubens," has published the following account of Pope John Paul II's interview with a small group of German Catholics on the occasion of his visit to Fulda, in November of 1980.

Question: "Holy Father, what has become of the 3rd Secret of Fatima? According to Our Lady's instructions, wasn't it supposed to be revealed in 1960? And what will happen in the Church?"

The Holy Father's Response: "Because of the seriousness of its contents, in order not to encourage the world wide power of Communism to carry out certain coups, my predecessors in the Chair of Peter have diplomatically preferred to withhold its publication.

"On the other hand, it should be sufficient for all

Fire From Heaven

Christians to know this much: if there is a message in which it is said that the oceans will flood entire sections of the earth; that, from one moment to the other, millions of people will perish . . . there is no longer any point in really wanting to publish this secret message.

"Many want to know merely out of curiosity or because of their taste for sensationalism but they forget that 'to know' implies for them a responsibility. It is dangerous to want to satisfy one's curiosity only, if one is convinced that we can do nothing against a catastrophe that has been predicted."

At this point, the Holy Father, took hold of his Rosary and said: "Here is the remedy against the evil! Pray, pray and ask for nothing else. Put everything in the hands of the Mother of God!"

Then he went on to say; "We must be prepared to undergo great trials in the not too distant future, trials that will require us to be ready to give up even our lives and a total gift of self to Christ and for Christ. Through your prayer and mine, it is possible to alleviate this tribulation but it is no longer possible to avert it, because it is only in this way that the Church can be effectively renewed.

"How many times, indeed, has the renewal of the Church been effected in blood? This time again, it will not be otherwise,

"We must be strong, we must prepare ourselves, we must entrust ourselves to Christ and to His holy Mother, and we must be attentive to the prayer of the Rosary?"

There is a message in this third part of the secret, according to this, which was not present in the official Vatican release.

The publication *Our Sunday Visitor*, July 9, 2000, on page 5 states: "The newly revealed third part of the secret picks up where the second left off, with a vision of the Virgin set against an 'angel with a flaming sword' threatening to 'set the world on fire' unless the people of the earth do penance." The secret stated that pointing to the earth with his right hand, the Angel cried out in a loud voice: 'Penance, Penance, Penance.'

In this current Marian Era this call for penance has been urgently requested in all the other apparitions and locutions around the world.

From *Catholic New York*, June 29, 2000, Volume XIX, No. 39, on page 7, in an article **Rome Comments, Vatican calls Fatima secret a prophecy of triumph over evil**, by Cindy Wooden, Catholic News Service:

"Archbishop Bertone [secretary Congregation for the Doctrine of the Faith] said the pope, who was elected in 1978, first read the contents of the wax sealed envelope in May 1981 while in Rome's Gemelli Hospital recovering from the attack.

Fire From Heaven

"The archbishop's insistence that the pope first read
the secret in the hospital deflated another Fatima
myth: that during a semiprivate meeting in Fulda,
Germany, in November 1980, Pope John Paul referred
to the Fatima secret and its supposedly apocalyptic,
end-of-the-world vision.

"Cardinal Ratzinger said the story 'really was apocry-
phal; it never really happened.'"

Later according to the article Cardinal Ratzinger also
said: "Naturally [there is] a margin of error" when interpreting visions, which is one reason why "the Church is
not imposing an interpretation."

What do various current apparitions, visions and locutions of the twentieth century and the prior centuries tell us which could help us understand this vision in the third part of the secret of Fatima? The
Church's spokesman in this document have ignored
these in making their interpretation, since they are according to them only private revelation. When there are
so many private revelations in the twentieth century and
preceding centuries which can be used to explain this
important event in Church and world history they
should be used.

The many current and recent apparitions, visions and
locutions from around the world paint a picture of what
has been happening and what will happen to humanity,
the Church and the Pope in the near future.

The entire Church — Pope, Cardinals, Bishops, Priests, Religious and lay people, rich and poor are climbing Calvary with immense physical and spiritual suffering along the Way of the Cross. Many will be physically killed or suffer from calumny along the way and when they have reached the summit of their ascent. Pope John Paul II is more and more ridiculed, mocked, isolated and abandoned. There have been and will be many martyrs along this Way of the Cross. The 20th century has been a century of Martyrs. These events in this vision are past, present and future, <u>and not all in the past</u>, as we see when we review visions and messages from Heaven's extraordinary attempt in this current Marian Era to bring our prodigal humanity back to the Father. Details predicted, prophesied, for the future are filled in by the visions, messages and locutions given by Heaven to other visionaries and locutionists.

Why Pope John XXIII Did Not Release The Third Secret In 1960

According to Fr. Malachi Martin in *The Keys of This Blood,* Pope John Paul XXIII had the opportunity with the opening of Vatican II on October 11, 1962, but didn't organize the collegial consecration of Russia to Mary.

"In 1960, Pope John [XXIII] held a conversation in the Vatican with Nikita Krushchev's son-in-law, Aleksei Adzhubei, editor of Izvestia. In addition, John accepted an agreement with Krushchev himself, by which a trade-

23

Fire From Heaven

off was made concerning the Second Vatican Council:
The Council would issue none of the usual statements
condemning the Soviet Union's Leninist Marxism; and
in return, two prelates of the Russian Orthodox Church,
Metropolitans Borovoy and Kotlrov, both with KGB
status, would attend Vatican II as observers..."[23]

This agreement offers an insight as to a possible reason
why Pope John XXXIII did not want the third secret revealed in 1960. Reflect upon the implications with this
agreement for Vatican II, if he did release the Third Secret at that time.

We had been told about the role of Russia in the
events of the twentieth century when the Church released the first two parts of Lucy's three part secret...."

In the past we also had been told that Pope John
XXIII did not release it since he said it did not relate
to his pontificate and thus archived it.

Cardinal Ratzinger said that the reason the succes-
sive popes since the 1940's have not disclosed the secret is because it could not be fully understood until
the close of the 20th century. "There was no sense in
offering humanity an indecipherable image which
would have created only speculation."

Our Blessed Mother in order to get this suppressed
message out to the faithful through the remainder of

24

the 20th century increased the frequency and urgency of her apparitions and messages. Jesus, God The Father, St. Joseph, many saints and the Archangels have frequently appeared and given urgent messages to give us the means to be used to avert or mitigate the prophesied great apostasy and great chastisement.

Our Blessed Mother and St. Michael began to appear in Garabandal, Spain from 1961 to 1965. In 1961 they began to release the third part of the secret in the visions and messages of Garabandal.

Garabandal was ignored.

Our Lady released this third part of the secret of Fatima at Akita, Japan. On October 13, 1973 Our Lady gave us this hidden third secret:

"My dear daughter, listen well to what I have to say to you. You will inform your superior. As I told you, if men do not repent and better themselves, the Father will inflict a terrible punishment on all humanity. It will be a punishment greater than the deluge, such as one will never have seen before. Fire will fall from the sky and will wipe out a great part of humanity, the good as well as the bad, sparing neither priests nor faithful. The survivors will find themselves so desolate that they will envy the dead. The only arms that will remain for you will be the rosary and Sign left by My Son. Each day recite the prayers of the rosary. With the rosary pray for the Pope, the bishops, and the priests.

25

Fire From Heaven

"The work of the devil will infiltrate even the Church in such a way that one will see cardinals opposing cardinals, bishops against other bishops. The priests who venerate Me scorned and opposed by their confreres ...churches and altars sacked, the Church will be full of those who accept compromises and the demon will press many priests and consecrated souls to leave the service of the Lord. The demon will be especially implacable against souls consecrated to God. The thought of the loss of so many souls is the cause of my sadness. If sins increase in number and gravity, there will be no longer pardon for them.

"With courage, speak to your superior. He will know how to encourage each one of you to pray and to accomplish works of reparation."[32]

In 1972, at Fatima on May 8 Our Lady began preparing for the Marian Movement of Priests choosing Fr. Gobbi for the interior locutionist to reveal the messages of her plan.

On October 13, 1972 Fr. Gobbi and two other priests launched the movement. Our Lady in the years that followed has revealed her secret in detail both as to the Apostasy in the Church and the Great Chastisement of humanity, as well as the secret of the wonderful, glorious outcome. This has been revealed through her many messages for her Movement of Priests. The message of March 11, 1995 is most explicit concerning this secret. A reading of the messages of each

May 13 from 1990 through 1996 and the message of May 8, 1997 is very instructive.

On March 11, 1995, at Fatima, Our Lady told Fr. Gobbi: "I want you spiritually here with me, because as of now you are entering into <u>the last period of time of this century of yours, when the events which I have predicted to you will come to complete fulfillment</u>. For this reason, here in the very place where I appeared, I want today to reveal to you *my secret.*

"My secret concerns the Church.
"In the Church, **the great apostasy**, which will spread throughout the whole world, will be brought to its completion; the **schism** will take place through a general alienation from the Gospel and from the true faith. There will enter into the Church **the man of iniquity**, who opposes himself to Christ, and who will bring into her interior **the abomination of desolation**, thus bringing to fulfillment the horrible sacrilege, of which the prophet Daniel has spoken. (cf. Mt 24:15)

"My secret concerns humanity.
"Humanity will reach the summit of corruption and impiety, of rebellion against God and of open opposition to his Law of love. It will know the hour of its **greatest chastisement**, which has already been **foretold to you** by the prophet Zechariah. (cf. Zec. 13:7-9)

"Then this place will appear to all as a bright sign of my motherly presence in the supreme hour of your **great tribulation**. From here my light will spread to every part of the world, and from this fount will gush the water of divine mercy, which will descend to irrigate the barrenness of a world, now reduced to an immense desert.

"And in this, my extraordinary work of love and of salvation, there will appear to all the triumph of the Immaculate Heart of her who is invoked as the Mother of Mercy."[2]

In message # 482, November 22, 1992 Our Lady told Fr. Gobbi: ".... The times which were foretold to you by the prophet Zechariah have now come.

"An oracle of the Lord: I will strike the shepherd, and the sheep will be completely scattered; and then I will turn my hand against the little ones.

"An oracle of the Lord: In all the land, two thirds of them will be cut off and perish; and one third shall be left.

"'I will pass this third through fire; I will refine it as silver is refined, test it as gold is tested.

"It will call upon my Name, and I will hear it; I will say: "This is my people." And it will say: "This is my God."' (cf. Zec. 13:7-9)[2]

Chapter 2

CHASTISEMENTS

Plague

Plague is defined as:
a noun:
1.A pestilence, affliction, or calamity.
2.A cause for annoyance; nuisance.
3.A highly infectious, usually fatal epidemic disease, especially bubonic plague.
a verb: plauged, plaguing.
　　　To harass, pester, or annoy

The Hour Of Great Tribulation

On October 13, 1989 in message # 412 Our Lady told Fr. Gobbi in locution: "The times of the decisive battle have come. The hour of great tribulation has now descended upon the world, because the angels of the Lord are being sent, with their plagues, to chastise the earth...

Fire From Heaven

"This is the time when the Lord our God is being continually and publicly offended by sins of the flesh. Holy Scripture has already warned you that those who sin by means of the flesh find their just punishment in that same flesh. And so the time has come when *the Angel of the first plague* is passing over the world, that it might be chastised according to the will of God.

"*The Angel of the first plague* cuts -- into the flesh of those who have allowed themselves to be signed with the mark of the monster on the forehead and on the hand and have adored his image -- with *a painful and malignant wound,* which causes those who have been stricken by it to cry out in desperation. This wound represents the physical pain which strikes the body by means of grave and incurable maladies. The painful and malignant wound is a plague for all humanity, today so perverted, which has built up an atheistic and materialistic civilization and has made the quest for pleasure the supreme aim of human life. Some of my poor children have been stricken by it because of their sins of impurity and their disordered morals and they carry within their own selves the weight of the evil they have done. Others, on the other hand, have been stricken, even though they are good and innocent; and so their suffering serves for the salvation of the many wicked, in virtue of the solidarity which unites you all.

"The first plague is that of malignant tumors and every kind of cancer, against which science can do nothing notwithstanding its progress in every field, maladies which spread more and more and strike the human body, devastating it with most painful and malignant wounds. Beloved children, think of the spread of these incurable maladies, throughout every part of the world, and of the millions of deaths which they are bringing about.

"The first plague is the new malady of AIDS, which strikes above all my poor children who are victims of drugs, of vices and of impure sins against nature....."[2]

Michael H. Brown in *The Bridge To Heaven*, 1993 reports that Maria Esperanza told him: "Before AIDS appeared Our Lady told me, pray, pray, pray, because an illness is going to be discovered, and there won't be a cure at the beginning, but after they will find a way so that the virus will be contained, enclosed in a way that won't harm. It will be a terrible sickness, and it will come through sex.

"That is because people are abusing passions. They have no control. And now [Mary] told me another sickness will come, that the person will only last for a month. How can you avoid this? ...

"There are rare sicknesses emerging that have not been seen before. Every day there is a new virus...."[31]

Fire From Heaven

Results Of The Plague Of AIDS

According to a Washington Post article, Wednesday, July 5, 2000 a U.N. epidemiologist predicted in 1991 that by the end of the decade, 9 million people in sub-Saharan Africa would carry the HIV virus, which causes AIDS. Current figures are 2 and ½ times that high. Unless large-scale anti-HIV/AIDS campaign is launched, experts fear that 50 million people worldwide could be living with HIV by 2005. Infection rates of adults in Africa are for example, 5.06% in Nigeria, i.e., 2.7 million infected people, 35.8% in Botswana, i.e., 290,000 infected people and in neighboring South Africa, 19.94% or 4.2 million infected people. The adult population along the Mediterranean coast of Africa i.e., Morocco, Algeria, Libya, Egypt is 0 to 0.1%. In the United States the rate for adults is 0.61% and in Brazil it is 0.57%. AIDS has created 13.2 million orphans, 12.1 million in sub-Saharan Africa and 1.1 million in the rest of the world. UNAIDS estimates that by 2010 there may be 42 million orphans.

HIV/AIDS worldwide affects 34.3 million living people, 15.7% women, 17.3 % men, and 1.3% children under 15. Since the beginning of this pandemic, 11.5 million people have died in sub-Saharan Africa and 7.3 million elsewhere.

AIDS last year surpassed all other causes of death in Africa. 5,500 people die of AIDS in sub-Saharan Africa every day. This figure is expected to climb to 13,000 daily by the year 2010.

In populations with high HIV infection rates, AIDS deaths will shrink the proportion of women older than their early 20's and men older than their early 30's.

An internal study June 1992 at the World Bank by this bank's population and human resources department found: "If the only effect of the AIDS epidemic were to reduce the population growth rate, it would increase the growth rate of per capita income in any plausible economic model." The World Bank report noted that is exactly what happened in the 14th century with the bubonic plague. South African economist Alan Whiteside said: "Only the World Bank would put that on paper."

New infections with HIV is estimated at 15,000 a day.

Sandra Thurman, director of the White House Office of National AIDS Policy stated: "We are at the beginning of a pandemic... We certainly know that before we are able to stop this pandemic we'll have hundreds of millions of people infected and dead, and that's the best case scenario."

Diseases and Pestilence

On October 13, 1997 Our Heavenly Mother said to Denise Curtin and Joseph DellaPuca: "Major earthquakes, a famine, and world-wide pestilence will cause my children to fall to their knees and ask for forgiveness of God. You shall now see the sins of your souls in the judgment of our Lord and Savior, Jesus Christ...." [4]

Fire From Heaven

The Scourge Of Epidemics, Hunger And Of Fire

At Fatima, on March 15, 1993, in message # 489, Fr. Gobbi received the inner locution from Our Blessed Mother: *"Humanity* will know the bloody hour of its chastisement: it will be stricken with the scourge of epidemics, of hunger and of fire; much blood will be spilt upon your roads; war will spread everywhere, bringing down upon the world incommensurable devastation.

"You, my poor children, must all bear the weight of great sufferings and of unspeakable sorrows, so that the great miracle of divine justice and mercy may manifest itself to all."[2]

Pope Leo XIII And A Fatal Plague

The Masons hold all religions to be alike, and the Catholic religion as equal to other religions. They have plotted the destruction of the papacy, holding that the sacred power of the Pontiffs must be abolished, and the Pontificate must be utterly destroyed. Pope Leo XIII calls this a "fatal plague."[41]

Despair Is The Final Plague Of Satan

On October 7, 1997 the Lord gave Joanne Kriva the message: "Now in my name say to my dearly beloved children: Satan is reaching the summit of his power that I permit for this time. All must be purged and made clean; therefore, I ask all you, my faithful ones, to understand that severe and unprecedented suffering is coming to the earth. It is by suffering that you are made clean to enter into salvation. You are cleansed and purified as is all of nature so that no evil may find a dwelling place in the new heavens and the new earth. The slate will be wiped clean and you will enter into the Era of the New Eden. Forsake no effort to make yourself worthy to enter in where all shall be peace. Accept any suffering that comes to you for in the time of the eclipse of the Church, the sacraments of purification will be taken from you and you will be helpless and at the mercy of godless men. Prayer will be your only refuge, therefore, I beseech you to pray unceasingly. Do not grow weary of praying; it is your weapon against the enemy, it is your protection in the face of evil, and it will keep you strong in faith and hope for the final triumph.

Do not despair for there will be despair everywhere -- this is the final plague of Satan, for those who have turned from me have no hope. Thus it will be. Listen for my words given to my faithful messengers for this time for they will lead you through the dark and desperate times that now bring this age of evil to an end.

That is all I wish to say for this day. Thank you my little one for your faithfulness to my will for you. That is all.[9]

The Chastisement Is Already Upon The World.

On September 23, 1994 St. Joseph said to Janie Garza: "My little one, the chastisement is already upon the

Fire From Heaven

world. You can see its manifestation in the sinfulness
of the world, the great apostasy, the schism that is destroying many priests and consecrated souls, the violence in the family, the bloody massacre of the innocent
infants, the increase in false prophets that are misleading many, the destruction of the youth through drug
abuse and unhealthy relationships, the deadly plague,
the pestilence that sweeps throughout the world taking
the lives of many, the increase in homosexuality, the broken marriages that end in divorce, the destruction in
natural disasters, the corrupted world leaders who are
bringing destruction upon their countries, and the blasphemies against God by those who hate God. These are
some of the signs of the chastisement and the only
refuge is the refuge that you will find in the Immaculate Heart of Mary." [8]

Messages To Denise Curtin And Joseph DellaPuca
About Chastisements

On August 13, 1996 our heavenly mother in a message
to Denise Curtin and Joseph DellaPuca said: "My children, your sins are scorching the Earth with evil, as the
lifeblood of your faith is being tested. Your chastisements on the land will force people to move to new
lands. Your current farms are suffering droughts and
floods as never witnessed before. Soon growing food
will be difficult and it will be desperately needed. My
children, you have been turned into evil waters that are
leading you away from my Son, Jesus Christ.

My children, you will soon perish in the hands of the Evil One. I keep sending you many messages to awaken the spirit., graces that will lead you to Eternal Salvation." [4]

On August 13, 1997 Mary in a message to Denise Curtin and Joseph DellaPuca said: "You will soon see cataclysmic events that will never be understood by mankind, and disruptions of every nation on Earth. Can you not see the warnings that already befell the Earth? Why are my children's hearts so hardened and their souls so cold? Because they are being deceived by the Evil One.

Pray, pray, pray, my children, the Rosary daily. Recite the Divine Mercy, in reverence to my Son and receive His Body, Blood, Soul and divinity each day to nourish your souls.

Please, my children, have a deep conviction of love and a total confidence in me, your heavenly mother." [4]

On April 15, 1996 our heavenly mother in a message to Denise Curtin and Joseph DellaPuca said: "As I have foretold you, the natural disasters which you are witnessing will increase in number, day after day after day, and they shall come to know that these are events from our Father in Heaven." [4]

On September 3, 1998 our heavenly mother in a message to Denise Curtin and Joseph DellaPuca said: "My dearest little children, as I speak to you the world is on the brink of economic crisis. I have foretold you this

Fire From Heaven

and it shall come to being. It is here that the Antichrist shall make himself known. You must be prepared, my dearest little children, for the times of which I have spoken to you privately are now about to be unveiled to all my children of the world. Look at the natural disasters that have happened to your country, and yet my children still have remained blinded by the ways that they have chosen to live. Disasters will increase in intensity, lives will be taken. Why have my children not listened to my pleas. Why have my children turned against their God? [4]

Chastisements Because Of The Sin Of Abortion

Joanne Kriva on July 22, 1992 received a message from the Lord God: "Now for today say in My name: I wish to speak to the inhabitants of the American states. This I say to you: Unless this people once again turn back to Me, return to prayer, return to belief and faith, this mighty nation will crumble and fall never to rise from the ashes. I warn this people that death and violence will overtake them. I warn them that the voices of their children, stilled before their births, cry out for justice before the throne of justice... For this massacre of the innocents just retribution is about to be exacted from this people who flaunt My law in the dung heap of carnal desires and unrestrained passions. The proud land grovels in the ashes of its lost heritage. Its voice is but a whisper in the affairs of nations. So I decree. So shall it be. Thus say I, the Lord God." [10]

38

Joanne Kriva on July 20, 1993 received a message from the Lord God: "I speak to you the message of the First Trumpet... I say and proclaim that truly <u>one-third of creation shall perish.</u> Already this judgment has begun. Humans perish in greater and greater numbers from <u>plagues, incurable disease, war, starvation, torture at the hands of despotic rulers, and self-immolation. That abomination of abominations -- the holocaust of the unborn generation -- claims this number (1/3) of your future.</u> Everywhere does mankind fall in greater and greater numbers, and so it shall continue until the fulfillment of the prophecy is accomplished...."[10]

Financial Chastisement

Appearing as Our Lady of Guadalupe on March 12, 1995, Our Lady said to Maureen Sweeney-Kyle: "Dear children, today I invite you to recognize the season of tribulation that is upon you. As in any season there are signs. <u>Recognize the cataclysmic natural events as from God. These occur in order to return souls to God, Who is King of Heaven and Earth. In the next season of tribulation you will find money systems failing and collapsing. This will occur as a means of stripping people from the idol of money. The next</u> season I reveal to you my dear daughter, my dear people, is the apostasy, which will occur in the Church. It will be as a winnowing fan separating the wheat from the chaff, and will take place mainly in the <u>West. Then the season of the Antichrist. He will be in the world and hearts.</u> Dear children, I reveal these things to you now, so that as these events unfold, you will recognize God's Hand in your midst. Just as in nature, the seasons will overlap one another. There will be no clear line of demarcation, but you will recognize them through Holy Love. I am blessing you now."[38]

On December 24, 1996 at 6:00 p.m., Christmas Eve, Mary told Sadie Jaramillo: "Catastrophic events await this United States, events that will bring many to their knees in fear... The horsemen of the Apocalypse are sent forth in this time of plagues, famine, war and strife, and will bear the justice of God. For this sinful nation will be brought low to its knees. This nation will know captivity and economic collapse. Only those who have entered into the Ark of My Immaculate Heart, will know peace, protection and guidance.

"The last grain of sand has gone through the hourglass, and the time of all times to accomplish The Triumph of My Immaculate Heart and The Eucharistic Reign of Christ is here."[6]

Sadie Jaramillo received a message from Jesus on November 8, 1996 –8:10 A.M. which was interrupted and continued on November 9, 1996 at 4:30 A.M.

On November 8, 1996 –8:10 A.M. Jesus said to Sadie Jaramillo: "The hold of the enemy is such that this world cannot be touched but by a supernatural act of God. The world closes its eyes and ears of their seared-by-sin consciences, so that they elect a man to rule who has continued to ignore the very basis for which this nation, once under God, became a beacon of light and hope. For God's very hand used good men, holy men, to implement His laws of love and justice. That was long ago and the insatiable hunger for power, money, and man's own self-indulging vices have corrupted this society.

"What happens now is prophecy fulfilled. The pockets of many now full will become empty The floor of the financial market will crash and the repercussions will resound worldwide. The despair of many will cause their own self-destruction. The world has not seen anything like this to be. Why, do you have eyes, but yet are blind to the truth? Why do you have ears and fail to hear the truth?"

On Tuesday, November 4th, 1996, election day Jesus instructed Sadie Jaramillo to write the message: "Once again this nation has looked to a man (Clinton) for the answers to their financial woes. Now I tell you to pray, child, for the financial crisis that comes quickly to man will surpass that of anything seen up to now. Pray for the children of God."

(Sadie said: The infused understanding; there will come a crash of the stock market so severe many people will despair to the point of suicide. I am given the understanding that this crash will far surpass anything that has ever happened. Our Lord asks me to pray that His justice pass swiftly over the children of God, the believers.)

41

Fire From Heaven

Jesus said: "For Justice will swiftly come! And for My Church once (continued November 9, 1996 at 4:30 A. M.) resplendent, (it) is now stained and spotted and full of wrinkles. This is not the Church I am coming back for! The Church of My Heart will be cleansed and purified. It will be holy and one, brilliant like the sun!"

"Now the thunder of God's justice will resound. Nature will mirror the fury of God's anger and many will be brought to their knees. Great confusion and chaos will abound. This nation will soon be under martial law and many even now see the signs.

"The persecution of ethnic groups will increase, but I have My own in the eye of the storm and it will not overtake you!....

"But you, oh enemies of God!, tremble, for God will seek you out and destroy you! Repent before it is too late! Great mercy have I shown you for justice to be postponed so many times, but no longer will this be. Mercy will be fulfilled and justice will reign!" [6]

Prizes and Possessions Disappear In An Instant

Jesus told Sadie Jaramillo on January 5, 1997 at 7:00 p. m.: "My Father's Will for your life will be brought about because of your fidelity and perseverance. For what you consider your treasure, is what you should feel.

"But contrary is true, and many now face the trial of seeing their prizes and possessions disappear in an instant. It will not stand as their idols any longer, not their homes, nor their jobs, nor their money, nor their pleasure idols, nor their perverted ideas.

"None of it will stand in the fury of My Justice nor in the fury of the control from the one who opposes Me, that he will show to those who live through his reign.

"I am asking you to prepare by fasting and prayer, for My Divine Intervention will prevail over My vineyard, My harvest, My shepherd, My flock....

"I do not exist in your measure of time, but I do say, your time is now. Prepare, for nothing will be the same. What exists today will cease to exist and control, total and final will be in force."[6]

Chapter 3

Satan Reigns In The Highest Places in the Church and the World

Pope Leo XIII is reported to have had an ecstasy on October 13, 1884, in which he heard Satan ask God for permission to try to destroy the Church and heard God grant to Satan 100 years to try to accomplish this.

On November 5, 1983, Mirjana, a visionary at Medjugorje, Yugoslavia, confided to Fr. Tomislav Vlasic revelations received prior to December 26, 1982. He in turn on December 16, 1983 confided them in a letter to Pope John Paul II: "I am reporting here what Mirjana told me in a conversation of November 5, 1983. I summarized the essentials of her account, without literal quotation."

Father Vlasic said that the Blessed Virgin gave Mirjana the following message in substance, "Excuse me for this, but you must realize that Satan exists. One day he appeared before the throne of God and asked permission to submit the Church to a period of trial. God

44

gave him permission to try the Church for one century. This century is under the power of the Devil, but when the secrets confided to you come to pass, his power will be destroyed. Even now he is beginning to lose his power and has become aggressive. He is destroying marriages, creating division among priests and is responsible for obsessions and murder. You must protect yourselves against these things through fasting and prayer, especially community prayer. Carry blessed objects with you. Put them in your house, and restore the use of holy water."

The Red Dragon, Freemasonry and Islam

On June 14, 1998 Mary said to Sadie Jaramillo: " I tell you again, the Mercy will descend amidst fire and turmoil! The symbols shown to you on your trip indicate the red dragon will rear its ugly head and align itself with those of the race of the Orient! So too will the Freemasons make their move to accomplish their one-world order. Islam is a sleeping giant ready to awaken. Thus for many in the coming days; they will pray for death, for these have not prepared for this battle of all battles! The preparations are spiritual ones and many have spent precious time in only the cares of the world. They will find, as with the princes of the Church, that there is a God. A God of Love who only asked for their heart! All that has been foretold to you and many others is on the point of being fulfilled. Know that I your Mother and the Mother of God, ask now from you the total focus of your heart on My Son Jesus, for this apos-

tasy which is eclipsing the Church will soon bring
darkness and the fulfillment of Daniel's prophecy.
(Daniel Chapter 12). The one who has prepared snares
and traps for humanity prepares for his unveiling to the
world. Peace, security and wealth, he will promise, order
to a world filled with disorder! The message you proclaim is to awaken the dead souls of my children to the
truth...." [3]

Satan Was The Uncontested Dominator Of The Events Of The 20th Century

At Fatima on May, 13, 1990, the Anniversary of the
First Apparition, in message # 425 Our Blessed Mother
told Fr. Gobbi, Marian Movement of Priests, in locution:
"... The very painful events which followed have,
through their occurrence, given complete fulfillment
to the words of my prophecy....

"Satan has been the uncontested dominator of the
events of this century of yours, bringing all humanity
to the rejection of God and of his law of love, spreading
far and wide division and hatred, immorality and
wickedness and legitimating everywhere divorce,
abortion, obscenity, homosexuality and recourse to
any and all means of obstructing life.

"Now you are beginning the last decade of this century of yours.

"*I am coming down from heaven,* so that the final secrets may be revealed to you and that I may be able thus to prepare you for what, as of now, you must live through, for the purification of the earth.

"My third secret, which I revealed here to three little children to whom I appeared and which up to the present has not yet been revealed to you, will be made manifest to all by the very occurrence of the events.

"The Church will know the hour of its greatest apostasy. The man of iniquity will penetrate into its interior and will sit in the very Temple of God, while the little remnant which will remain faithful will be subjected to the greatest trials and persecutions.

"Humanity will live through the moment of its great chastisement and thus will be made ready to receive the Lord Jesus who will return to you in glory.

"For this reason, *especially today, I am coming down again from heaven:* through my numerous apparitions; through the messages which I give; and through this extraordinary Work of my Marian Movement of Priests, to prepare you to live through the events which are even now in the process of being fulfilled, in order to lead you by the hand to walk along the most difficult and painful segment of this your second advent, and to prepare the minds and the hearts of all to receive Jesus at the closely approaching moment of his glorious return." [2]

Fire From Heaven

On May 13, 1993 Our Lady told Father Gobbi, in message #495: "Satan has succeeded in entering into the Church, the new Israel of God. He has entered with the smoke of error and sin, of the loss of faith and apostasy, of compromise with the world and the search for pleasure. During these years, he has succeeded in leading astray bishops and priests, religious and faithful.

"The forces of Masonry have entered into the Church, in a subtle and hidden way, and have set up their stronghold in the very place where the Vicar of my Son Jesus lives and works...."[2]

On May 13, 1994 Our Lady told Father Gobbi, at Fatima, in message #520, *An Apocalyptic Message:* "... It is within your time that the fulfillment of the message is taking place, the message which I have given you at Fatima and against which my Adversary has thrown himself in fury, but which will now appear in all its extraordinary importance for the Church and for all humanity.

> It is an apocalyptic message.
> It has regard to the end times.
> It announces and prepares for the return of my
> Son Jesus in glory....

"Upon this Church, darkened and wounded, stricken and betrayed, I am causing the rays of love and light from my Immaculate Heart to come down. When there will have entered into her the man of iniquity who will bring to fulfillment the abomination of desolation which will reach its climax in the horrible sacrilege, as the great apostasy will have spread everywhere, then my Immaculate Heart will gather together the little faithful remnant which, in suffering, in prayer and in hope, will await the return of my son Jesus in glory...

"Mine is an apocalyptic message, because you are in the heart of that which has been announced to you in the last and so very important book of Sacred Scripture.

"I entrust to the angels of light of my Immaculate Heart the task of bringing you to an understanding of these events, now that I have opened the sealed Book for you." [2]

At La Salette, on September 19, 1846, in an apparition approved by the church, Melanie was told by Our Blessed Mother: "Rome will lose the faith and become the seat of the Antichrist.... The Church will be in eclipse.... Pagan Rome will disappear." [7]

Marie-Julie Jahenny, born February 12, 1850, died 1941, a stigmatist from La Fraudais near Blain in Brittany. During her ecstasy of the 3rd of June 1880, Our Lord describes how Lucifer will proceed. He will address priests: "You will dress in a large red cloak... We will give you a piece of bread and a few drops of water. You can do with everything that you did when you belonged to Christ... ("But," says Our Lord, "they do not

Fire From Heaven

add: *Consecration* and *Communion"*).

And hell had added: "We will permit you to say it in all houses and even under the firmament." [42]

Marie-Julie saw that "there will not remain any vestige of the Holy Sacrifice, no apparent trace of faith. *Confusion* will be everywhere."

'The preceding 1st of June: "All the works approved by the infallible Church will cease to exist as they are today for a time. In this sorrowful annihilation, brilliant signs will by manifested on earth. If, because of the wickedness of men Holy Church will be in darkness, the Lord will also send darkness that will stop the wicked in their search of wickedness..." [42]

At Akita Japan, on September 15, 1987, the Feast of Our Lady of Sorrows, Fr. Gobbi, received the interior locution from Our Blessed Mother: "A chastisement worse than the flood is about to come upon this poor and perverted humanity. Fire will descend from heaven and this will be the sign that the justice of God has as of now fixed the hour of his great manifestation. I am weeping because the Church is continuing along the road of division, of loss of the true faith, of apostasy and of errors which are being spread more and more without anyone offering opposition to them. Even now, that which I predicted at Fatima and that which I have revealed here in the third message confided to a little daughter of mine is in the process of being accomplished. And so, even for the church the moment of it's great trial has come, because the man of iniquity will establish himself within it and the abomination of desolation will enter into the holy temple of God." [2]

In message # 485, on December 31, 1992, The End of the Times, Our Lady told Fr. Gobbi in locution: "I have announced to you many times that the end of the times and the coming of Jesus in Glory is very near. Now I want to help you understand the signs described in the Holy Scriptures, which indicate that his glorious return is close.

"These signs are clearly indicated in the Gospels, in the letters of Saint Peter and Saint Paul, and they are becoming a reality during these years:
- "The first sign is the spread of errors, which lead to the loss of faith and to apostasy...
- "The second sign is the outbreak of wars and fratricidal struggles, which lead to the prevalence of violence and hatred and a general slackening off of charity, while natural catastrophes, such as epidemics, famines, flood and earthquakes, become more and more frequent....
- "The third sign is the bloody persecution of those who remain faithful to Jesus and his Gospel and who stand fast in the true faith. Throughout this all, the Gospel will be preached in every part of the world....
- "The fourth sign is the horrible sacrilege, perpe-

Fire From Heaven

trated by him who sets himself against Christ,
that is, the Antichrist. He will enter into the holy
temple of God and will sit on his throne, and have
himself adored as God.

"This one will oppose and exalt himself against everything that men adore and call God. The lawless one
will come by the power of Satan, with all the force of
false miracles and pretended wonders. He will make use
of every kind of wicked deception, in order to work
harm.' (2 Thes 2,4.9)

"One day, you will see in the holy place he who com-
mits *the horrible sacrilege.* The prophet Daniel spoke of
this. Let the reader seek to understand.' (Mt 24,15)

"Beloved children, in order to understand in what
this *horrible sacrilege* consists, read what has been
predicted by the prophet Daniel: 'Go, Daniel; these
words are to remain secret and sealed until the end time.
Many will be cleansed, made white and upright, but the
wicked will persist in doing wrong. Not one of the
wicked will understand these things, but the wise will
comprehend.

"Now, from the moment that the daily sacrifice is
abolished and the horrible abomination is set up,
there shall be one thousand two hundred and ninety
days. Blessed is he who waits with patience and at-
tains one thousand three hundred and thirty-five
days.' (Dn 12,9-12)

52

"The Holy Mass is the daily sacrifice, the pure oblation which is offered to the Lord everywhere, from the rising of the sun to its going down.

"The sacrifice of the Mass renews that which was accomplished by Jesus on Calvary. By accepting the protestant doctrine, people will hold that the Mass is not a sacrifice but only a sacred meal, that is to say, a remembrance of that which Jesus did at his last supper. And thus, the celebration of Holy Mass will be suppressed. In this abolition of the daily sacrifice consists *the horrible sacrilege* accomplished by the Antichrist, which will last about three and a half years, namely, one thousand two hundred and ninety days.

- "The fifth sign *consists in extraordinary phenomena,* which occur in the skies. The sun will be darkened and the moon will not give its light; and the stars will fall from the sky; and the powers of the heavens will be shaken.' (Mt 24,29)
....

"My beloved ones and children consecrated to my Immaculate Heart, I have wanted to teach you about these signs, which Jesus has pointed out to you in his Gospel, in order to prepare you for the end of times, because these are about to take place in your days...."[2]

At Fatima, on March 15, 1993, in message # 489, Fr. Gobbi received the inner locution from Our Blessed Mother: "... *I have wanted you here,* to tell you that you must now all enter right away into the safe refuge of my Immaculate Heart. Just as Noah, in the name of the Lord,

53

called into the ark those who were to be saved from the flood, so now must you, my littlest child, in the name of your heavenly Mother, call into the refuge of my Immaculate Heart those who must be protected, defended and saved from the great trial which has now come for the Church and for all humanity.

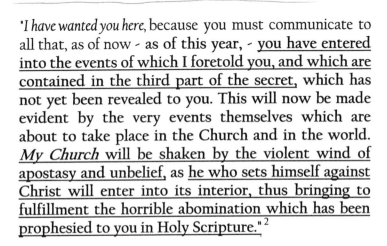

'*I have wanted you here*, because you must communicate to all that, as of now - as of this year, - you have entered into the events of which I foretold you, and which are contained in the third part of the secret, which has not yet been revealed to you. This will now be made evident by the very events themselves which are about to take place in the Church and in the world. *My Church* will be shaken by the violent wind of apostasy and unbelief, as he who sets himself against Christ will enter into its interior, thus bringing to fulfillment the horrible abomination which has been prophesied to you in Holy Scripture."[2]

The Loss Of The Faith Is Apostasy

Fr. Gobbi, in the locution of June 13, 1989 from Our Blessed Mother, was given the message: "Thus errors are spread in every part of the Catholic Church itself. Because of the spread of these errors, many are moving away from the true faith, bringing to fulfillment the prophecy which was given to you by me at Fatima: 'The times will come when many will lose the true faith.' The loss of the faith is apostasy."[2]

Chapter 4

Apostasy in the Church

In message #362, September 15, 1987, Akita (Japan), Our Blessed Mother told Father Gobbi, "I am weeping because the Church is continuing along the road of division, of loss of the true faith, of apostasy and of errors which are being spread more and more without anyone offering opposition to them...".[2]

In message # 486, January 1, 1993, *The Time of the Great Trial,* Our Blessed Mother told Father Gobbi: "The great trial has come for the Church, so violated by evil spirits, so divided in its unity, so darkened in its holiness. See how error has flooded throughout it, error which leads to the loss of the true faith. Apostasy is spreading everywhere."[2]

On December 17, 1993 St. Joseph said to Janie Garza: "My little one, you have a generous heart, and your heart is full of love for priests. Pray for all priests, for these are hard times for the Church. The Church is in the midst of great turmoil. Many priests are struggling with their faith. Priests in great numbers are separating themselves from the Vicar on earth. There is much division in the Church among the priests and religious.

"Many priests are not living their priestly vows of poverty, chastity, and obedience. Many priests have separated from God and have lost reverence and love for the Eucharist. <u>The apostasy is growing strong within the Church.</u> Holy priests suffer much because of all the turmoil and <u>the apostasy in today's Church.</u>

"<u>Many priests have stopped practicing the sacrament of Reconciliation.</u> Their souls are stained and dark with sinfulness. The world is in need of holy priests that will help guide their people back to God. Many priests alienate themselves from God due to their lack of commitment to follow the true doctrine of the Church. They choose to be a part of the world instead of being holy and belonging to God's Kingdom.

"<u>Many priests are not feeding the flock entrusted to them,</u> and the flock leaves their shepherd, looking elsewhere to be fed. <u>Many priests have been responsible for their flock leaving the Catholic faith.</u> The Church is in need of much prayer.

"My little one, offer up all your sufferings and prayers for the purification of the Church. Pray unceasingly for all priests. Invite others to pray and fast for the Church. Pray and ask the intercession of St. Michael for the protection of the Church. Share this message, for <u>the Church is in need of purification and conversion.</u> Many priests live in darkness and much prayer is needed for enlightenment of the Holy Spirit. Now, my little one, you know what you must do to help the priests...." [8]

On October 13, 1996 Our Heavenly Mother said to Denise Curtin and Joseph DellaPuca: "My dear, dear children, can you see, my little ones, how the natural disasters have been increased all over the world, as well as wars and diseases? There is much apostasy in my Church, the very Church my Son gave to all His children. Please pray for my beloved Church and priests. I love them so. Live the Gospel and live according to the teachings of my Church. Your prayers, fasts, vigils, and sacrifices will help things according to Heaven's plan." [4]

On July 9, 1998 Mary said to Denise Curtin and Joseph DellaPuca: "At Fatima, I have foretold to you when the True Faith would be lost. These are the times. And as my Adversary deceives many, the darkness will grow deeper and deeper, and sin will cover everything, but you must clothe yourselves in divine grace.

"Satan will seduce you by pride, doubt, unbelief and discouragement, resulting in much confusion. Avoid everything that disturbs the spirit and focus on the Cross, the sign of your salvation....

"Even in my Son's Church, the crisis has become more acute as many of my beloved priests do not heed my voice. They scatter the flock along the roads of insecurity and division, of error and apostasy." [4]

Apostasy Leads To Schism

On January 27, 1995 St. Joseph said to Janie Garza: "I, St. Joseph, wish to invite all families to pray everyday for the conversion of the world. **Through your prayers you will stamp out much of the evilness that exists in the world.** Learn to forgive your loved ones and love those who wound you the most.

"The world is in need of much prayer and love. **Pray especially for <u>the apostasy and schism that is growing strong within the Church and that is destroying and dividing the Church of God.</u>**" [8]

On September 23, 1994 St. Joseph said to Janie Garza: "My little one, <u>the chastisement is already upon the world.</u> **You can see its manifestation in the sinfulness of the world, <u>the great apostasy, the schism that is destroying many priests and consecrated souls,</u> the** violence in the family, the bloody massacre of the innocent infants, **the increase in false prophets that are misleading many,** the destruction of the youth through drug abuse and unhealthy relationships, the deadly plague, the pestilence that sweeps throughout the world taking the lives of many, the increase in homosexuality, the broken marriages that end in divorce, the destruction in natural disasters, the corrupted world leaders who are bringing destruction upon their countries, and the blasphemies against God by those who hate God. <u>These are some of the signs of the chastisement and the only refuge is the refuge that you will find in the Immaculate Heart of Mary.</u>" [8]

On July 9, 1997 Joanne Kriva was told by Our Lord in locution: In my name speak these words to my people. Courage, my beloved children. As you enter this final hour of the tribulation, I call you to great courage and perseverance. The furies of hell roam freely upon the earth and cause great suffering and anguish throughout the earth. The Church is divided; my shepherds are divided; there is widespread apostasy, heresy, and schisms that are manifest in the Church throughout the world. There is no peace in the world, but least of all in the hearts of those who reject my Word and the Father's plan of salvation.

"Hear me well, my children, the world and my Church have become infected sores -- infected with hatred; lusts for power, riches, the perversions of the flesh; paganism and Satan worship; loss of faith, hope, and charity; and most of all a failure to love as I have commanded you to love...." [9]

Apostasy Leads to A False Pope [Antipope] and Schism

On May 31, 1996 the Lord God said to Joanne Kriva: "...What grave evil is afoot within My Church in this time.

"Pray for the Church, my faithful ones. Pray for the shepherds. They must be faithful guardians of my truth and courageous leaders of my flock. Let them follow the example of my Pope John Paul II, who fearlessly defends

the faith before the whole world. He is a shining example of priestly holiness. Follow him, I say to you, for he is
your 'papa', the father of the Church on earth. Soon
you will have no 'papa'. His light will be extinguished
and **the Church will be without Peter**. Thus say I the
Lord God. That is all." [9]

Sadie Jaramillo was told on September 8, 1997 by
Mary: "... I have asked you specifically to pray for the
Princes of the Church, for soon they will stand one
against another openly. Whereas now, the division
occurs where the heart of that shepherd is closed to
the Vicar of Christ.... Pray for my Son's Vicar, for soon
he will fall under the oppositions force,..." [6]

Message To Sadie Jaramillo. January 30, 1998, 7:00 a.
m. (S.J., after morning prayer, I hear Our Lady, I test,
and she asks me to take up my pen and paper to
write. During the Rosary at the Thursday night cenacle,
I was shown the following visions:

I was shown a procession of Cardinals. At the head
was one dressed in pontifical garb, but he was all in
black. I could see a very ornate red chair that was
empty. This man dressed as a Pope, but in black, was
walking toward the empty chair.

I was then shown the graph that indicates the activity of
the stock market. I saw it at a certain point, then the
line began to go down until it was no longer visible. I
then saw the Stock Exchange, and their bodies were lying on the floor.

Then I was shown an image of Our Lady embracing the Holy Father, John Paul II, as he seemed to be resting his head on her shoulder. Our Lady was dressed in a white gown and she wore a very ornate crown on her head.)....

You were shown he, who opposes my True Vicar, will take this seat left empty when the Pope of my Heart is forced to flee. I wear a crown, for he (John Paul II) will crown me with the title Co-Redemptrix, Media-trix, Advocate of all graces!

The warning of God's Love will be upon you and the whole world! In the crucible of Truth and His Love the lost will be found; the lukewarm will be fanned into flame; the fervent will rise to the degree of the heroics needed for the Truth of the Church to flourish once again!

This sign of my beloved daughter's healing is a sign for my remnant! You will see greater than this in days ahead!

(S. J., I had been praising God, Jesus and Our Lady for Mother Angelica's physical healing!)

Mary: There is no turning back the events even now in progress. This nation will be brought to its knees. See the leader of your country and how his moral behavior is condoned and accepted! His unwillingness to end the scourge of the slaughter of the innocents brings now the wrath of God to him and to this nation!..."[6]

God our Father gives me the following message to

Fire From Heaven

Sadie Jaramillo on January 8, 1999, 7:30 a.m.: "I AM the Father of Love (Jesus). My Son and My Spirit give testimony to ME. I WAS, I AM, I WILL ALWAYS BE, and Praises are given to the Trinity!

My daughter,... However, as you look all around my creation, humanity has become pagan again and fallen to levels of degradation never before known! I hear the cries of the faithful and long to gather you all in my arms...

So now tell My children:

"You will pass through the Trial of Fire; the Fire of My Love; the Fire of My Justice; the Fire of My Purification!

- The Fire of My Love is your illumination of conscience (the Warning)!
- The Fire of My Justice will see fire consume the idols of my children.
- The Fire of My Purification is the Fire that will descend from the heavens to purify and cleanse the earth to prepare for the Time of Peace! It will cover the world with blackness, but those who believe will be prepared (the 3 Days of Darkness)!"

Thus, Mankind will be purified! The Church that extends My Life of Grace will be purified! The world will be purified, cleansed from the stench of sin and bloodshed of the innocents!

Prayer has been your power and my weakness: for many

who have tired and fallen away; for many who have dis-
believed; for many who have tried to destroy (projects,
discredit authentic apparitions etc.)! Now will their
moment of decision come! The hour of decision is
come!...

You have prayed that My Justice pass quickly over
My people, so I have extended The Time of Mercy
and shortened the Time of My Wrath!

No longer will my children be left without shepherds to
lead (them); no longer will the Church block the flow of
grace; no longer will they betray My Son! The Vicar of
My Son (Pope John Paul II) will give his immolation
with many more to follow!...."[3]

On October 13, 1997 Our Heavenly Mother said to
Denise Curtin and Joseph DellaPuca: "Pray, Pray, Pray,
my beloved children for yourselves, and your beloved
ones. Pray for my beloved Pope, in the battle for my
Son's Church. Pray for his continued health and
strength against the schisms that continue in the
House of God. Pray for my beloved priests, whom Satan is now attacking in order to obtain their souls, for
this will be a time of much confusion of mind, heart and
soul for my children." [4]

On June 13, 1998 Mary said to Denise Curtin and Joseph DellaPuca: "My motherly soul is pierced as my
Son's Church prostrates beneath the weight of the agony
of pain. My beloved Pope becomes more and more
and more ridiculed, mocked, isolated, --and abandoned. Many bishops and priests have taken the road

of unholiness. These wolves in sheep's clothing inflict slaughter upon the sheepfold of my Son, Jesus Christ." [4]

False Ecumenism And A One World Religion

On September 13, 1992 Josyp Terelya had an apparition from Our Blessed Mother in Marmora, Ontario. She told him that the final times are near. You are on the threshold of the day of judgment. She said, "Remember Satan has infiltrated the very womb of the Church, and is spreading the idea of his ecumenical Christianity, of his new interpretations of the faith. This has led to today's indifference and neglect in the religious education of children and the youth. There is a loss of awareness of the true Catholic faith. The dangerous ideology of a modern ecumenical Christianity is spreading. Satanists are attempting to destroy Holy Sunday, so that modern Christians cannot discern between good and evil. Sunday is the greatest day in the Church of Christ. Defend it against Satan."

Our Lady told Fr. Gobbi in message #406 *The Beast Like a Lamb*, on June 13, 1989: "....*The Church is truth*, because Jesus has entrusted to it alone the task of guarding, in its integrity, all the deposit of faith. He has entrusted it to the hierarchical Church, that is to say, to the Pope and to the bishops united with him. Ecclesiastical Masonry seeks to destroy this reality through false *ecumenism*, which leads to acceptance of all christian Churches, asserting that each one them has some part of the truth. It develops the plan of founding a universal ecumenical

Church, formed by the fusion of all the christian confessions, among which, the Catholic Church."[2]

Some Attempts To Form A United World Religion

1893 The World's Parliament of Religions: The idea of
a united religions came along with many other propos-
als.

1920 The International Congress of Religious Liberals
(known now as the IARF) called for a League of Religions: "Let us lay the foundation at least of a League of
Religions which shall be the counterpart and ally of the
political League of Nations"

Early 1920s Rudolph Otto Suggested the creation of
an Inter-Religious League as a parallel to the League
of Nations.

1930s - Dr. Norman Bentwich: In his book, *The Religious
Foundation of Internationalism,* he called for a League of
Religions and said the idea had a long history including
such proponents as Leibnitz and Rousseau.

World Congress of Faiths: Founded in the 1930s by
Sir Francis Younghusband who wrote that "a religious
basis is essential for the new world order"

1950s - World Parliament of Religions: Founded at
Presbyterian Labor Temple in New York to establish a
permanent group "to work with a permanent United

Nations to stop war and the causes of war and to extend the more abundant life among all peoples on earth."

1996 - San Francisco Summit Meeting for a Global United Religions Initiative: Proposal of a United Religions that would begin with the purpose of pursuing peace among religions for the sake of wholeness for the entire order of life. This United Religions had a target date of the year 2000 for its charter signing. Primarily from a paper presented by the Rev. Marcus Braybrooke in April 1996 at Westminster College, Oxford, at the International Interfaith Centre Conference

The United Religions Initiative (URI) started in San Francisco in the context of the United Nations 50th Anniversary Service at Grace Cathedral.

The United Religions Initiative was started by **The Rt. Rev. William E. Swing** [Episcopal Bishop, San Francisco] **issued an invitation to share a vision:** "that the religions of the world can come together in prayer, dialogue, and action for global good. And you are invited to share in the creation of United Religions, an organization to make that vision a reality.

In this vision, the United Religions (UR) can provide the world's religious traditions with a conspicuous, permanent gathering place. Here, through daily prayer, dialogue, and action, they may use their spiritual and moral resources for the good of all life on this earth.

THE PROPOSED FOUR BASIC PRINCIPLES

1) The United Religions as a symbol of unity in a world of disunity.

> In the face of seemingly intractable problems and bitter divisions, the UR will be a symbol that people of faith share a profound belief that all of life is interconnected and that unity is worth striving for.

2) The United Religions as a spiritual resource for a world in need.

Each religious tradition is blessed with rich spiritual gifts: prayer, meditation, pondering truth, moral teaching, and the basic desire to commune with the Eternal. These spiritual resources have the power to transform individual lives and to change the course of human history by leading us to discover the Ultimate and each other on deeper and deeper levels. The United Religions will be founded on sharing spiritual practice and finding in that practice the wisdom and inspiration to acknowledge and celebrate our mutual humanity and to discover compassionate solutions to issues of hard realities. Also, United Religions will help make these spiritual resources available, beyond individual faith communities, to the whole world. For this to happen, religions have to be willing to be quiet together, to wait together, to pray together, to repent together, and to honor the Ultimate in the midst of their immediate struggles.

3) United Religions as an informed voice in the midst of protracted injustices.

The United Religions will provide an assembly of workable size and representation where all participants can strive to discover a shared moral voice that sounds the depths of justice common to all religious traditions.

This emerging moral voice will help the world's religions be effectively pro-active in creating a more just world, and effectively reactive in responding to existing injustice.

4) The United Religions as a channel of effective action.

The primary action of the United Religions will be the prayer and dialogue of its regular assembly. From that assembly will come other action to help the UR move beyond being only a symbol of unity, to being an active agent of unity and global good....

The UR will establish and operate a "Value Bank" to provide people with an opportunity to invest their financial resources in an institution that furthers their spiritual values and promotes global good. This bank will invest in companies, nations, organizations, and projects that empower people and promote the values of the UR. An institute, connected with the bank, will conduct the research necessary to guide the bank's investments and make the fruits of that research available in a variety of formats (e.g., database, studies, reports).

As a result of this work by Bishop Swing, Episcopal Bishop of San Francisco and Mikhail Gorbachev at the Presidio in San Francisco among others [Mikhail Gorbachev, who the day after the release of the Third Secret of Fatima, at the Vatican along with Cardinal Sodano, gave a press conference without questions allowed] there has been developed:

The United Religions Initiative Charter

November 18, 1999

The United Religions Initiative (URI) is a growing global community dedicated to promoting enduring, daily interfaith cooperation, ending religiously motivated violence and creating cultures of peace, justice and healing for the Earth and all living beings.

Working on all continents and across continents, people from different religions, spiritual expressions and indigenous traditions are creating unprecedented levels of enduring global cooperation. In time, the URI may have the visibility and stature of the United Nations. Today, at its birth, people's hopes are rising with visions of a better world. It is a world where the values and teachings of the great wisdom traditions guide people's service, where people respect one another's beliefs, and where the resourcefulness and passion of ordinary people working together bring healing and a more hopeful future to the Earth community.

Since June of 1996 thousands of people have shared their visions and worked together to create the URI. It is a new kind of organization for global good rooted in shared spiritual values. People from many different cultures and perspectives have worked to create an organization that is inclusive, nonhierarchical and decentralized; one that enhances cooperation, autonomy and individual opportunity. This co-creative work offered by people of many cultures has produced a unique organization composed of self-organizing groups which operate locally and are connected globally.

The URI's Charter has been spoken into being by a myriad of voices from around the world. Its essential spirit, values and vision are expressed in the Preamble, Purpose and Principles. Taken together, they inspire, ground and guide all URI activity. The Charter includes:

Preamble – the call that inspires us to create the URI now and continue to create it everyday;

Purpose – the clear statement that draws us together in common cause;

Principles – the fundamental beliefs that guide our structure, decisions and content;
Organization design – the way of organizing that enhances cooperation and magnifies spirit;

Guidelines for Action – an action agenda to inspire and guide the worldwide URI community.

The global URI organization will be born in June 2000. "

In the plan for developing the URI there were three phases.

Phase III is completing the network:
1)   June 2005 — Full scale program in operation.
2)   June 2005 — Facilities completed and open to the world.
3)   June 2005 — Ongoing expansion of world wide interfaith network.

Chapter 5

Modernism, Freemasonry and the Great Apostasy

Modernism

Pope St. Pius X in 1907 condemned Modernism in the encyclical *Pascendi Dominici Gregis*. He defined Modernism as "the synthesis of all heresies." He told us that the trinity of parents responsible for the perversion known as modernism are: 1) Its religious ancestor is the Protestant Reformation; 2) Its philosophical parent is the Enlightenment; 3) Its political pedigree comes from the French Revolution. The Enlightenment produced rationalists who placed reason over faith.

He recognized Modernism as the most dangerous revolution the Church has ever had to face and that it was scourging her severely.

He stated that Modernism leads to **pantheism and atheism**. Modernists place the foundation of religious philosophy in that doctrine called **agnosticism**.

The modernists hold dogma (religious formulas) as arising as secondary propositions based on primitive and simple formulas. They consider them to be **symbols and instruments**; that is, images and vehicles of truth which are subject to change and ought to evolve and be changed.

Pope St. Pius X states that they admit that all religions are true.

He recognized that they seize upon chairs in the seminaries and universities, gradually making them chairs of pestilence. Pope Pius X stated that Modernists try in every way to diminish and weaken authority.

They propose to remove the ecclesiastical Magisterium itself by sacrilegiously falsifying its origin, character, rights, and by freely repeating the calumnies of its adversaries.

Pope St. Pius X suppressed Modernism in the seminaries and universities, where it went underground to resurface after Vatican II as neo-modernism, which masquerades under "The Spirit of Vatican II," feminism in the Church, liberation theology, and the conciliar Church.

Modernism In the Church

On April 20, 1994, Our Lord in a locution told Joanne Kriva that the powers of the Antichrist grow bold in their efforts to dismantle His Church. Our Lord stated that slowly but surely the foundation upon which his Church was founded "is subjected to the chisel of false teachers and the heresy of Modernism.... However strong this new (false) church may seem, it will collapse upon itself for it is founded upon lies, deceptions, false doctrines, and the egos of those who seek only their own importance and power." [10]

Freemasonry

The Religion of Freemasonry

Masonry is a religion with the characteristics of a religious cult. Worship is practiced in separate phases or periods:
• Adoration of the Great Architect of the Universe. (the true Masonic Divinity is concealed)
• Adoration of Nature. The idea of the Great Architect of the Universe is translated into that of the God-Nature, universal cause of things, as conceived by the materialist, the pantheist, or the theosophist, who only disagree on the name but not on the idea which is formed of the first principal cause of things. Albert Pike, the author of *Morals and Dogma of the Ancient and Accepted Scottish Rite of Freemasonry*, written in 1871, called by Haywood "the Scottish Rite Bible", states of the worship of Nature. "There is merely formal Atheism, which is the negation of God in terms, but not in reality." There is a worship of the flesh which Masonry has inherited from

the ancient pagans.

In the worship of Nature, the sun is taken as its repre-sentative and most characteristic symbol of the God-Nature, which Masons adore. This worship is referred to in the many symbols or ceremonies in the lodges. The circumambulation or procession around the altar in the lodges according to Albert G. Mackey, author of *Encyclo-pedia of Freemasonry* is an imitation of the course of the sun. The worship of the sun represents a restoration from death to life. To the sun also, as a regenerator and vivifier must be attributed the phallic cult of worship which formed a principal part of the mysteries.

• **Worship of Satan or Lucifer in some lodges at least.** According to the Masonic laws Satan is the good god or angel of light who came to teach Eve the secret which was to make human beings like God, seducing her carnally, a knowledge which she shared afterwards with Adam. [11]

Illustrious Masons speak of the goddess-reason. [11]

Freemasonry is the modern-day continuation of Gnosticism and of the ancient secret societies.

Albert Pike on page 626 of Morals and Dogma stated: "The Kabalah is the key to the occult sciences and the Gnostics were born of the Kabalists."

The Kabalah is found principally in two books called the *Book of Creation* and *Aohar*, [11]

Masonry has or pretends to have a relationship with the more ancient sects, the Egyptian, the Chaldeans, the Indo-Brahmins, the Greeks, the Persians, etc... From these sources comes also its doctrines of pantheism, materialism, the dualism or bisexualism of God, the emanation of souls, etc. "In the Masonic legends of certain degrees it is customary to say that Masonry... comes from Satan himself, who for them is the good God, the eternal enemy of Jehovah, the God of the Bible and of the Christians."[11]

The Knights Templar, a military and religious order was first established in 1118 AD in Jerusalem. It grew rapidly and in the year 1128 was taken under the special protection of the Pope. They became extremely wealthy through gifts of land and money.

After embracing Gnosticism while in Palestine, and having been in touch with the sect of the Assassins from whom they received many of their organizational traits, the order of Knights Templar degenerated. In 1312 Pope Clement V abolished the Order. [12]

"Evidence suggests that the surviving Knights either founded or merged with an existing secret order in the early 1300s, later referred to as the Order of the Rose Croix (The Rosecrucians)." [12]

The Rosecrucians in progressing to their goal of establishing a New World Order "decided to take on the appearance of a benevolent organization of good works in order to continue their occult traditions within. They merged with and finally took over the stone mason guilds of Europe, retaining many of their symbols from the building trade." The stone masons who were actually employed in the building profession were known as <u>Operative Masons</u>, unlike the occult adepts who took over their guilds, who became known as <u>Speculative Masons</u>. [12]

The transition from Operative to Speculative Masonry took several decades, the move beginning in the 1640s and culminating in the formation of the world's first Grand Lodge in London in 1717. In this gradual takeover, "the torch was passed to the Masonic Order, with <u>the Rosecrucians</u> embedding themselves deep within its structure and hierarchy to <u>become the Adepts, or the Princes of Freemasonry</u>." [12]

<u>This "new" order expanded rapidly</u>. [12]

The Illuminati

A new ultra secret society known as the Illuminati was formed as an Order within the Masonic Order.

Albert G. Mackey, describes the Illuminati as a "secret society founded on May 1, 1776, by Adam Weishaupt, who was professor of canon law at the University of Ingolstadt."... "John Robinson, an 18th century historian and a prominent Mason, was entrusted with some of the original documents and correspondence of the Illuminati." In his book *Proofs of a Conspiracy*, 1798, he

Fire From Heaven

wrote: "The express aim of the Order was to abolish Christianity, and overturn all civil government." He quoted Weishaupt as saying that the plan for a New World Order can succeed "in no other way but by secret associations, which will by degrees, and in silence, possess themselves the government of the States, and make use of those means for this purpose..." Mackey commented that the order extended rapidly into other countries, and its Lodges were found in France, Belgium, Holland, Denmark, Sweden, Poland, Hungary, and Italy. [12]

At the Masonic Congress of Wilhelmsbad on July 16, 1782, the Illuminati solidified itself as the undisputed leader of the occult one-world movement. The decision was made to move the headquarters of illuminized Freemasonry from Bavaria to Frankfurt, which was already becoming the stronghold of the Rothschilds and the international financiers. An alliance was forged between illuminized Freemasonry and the growing Rothschild network. [12]

After the exposure of the Illuminati plot by the Bavarian government after only 10 years of existence, and revelation of it to the leaders of Europe, some of whom were under the Order's influence, most of the initiates got away and were taken in by various European leaders. Although the Illuminati officially ceased to exist the continuation of its efforts were ensured through the Grand Orient Lodge of France. Working through the Grand Orient and the network of illuminized Masonic Lodges already put in place by Weishaupt, high-Freemasonry continued its agenda for world domination. [12]

The first major "accomplishment" of illuminized Free-masonry was the French Revolution through the Jacobin Society and Napoleon Bonaparte who was one of their men. Illuminized Freemasonry received help from Voltaire, Robespierre, Danton and Maat, all of whom were prominent Masons. The Jacobin Society named Weishaupt as its "Grand Patriot."

William T. Still tells us that "Weishaupt was as much the founder of revolutionary Communism as was Karl Marx.... Weishaupt adopted the teachings of radical French philosophers such as Jean Jacques Rousseau (1712-1778) and the anti-Christian doctrines of the Manicheans. He was indoctrinated in Egyptian occultism in 1771 by a merchant of unknown origin named Kolmer, who was said to have traveled Europe in search of converts. For the next five years Weishaupt formulated a plan by which all occult systems could be reduced to a single, powerful organization. On May Day, 1776 Weishaupt launched his order of the Illuminati." [13]

"The plan of the Illuminati was to replace Christianity by a religion of reason." [13]

"British historian, Nesta Webster, author of *World Revolution*, observed that Rousseau's writings embodied all of the principles which would later be known as Communism." [13]

The tenets of Illuminati were summarized by William T. Still as:

- Abolition of monarchies and all ordered government.
- Abolition of private property and inheritance.
- Abolition of patriotism and nationalism.
- Abolition of family life and the institution of marriage, and the establishment of communal education of children.
- Abolition of all religion. [13]

The novice in the Illuminati was taught that "the ends justify the means, that evil methods were justifiable if the ultimate outcome was for good." In the higher degrees he was told that: "This is our 'Great Secret.' Once the impediment of religion is dispensed with, the way is open for a world dictatorship, ruled by Illuminism." [13]

"Weishaupt had already decreed bringing women into the order should be a goal, so that the philosophy of the new liberated women could be developed. This concept was devised to aid in his plan for the breakup of the family by generally developing rationales which would sow discord between men and women. He initially achieved this by painting the plight of women as a downtrodden class." [13]

Although the Illuminati's efforts had officially ceased to exist, unofficially its agenda continued to move forward throughout the network of illuminated Masonic Lodges that had already been set in place. The main catalyst for this continued drive seemed to come from the Grand Orient Lodge of France, and later on, from the Masonic leaders of Italy and the United States.

On July 14, 1889 Albert Pike as the leader of Freemasonry, issued his instructions to the 23 Supreme Councils of the World:

"To you, Sovereign Grand Inspectors General, we say this, that you may repeat it to the Brethren of the 32nd, 31st, and 30th degrees -- <u>The Masonic religion should be, by all of us initiates of the high degrees, maintained in the purity of the Luciferic Doctrine</u>...

"That is why the intelligent disciples of Zoroaster, as well as, after them, the Gnostics, the Manicheans and the Templars have admitted, as the only logical metaphysical conception, the system of two divine principles fighting eternally, and one cannot believe one inferior to the other. Thus, the doctrine of Satanism is a heresy; and <u>the true and pure philosophic religion is the belief in Lucifer, the equal of Adonay; but Lucifer, God of Light and God of Good, is struggling for humanity against Adonay, the God of Darkness and Evil.</u>" [13]

Communism, Illuminized Freemasonry and International Banking

In the Stalin Showcase Trials of 1938-1939 the role of

the financiers of Communism was revealed. The role
of They, Wall Street was revealed. In 1938, the Russian
Ambassador to Paris, Christian G. Rakovsky, a founding
member of the Russian Communistic State, a member of
Them, the hidden forces behind Freemasonry was ar-
rested. Gavriil G. Kusmin (known as Gabriel) was sent
by Stalin to question him. [14]

The interview was witnessed by Dr. Landowsky, a Rus-
sianized Pole who lived in Moscow. He kept a copy of
the interview which was published in the booklet, *The
Red Symphony*, by J. Landowsky, Excerpts from this interview were published in *Towards World Government, New
World Order* by Deirdre Manifold. [14]

Rakovsky said: "You know that according to the un-
written history known only to us, the founder of the
First Communist International is indicated -- of
course secretly -- as being Weishaupt... he was ordered to found a secret organization which was to
provoke and push the French Revolution to go further than its political objectives with the aim of
transforming it into a social revolution for the establishment of Communism.... [14]

Rakovsky said what is not known are the relations between Weishaupt and his followers with the Rothschilds. The secret of acquisition of wealth of the best
known bankers could have been explained by the fact
that they were the treasurers of the first Comintern.
There is evidence that when the five brothers spread
out to the five provinces of the financial empire of

Europe, they had some secret help for the accumulation of these enormous sums; it is possible that they
were the first Communists from the Bavarian Cata-
combs who were already spread all over Europe. But
others say, and I think with better reason, that the
Rothschilds were not the treasurers, but the chiefs of
that first secret Communism. The opinion is based on
the well known fact that Marx and the highest chiefs
of the First International -- already the open one --
were controlled by Baron Lionel Rothschild, whose
revolutionary portrait was done by Disraeli, the English Premier, who was his creature.... He described
him in the character of Sidonia, a man who, according
to the story, was a multimillionaire, knew and controlled spies, Carbonari, Freemasons, ..., Gypsies,
revolutionaries, etc.. [14]

Rakovsky brought out that he thought we could determine that the inventor of the Financial International and the Revolutionary International was the
same person. He stated it is an act of genius: to create,
with the help of Capitalism, accumulation of the highest
degree, to push the proletariat towards strikes, to sow
hopelessness, and at the same time create an organization which must unite proletarians with the purpose of
driving them into revolution. This is to write the most
majestic chapter of history. Even more -- remember the
phrase of the mother of the five Rothschild brothers:
"If my sons want it, then there will be no war." This
means they were the arbiters of peace and war, but
not emperors.... Is not war already a revolutionary func-
tion? War -- the Commune. Since that time every war

was a giant step towards Communism. [14]

The Alta Vendita

When Weishaupt passed away, the Alta Vendita or highest lodge of the Italian Carbonari exercised the supreme government of all the secret societies of the world. It ruled the blackest Freemasonry of France, Germany and England until Mazzini wrenched the scepter away. [15]

Alta Vendita and The Conspiracy To Take Over The Church

In the permanent instructions of the Alta Vendita we have the conspiracy to take over the Church. They were to give bad names to faithful Prelates who may be too knowing or too good to do the work of the Carbonari against conscience, God and the souls of men. The instruction stated, the Pope, whoever he may be, will never come to the secret societies. It is for the secret societies to come first to the Church, in the resolve to conquer the two. The work which we have undertaken is not the work of a day, nor of a month, nor of a year. It may last many years, a century perhaps, but in our ranks the soldier dies and the fight continues... That which we ought to demand, that which we should seek and expect, as the Jews expected the Messiah, is a Pope according to our wants.... It is to the youth we must go. It is that which we must seduce; it is that which we must bring under the banner of the secret societies.... Now then, in order to secure to us a Pope in the manner required, it is necessary to fashion for that Pope a generation worthy of the reign of which we dream. The instructions told them to never speak in the presence of the youth a word of impiety or impurity. You ought to present yourself with all the appearance of a man grave and moral. Once your reputation is established in the colleges, in the gymnasiums, in the universities, and in the seminaries -- once that you have captivated the confidence of professors and students so act that those who are principally engaged in the ecclesiastical state should love to seek your conversation. Nourish their souls with the splendors of ancient Papal Rome... Offer them at first, but always in secret, inoffensive books, poetry resplendent with national emphasis; then little by little you will bring your disciples to the degree of cooking desired... you will obtain for yourselves the reputation of good Catholics and pure patriots. That reputation will open the way for our doctrines to pass to the bosom of the young clergy, and even to go into the depths of convents. In a few years the young clergy will have, by the force of events, invaded all the functions. They will govern, administer, and judge. They will form the council of the Sovereign. They will be called to choose the Pontiff who will reign; and that Pontiff, like the greater part of his contemporaries, will be necessarily imbued with the Italian and humanitarian principles which we are about to put in circulation. It is a little grain of mustard which we place in the earth, but the sun of justice will develop it even to be a great power; and you will see one day what a rich harvest that little seed will produce. [15]

"Let the clergy march under your banner in the belief always that they march under the banner of the Apostolic Keys... Lay your nets like Simon Barjona. Lay them in the depths of sacristies, seminaries, and convents, and if you precipitate nothing you will give yourself a draught of fishes more miraculous than his. The fisher of fishes will become fishers of men. You will bring yourselves as friends around the Apostolic Chair. You will have fished up a Revolution in Tiara and Cope, marching with Cross and banner -- a Revolution which it will need but to be spurred on a little to put the four corners of the world on fire..." [15]

The first leader of the Alta Vendita was a corrupt nobleman who took the name Nubius. He was sacrificed by the party of Mazzini, and managed in revenge to communicate documents to the authorities of Rome. Piccolo Tigre, a member of the Alta Vendita, was the most active agent of Nubius. The letter of Piccolo Tigre stated that they should isolate a man from his family, to cause him to lose his morals. They were to then recruit him for affiliation with the nearest lodge. [15]

"The main advice of the permanent instruction is to seduce the clergy... The ecclesiastic is to be deceived, being led on by patriotic fervor, and blinded by a constant, though, of course false, and fatal popularity... The seduction of the foremost ecclesiastics, prelates, and bishops was the general, policy of the sect at all times." [15]

When Nubius passed away, Lord Palmerston of England for the greater part of his career was the real master, the Grand Patriarch of the Illuminati, and as such, the Ruler of all the secret societies of the world. [15]

There Have Been Attempts To Capture The Roman Catholic Church From Within

In the book *AA-1025-- The Memoirs of an Anti-Apostle* it was revealed how a French nurse in the 1960's attending an auto crash victim, who died with no identification on him, found in his briefcase biographical notes which contained information about how the Communist Party commissioned him to enter the priesthood to subvert and destroy the church from within. He was the 1,025[th] man in the program when he was recruited. [40]

In his book *The Keys of This Blood*, 1990, on pages 535-536 and page 678, Fr. Malachi Martin informs us that the Papacy was almost captured after the death of Pope Leo XIII when his Cardinal Secretary of State, in the Conclave of 1903, received the votes to pronounce the *Accepto*, but was never allowed to do so. Emperor Franz Joseph of Austria, at that time had the privilege from the Vatican of vetoing any pope-elect whom he did not fancy. The Emperor did not fancy him. The ostensible reason given was the Cardinal Secretary of State's record of political opposition to Austria and his support of France. So, on August 2, 1903, the Polish born Jan Cardinal Puzyna of Austria-Hungary stood up in the Conclave and announced the Emperor's veto of the Cardinal Secretary of State. [23]

The Church then elected Cardinal Sarto [Italian for tailor], whose father was a polish born tailor named Jan Krawiec [Polish for tailor] and his mother Margherita a seamstress. Cardinal Sarto took the name Pope Pius X. His father had moved to Italy for political asylum when Poland fell into Prussian hands. [23]

Pope Pius X was later declared a Saint. It was Pope Pius X who condemned Modernism as the Synthesis of All Heresies.

Freemasonry and Modernism have so much in common that they are of the same threat to the Catholic Church and to all of society.

In the United States the Order of the Skull and Bones at Yale University has been exposed as an Illuminati organization. Esquire September 1977, by Ron Rosenbaum in *Last Secrets of Skull and Bones*, and by the National Research Institute's *Trumpet*, October 1988, and in *Fame*, August 1989, by Steven M. L. Aronson.

Pope Leo XIII's April 20, 1884 Encyclical Humanum Genus

Pope Leo XIII April 20, 1884 wrote Humanum Genus an encyclical on Freemasonry, condemning it as

Popes before him had done. He said, "Let no man think that he may for any reason whatsoever join the Masonic sect, if he values his Catholic name and his eternal salvation as he ought to value them. Let no one be deceived by a pretense of honesty." The encyclical teaches that the fruit produced by Freemasonry is pernicious and bitter for it is nothing less than the overthrow of the Christian social and political order, and the substitution of a new state of things founded on Naturalism. This means in Masonry human nature and human reason are supreme, and that there are no truths revealed by God that men are bound to believe. The Pope notes that the Masons want to bring back after a lapse of eighteen centuries the manners and customs of the pagans. The Masons hold all religions to be alike, and the Catholic religion as equal to other religions. They have plotted the destruction of the papacy, holding that the sacred power of the Pontiffs must be abolished, and the Pontificate must be utterly destroyed. **Pope Leo XIII calls this a "fatal plague".** Pope Leo XIII ratified and confirmed by his Apostolic authority what the Roman Pontiffs Our predecessors had decreed for the purpose of opposing the undertakings and endeavors of the Masonic sect, and whatsoever they had enacted to deter or withdraw men from societies of this kind. [41]

Masons In the Church

On February 12, 1979, Our Lady as the Mother of all Peoples said to Mother Elena Leonardi: "Communism will triumph because of the godless rulers; many magistrates will perish; <u>freemasonry in the churches, prelates without dignity</u>... My daughter, the time has run out; this is the Apocalyptic hour; if they do not return to my Heart, they will know only desolation. Cardinals and bishops will confront the Pope who will be accused and mistreated, since the days of suffering are being prepared for the Holy Father. Speak to him and tell him to be prudent and strong; I protect and watch over him." [16]

The False Church of These End Times

Cardinal Wojtyla, now Pope John Paul II, on June 24, 1977 said, "We find ourselves in the presence of the greatest confrontation in history; the greatest mankind has ever had to confront. We are facing the final confrontation between the Church and the Anti-Church, between the Gospel and the Anti-Gospel."

On May 31, 1978, Ida Peerdeman, a visionary in Holland, at the Consecration heard: "Be faithful to its "True Doctrine. Bring My People to Me and I will feed their souls." At Holy Communion Ida had a vision of the whole world before her and heard, "They have ravaged My Church and chased My followers into wilderness." The Voice said, "Watch well, and understand rightly everything I'll show you." Ida saw several large buildings. She recognized them as the side wall of the Vatican. The other buildings were seminaries and universities. From all these buildings she saw priests and clergymen coming out. She became frightened because their faces looked like heads of foxes, wolves and hyenas. They came along skulking and moved around searching like these animals. Ida heard the Voice say, "They are those who have led My people into wilderness and have broken up My Church." [17]

Blessed Katherine Emmerick, in visions, saw the Church of St. Peter in ruins and so many of the clergy busying themselves in the work of this destruction, but not openly in front of others. She saw that everything that pertained to Protestantism was gradually gaining the upper hand, and the Catholic religion fall into complete decadence. She saw many pastors allowing themselves to be taken up with ideas dangerous to the Church. They were building a great, strange, and extravagant Church in which everyone 'was to be admitted in order to be united and have equal rights: Evangelicals, Catholics, sects of every kind; such was to be the new Church. [18]

The Beast Like a Leopard, Ecclesiastical Freemasonry

On June 17, 1989, in message # 406, The Beast Like a Lamb, Our Blessed Mother told Father Gobbi that she wanted to warn us of the grave dangers that threaten the Church today, because of the many and diabolical attacks which are being carried out against Her to destroy Her. To attain this end, there comes out of the earth, by way of aid to the black beast which arises out of the sea, a beast which has two horns like those of a lamb. The lamb, in holy scripture, has always been a symbol of sacrifice. To the symbol of the sacrifice there is intimately connected that of the priesthood: the two horns. The high priest of the Old Testament wore a headpiece with two horns. The bishops of the Church wear the miter -- with two horns -- to indicate the fullness of their priesthood. The black beast like a leopard indicates Freemasonry; the beast with two horns like a lamb indicates Freemasonry infiltrated into the interior of the Church, that is to say, ecclesiastical Masonry, which has spread especially among the members of the hierarchy. [2]

Our Blessed Mother, in message # 406, on June 13, 1989, said in locution to Father Gobbi: "This Masonic infiltration, in the interior of the Church, was already foretold to you by me at Fatima, when I announced to you that Satan would enter in even to the summit of the Church." [Editor's note: Pope Paul VI said that the Smoke of Satan had entered the sanctuary.]

The task of ecclesiastical Masonry is that of destroying Christ and his Church, building a new idol, namely a false christ and a false church.

Ecclesiastical Masonry works to obscure his divine word, by means of natural and rational interpretations and, in the attempt to make it more understandable and acceptable, empties it of all its supernatural content. Thus errors are spread in every part of the Church itself. This fulfills the prophesy made at Fatima that, "The time will come when many will lose the true faith,"

The loss of the faith is apostasy.

Ecclesiastical Masonry works in a subtle and diabolical way to lead all into apostasy. By favoring those forms of exegesis which gives the Gospel a rationalistic and natural interpretation, by means of the application of the various literary genres, in such a way that it becomes torn to pieces in all its parts.

Ecclesiastical Masonry leads in the end to one arriving at denying the historical reality of miracles and of the resurrection and places in doubt the very divinity of Jesus and his salvific mission.

Ecclesiastical Masonry, after having destroyed the historical Christ, seeks to destroy the mystical Christ which is the Church.

"The Church is truth, because Jesus has entrusted to it alone the task of guarding, in its integrity, all the deposit of faith. He has entrusted it to the hierarchical Church, that is to say, to the Pope and the bishops united with him. Ecclesiastical Masonry seeks to destroy this reality through false ecumenism, which leads to the acceptance of all christian Churches, asserting that each one of them has some part of the truth. It develops the plan of founding a universal ecumenical Church, formed by the fusion of all the christian confessions, among, which, the Catholic Church."

Ecclesiastical Masonry, in many and subtle ways, seeks to attack the ecclesial devotion towards the sacrament of the Eucharist. It gives value only to the meal aspect, tends to minimize its sacrificial value, seeks to deny the real and personal presence of Jesus in the consecrated Host ....

Ecclesiastical Masonry seeks to destroy the foundation of the unity of the Church, through a subtle and insidious attack on the Pope. It weaves plots of dissension and of contestation against the Pope; it supports and rewards those who vilify and disobey him; it disseminates the criticisms and contentions of bishops and theologians. In this way the very foundation of its unity is demolished and thus the Church becomes more and more torn and divided."

Our Blessed Mother through Father Gobbi has told us that 666, the number of the beast, indicated thrice, expresses the year 1998, a period of history in which Freemasonry assisted by its Ecclesiastical form will succeed in its great design: that of setting up an idol to put in place of Christ and his Church: a false christ and a false church. At this time of the great apostasy, which will have then become generalized because almost all will follow the false christ and the false church, the door will be open for the appearance of the man or the very person of the antichrist.

The Ecclesiastical Masons, the false prophets, and their leader the false pope, will force all to worship this statue, an idol. This is an idol so powerful, we are told by Our Blessed Mother through Father Gobbi, in the message # 407, The Number of the Beast, June 17, 1989, that it puts to death all who do not adore this statue of the beast. It is an idol so strong and dominating as to cause all, small and great, rich and poor, freemen or slaves to receive a mark on the right hand and on the forehead, without which no one can buy or sell; this mark is the name of the beast or the number of his name. [2]

On December 31, 1993, Our Blessed Mother through Father Gobbi, revealed that Masonry with its diabolical power has set up its center in the very heart of the church, where the vicar of her Son Jesus resides, and from there it is spreading its evil influence to every part of the world. [2]

Chapter 6

The Great Trial For The Church

Fr. Gobbi was told by Our Blessed Mother on November 15, 1990, at Malvern, Pennsylvania in message #437: "The great trial has arrived for your church. Those errors which have brought people to the loss of the true faith have continued to spread. Many pastors have been neither attentive nor vigilant and have allowed many rapacious wolves, clothed as lambs, to insinuate themselves into the flock in order to bring disorder and destruction.

"How great is your responsibility; O pastors of the holy Church of God! You continue along the path of division from the Pope and of the rejection of his Magisterium; indeed, in a hidden way, there is in preparation a true schism which could soon become open and proclaimed.

"And then, there will remain only a small faithful remnant, over which I will keep watch in the garden of my Immaculate Heart." [2]

On January 1, 1993, in message # 486, Our Blessed mother told Fr. Gobbi in locution *The Time of the Great Trial:* "The great trial has come for the Church, so violated by the evil spirits, so divided in its unity, so darkened in its holiness. See how error has flooded throughout it, error which leads to the loss of the true faith. Apostasy is spreading everywhere....

" The hour of its great trial has above all come for the Church, because it will be shaken by the lack of faith, obscured by apostasy, wounded by betrayal, abandoned by its children, divided by schisms, possessed and dominated by Freemasonry, turned into fertile soil from which will spring up the wicked tree of the man of iniquity, the Antichrist, who will bring his kingdom into its interior." [2]

Cardinals, Bishops, Priests And Religious

On August 13, 1997 Our Heavenly Mother said to Denise Curtin and Joseph DellaPuca : "My dear children,... Our Lord and Savior, Jesus Christ, is the Truth and the only way to Eternal Salvation. Today, I call you to a greater unity with each other and within my Son's Church. Pray, Pray, Pray, my children, for my beloved priests, bishops and cardinals, that they remain steadfast and obedient to my chosen Pope, who will lead His people into the new era." [4]

Cardinals Will Oppose Cardinals, Bishops Will Oppose Bishops, Satan Will Walk Among Them

On March 26, 1978 Our Blessed Mother told Mother Elena Leonardi: " .... The time of the great trial will come also for the Church: cardinals will oppose cardinals, bishops against bishops. Satan marches triumphantly in the midst of their ranks due to their hubris and lack of charity! My daughter, there will be death everywhere because of the errors committed by the obstinate followers of Satan! Awareness of the terrible reality is urgent. Everyone must pray, do penance with the Holy Rosary, Holy Masses and Confessions. No sacrilegious Communions!"[16]

At Garabandal, 1961-1965, St. Michael the Archangel gave to Conchita, one of the visionaries, the message from Our Blessed Mother on October 18, 1961, "Before the cup was filling up, now it is flowing over. Many cardinals, many bishops, and many priests are on the path of perdition and taking many souls with them. Less and less importance is being given to the Eucharist. . You should turn the wrath of God away from yourself by your efforts..." [19]

At Garabandal on June 18, 1965, St. Michael the Archangel appeared and delivered a message from Our Lady: "Because the message of October 18, hasn't been fulfilled, and the world doesn't know about it, I tell you that this is the last one. I said before the cup was filling up. Now it is overflowing. Many priests, bishops, cardinals are on the road to perdition and are taking many souls with them. Each day we give the Eucharist less and less importance. We should use all our efforts to avoid God's wrath. If you ask sincerely for pardon, He will forgive you. Your Mother, through the mediation of Saint Michael, the angel, asks you to correct your ways. You are now receiving the last warnings. Think of the passion of Jesus." [19]

On October 13, 1973 at Akita Japan, an apparition twice approved by the local Bishop and the Bishops of Japan, Sister Agnes Katsuko Sasagawa was told by Our Blessed Mother: "Each day recite the prayers of the Rosary. With the Rosary pray for the bishops and priests. The work of the devil will infiltrate even the Church in such a way that one will see cardinals opposing cardinal, bishops against other bishops. The priests who venerate me will be scorned by their confreres ...." [21]

In message # 170, February 11, 1979, Our Blessed Mother told Father Gobbi, "This interior division sometime even leads priests to set themselves against priests, bishops against bishops, and cardinals against cardinals, for never before as in these times has Satan so succeeded in finding his way into their midst, rending asunder the precious bond of their mutual love." [2]

Fire From Heaven

In His message of January 25, 1996, to Sadie Jaramillo, Jesus said: "Amongst those will be brother priests of Mine, for whom you suffer. The princes of the church now stand at odds, one against another, cardinal against cardinal, bishop against bishop and I behold all. The living fulfillment of prophecy becomes clearer and clearer with each passing moment." [6]

On November 7, 1996 St. Michael said to Janie Garza: "The sufferings in your country will be manifested in many forms: Satan's attacks on the family will increase in great strength, the persecution in the Church will be great, priests will turn against priests, bishops against bishops, cardinals against cardinals. The religious will also partake in this great division. There will be great slander and evil plots against the holy Vicar of Christ. Great will be his suffering.

"The spirit of disobedience toward the holy Vicar will increase. Only a few will remain obedient and united with the holy Vicar of Christ. These few holy souls will be the ones who will carry the suffering of the Church through their prayers. Pray and fast for these holy priests of the Mother of God." [8]

At Akita on October 13, 1973 regarding the Apostasy we were told: "Each day recite the prayers of the Rosary. With the Rosary pray for the bishops and priests. The work of the devil will infiltrate even into the Church. One will see cardinals opposing cardinals... and bishops confronting other bishops. The priests who venerate me will be scorned and condemned by their confreres; churches and altars will be sacked; the Church will be full of those who accept compromises and the demon will tempt many priests and religious to leave the service of the Lord... I alone am able still to help save you from the calamities which approach. Those who place their total confidence in me will be given necessary help." [21]

On February 12, 1979, Our Lady as the Mother of all Peoples, said to Mother Elena Leonardi, "... My daughter, the time has run out; this is the Apocalyptic hour; if they do not return to my Heart, they will know only desolation. Cardinals and bishops will confront the Pope who will be accused and mistreated, since the days of suffering are being prepared for the Holy Father. Speak to him and tell him to be prudent and strong; I protect and watch over him." [16]

In Rome There Will Be Changes

At La Salette, on September 19, 1846, in an apparition approved by the church, Melanie was told by Our Blessed Mother: "Rome will lose the faith and become the seat of the Antichrist.... The Church will be in eclipse.... Pagan Rome will disappear." [7]

The Man Of Iniquity Will Establish Himself Within The Church

At Akita Japan, on September 15, 1987, the Feast of Our

Fire From Heaven

Lady of Sorrows, Fr. Gobbi, received the interior locution from Our Blessed Mother: "Even now, that
which I predicted at Fatima and that which I have
revealed here in the third message confided to a little
daughter of mine is in the process of being accomplished. And so, even for the church the moment of
it's great trial has come, because the man of iniquity
will establish himself within it and the abomination
of desolation will enter into the holy temple of God." [2]

Time of Darkness

Patricia Talbot of Ecuador [Apparitions 18-month period from August 24, 1988 until March 3, 1990] was told
by the Holy Virgin that today there is great confusion
and tribulation of the faith... The times of darkness
have begun, the tribulation of your faith... The darkness of faith of my little ones inhabits the world...
Your faith is demonstrated not only in prayer but also in
actions." [22]

In message #450 on May 19, 1991 Our blessed Mother
told Fr. Gobbi: "When this Pope will have completed
the task which Jesus has entrusted to him and I will
come down from heaven to receive his sacrifice, all of
you will be cloaked in a dense darkness of apostasy,
which will then become general.

"There will remain faithful only that little remnant
which, in these years, by accepting my motherly invita-

102

tion, has let itself be enfolded in the secure refuge of my Immaculate Heart. And it will be this little faithful remnant, prepared and formed by me, that will have the task of receiving Christ, who will return to you in glory, bringing about in this way the beginning of the new era which awaits you." [2]

In message #484 on December 24, 1992 Our Blessed Mother told Fr. Gobbi: "...the darkness is now becoming deeper, as the moment of the return of Jesus in glory draws closer.

"It is the darkness of the lack of faith and the apostasy, which has spread everywhere.

"It is the darkness of evil and sin, which has now obscured hearts and souls.

"It is the darkness of faithlessness and impiety, of egoism and pride, of hardness of heart and impurity...." [2]

Chapter 7

THE WARNING

Heaven's Great Intervention Of Divine Mercy
The Illumination Of Consciences
(The Warning)

Anna Maria Taigi - The Warning

Anna Maria Taigi, Beatified in 1920 as a model of women and mothers, was not only a prophetess of our time, but one of the most extraordinary mystics in the history of the Church.

Blessed Anna Maria Taigi spoke of a great chastisement which would come to the world before which there would be <u>an illumination of the conscience of men by which suddenly everyone would see themselves as God sees them.</u> She indicated that this illumination of conscience would result in the saving of many souls because many would repent as a result of this "Warning" ... this miracle of "self illumination". [18]

St. Edmund Campion - The Warning

It is interesting that 300 years before Blessed Anna Maria this same revelation was given to St. Edmund Campion who went to his death affirming this same prophecy.

THE WARNING Garabandal, Spain, 1961-1965

During the apparitions from 1961 –1965 at Garabandal, Spain, four young children saw and received messages from Our Blessed Mother. These apparitions occurred during the period of **Vatican Council II**, and just after the failure of the Church to reveal **the Third Part of the Secret of Fatima**, which those of us who were living at the time and who had been following the Fatima apparitions expected would be done by Pope John XXIII in 1960.

At Garabandal, Conchita, Mary Loli and Jacinta received messages about The Warning. Mary Loli was told the year of the Warning. Within a year following the Warning there would be a Great Miracle. Conchita was told the date of the Great Miracle.

In June 1962 these three visionaries experienced the "Night of the Screams" [actually over two nights that so terrified the people of the hamlet that almost all went to confession and Communion]. During these two nights they were shown the Warning and the Great Chastisement. The first night, during which only Mary Loli and Jacinta were present, was about the Warning. On the second night, during which Conchita was present as well, they were shown the Chastisement (which at that time was conditional). Mary Cruz did not share in either event.

On January 1, 1965, at the pines, The Blessed Virgin Mary told Conchita about the Warning. She was told what the warning would be, but does not know the day or the date.

The Warning - Conchita

Conchita told us that the Warning will be like two heavenly bodies or stars colliding that make a lot of noise and a lot of light, but they don't fall. We are going to see it. It will horrify us because at that very moment we will see our souls and the harm we have done. In that moment we are going to see our conscience, everything wrong that we are doing, and the good that we are not doing. It will be as though we are in agony, but we will not die by its effects, but perhaps we will die of fright or shock to see ourselves. The Warning is like a purification for the Miracle. Conchita said that it is sort of a catastrophe. It will make us think of the dead, that is, we would prefer to be dead than to experience the Warning. Conchita revealed to us that it would be very fearful, a thousand times worse than earthquakes. <u>It will be like fire.</u> <u>It will not burn our flesh, but we will feel it bodily and interiorly.</u> <u>It is a thing from heaven.</u> People in every part of the world will suffer from it. None of us will escape this: the good, so that they may draw nearer to God; the evil, so that they may amend their lives. <u>Conchita said that if she did not know what the Chastisement was, she would say that the Warning was worse than the Chastisement</u>

During an interview **Conchita** said the duration of the Warning is about five minutes.

In an interview in October 1968, in answer to a question about the Warning, Conchita said: "The Warning is something supernatural and will not be explained by science. It will be seen and felt."

According to Conchita: <u>"The Warning will be a purification, a preparation for the Miracle,</u> and everyone will see it. It will make people aware of the evil that they do with their sins."

The Warning - Mary Loli

Mary Loli said: "When the Warning occurs everything will stand still, even planes in the sky, but just for a few moments. At the moment everything stops, the Warning will occur. The Warning will last just a few minutes. It is very close and it is important we prepare ourselves because it is a terrible thing. It will make us feel all the wrong we have done."

Mary Loli told us: "Everyone will experience it wherever they may be, regardless of their condition or their knowledge of God. It will be an interior personal experience. It will look as if the world has come to a standstill, however, no one will be aware of that as they will be totally absorbed in their own experience. It is going to be something like an interior feeling of sorrow and pain for having offended God. God will help us see clearly the harm we are causing Him and all the evil things we do. He will help us to sense this interior pain because often when we do something wrong we ask the Lord's forgiveness with our lips, but now He will help us sense physically that deep sorrow."

Mary Loli said that it would look like the Communists had taken over the world and it would be very hard to practice religion, for priests to say Mass or for people to open the doors of the churches at the time of the Warning. It would be as though the Church had disappeared.

The Warning - Jacinta

Jacinta stated: "The Warning is something that is first seen in the air everywhere in the world and immediately is transmitted into the interior of our souls. It will last for a very little time, but will seem a very long time because of its effect within us. It will be for the good of our souls, in order to see in ourselves our conscience, the good and the bad we've done. Then we will feel a great love toward our heavenly parents and ask forgiveness for all our offenses The Warning is for everybody because God wants our salvation. The Warning is in order for us to draw closer to Him and increase our faith. Therefore, one should prepare for that day, but not await it with fear because God doesn't send things for the sake of fear but rather justice and love and He does it for the good of all His children that they might enjoy eternal happiness and not be lost."

The Miracle and Its Relation To The Warning

Conchita knows the date of the Miracle, and eight days before the Miracle occurs she will announce the date to the world. The Miracle is to occur during the months of March, April or May, between the 8th and the 16th of the month, at 8:30 P.M. Garabandal time on a feast day of a little known Martyr of the Eucharist, at the time of a rare ecclesiastical event, unrelated to the Miracle. Only one individual associated with Conchita, as far as we can determine, has named the month of April as the month of the Miracle

Conchita was told what the Miracle would be, and said: "It will be a miracle of the love of God, something that will prove and manifest His love to us in an outstanding way." The Miracle, Conchita has stated, will coincide with an event in the Church, a singular event that happens very rarely and had not (as of 1974) occurred in Conchita's lifetime. Conchita said that it is not new or stupendous, only rare, like a definition of a dogma – something like that in that it will affect the entire Church. It will happen on the same day as the Miracle, but not as a consequence of the Miracle, but only coincidentally.

There will be healing of those present in Garabandal at the time of the Miracle. The sick who are present will be cured, the incredulous will believe, and the sinners will be converted.

Our Lord told Conchita, on July 20, 1963, that the purpose of this Miracle is: "to convert the whole world. Conchita asked Our Lord if Russia would be converted. Our Lord answered: "Yes, she will be converted, and thus everybody will love Our Hearts."

On February 7, 1974 Conchita said: "For the words of the Blessed Mother to be complete, there must be the Warning and the Miracle. It is all one message."

[The fourth visionary, Mary Cruz, who later denied that these apparitions occurred, will, we are told, again believe that she did have them, but only after the Miracle.]

The Permanent Sign At Garabandal After The Miracle

After the Miracle there will be a permanent sign left at Garabandal.

On September 14, 1965, Conchita said: "The Sign that will remain forever at the pines is something that we will be able to photograph, televise and see, but not touch. It will be evident that this is not a thing of this world, but from God.

Conchita revealed that although the sign can be compared to a "pillar of smoke" or to "rays of sunlight" it will not actually be either of these things.

At Garabandal we were told that after these events have occurred there will be a short period of time for mankind to convert. If mankind doesn't, then there will be a Great Chastisement.

The Illumination (Warning)

Janie Garza, Austin, Texas, Visionary And Stigmatist

May 13, 1994 *The illumination of the soul*

St. Joseph: I, St. Joseph, bring God's blessings to you and to your family.

Janie: Thank you, beloved St. Joseph. Praised be the Eternal Father for His goodness forever and ever. Amen.

St. Joseph: My little one, I, St. Joseph, know that you have been struggling with the seriousness of the messages that you have received from Most Holy Mary and St. Michael. I am here to help you to understand these messages. **You see, my little one, the people of God have ignored His warnings.** The world does not understand the darkness that surrounds them.

Many people continue to live in sin, and forget that <u>the day is coming when they will be allowed to see the state of their souls.</u> What a terrible time this will be for many, many souls. Many will die, for they will not be able to withstand knowing the truth about the condition of their souls.

Janie: St. Joseph, could you explain why many people will die when they see their souls? I don't understand this, please help me to understand.

St. Joseph: My little one, the soul is where all truth lies and no one can see or know your soul except the Eternal One. He alone knows all souls, and He alone will judge all souls. No one knows the truth except the Holy Trinity. If people knew the truth, they would choose not to sin, for the truth would enlighten their hearts to know how much sin separates them from the truth. **The Truth is the Eternal Father.**

You cannot live in sin and say you know the truth, for you cannot have two masters. You must choose to live in darkness or to live in the light. For those who believe that they live in the light but continue to break every Commandment given by God, to these souls, I, St. Joseph, say that these souls will not be able to see

What must I tell the people?   ☆ ☆☆

the state of their souls and live.

Janie: This is hard for me to know. Are you saying that people who do not live God's Commandments will die when they see their souls?

St. Joseph: Yes, my little one, that's how it will be for many unless they repent and decide for conversion. There is still time for repentance, but time is growing shorter with each day that goes by.

Janie: What must I tell the people?   ☆ ☆

St. Joseph: Share with them that the Eternal One is calling them to return to Him and to accept His love and mercy, to amend their lives and to live the messages of prayer, fasting and conversion. All who repent will receive special graces to enter into the Sacred Heart of Jesus and the Immaculate Heart of Mary. To all who repent, God will shower His mercy on them. No one will be turned away, for God loves all His children. Now, my little one, remain united to the Two Hearts and continue living as God's chosen family. Peace, my little one, peace.

Janie: Thank you, beloved St. Joseph, thank you![8]

September 9, 1995 *The Illumination*

Jesus: Good morning, Our humble servant. We are here to bless you and your family. We are here to comfort you in your suffering.

Janie: Good morning, My Lord and My Lady. Thank You so much for blessing us and for bringing comfort to my heart.

Our Lady: Our sweet angel, you are suffering, for you've seen all the evil in the world through the visions which God allows you to see. You have seen many of the things that are to come. You have seen the suffering in the families and the suffering in the Bride of my Son. These visions which you embrace with your heart and make reparation for, this is the reason for your great suffering.

Janie: Blessed Mother, I don't mind my suffering, but I am affected by knowing of all the suffering youth, the children and the killing of the unborn babies. Please pray so that I will pray unceasingly for the poor sinners in the world. Could you tell me about the illumination which St. Joseph talked to me about. Will people suffer much?

Jesus: Our humble servant, the illumination that will take place will be for a short period. During this time My Father will allow all of humanity to see the state of their souls as My Father sees their souls. This will be a time of great grace when many souls will repent and return to My Father. Those souls that die will die from great shock to see the state of the darkness which exists in their souls.

Janie: Beloved Savior, will the illumination scare people?

Jesus: The fear that will inflame their hearts is the holy fear of the immense power of My Father, especially for those many souls that have continued to deny the existence of My Father. These will be the souls that will experience tremendous fear.

Janie: Will all people convert?

Jesus: Many will convert, but many will not.

Janie: Oh, Jesus, will this happen very soon?

Jesus: Our humble servant, this will happen within a short period. Do not be distracted with dates, but prepare everyday with strong prayer. Many who worry about these times will not live to see these things take place. This is why Holy Scripture warns everybody not to be concerned about tomorrow, for tomorrow is promised to no one. The present day has enough trials and crosses.

Know that when We speak about such things to come; this is for the people to convert and abandon their evil ways. Everyday is an opportunity for souls to convert. People should not wait for such things to come to convert, but they should convert now, before it's too late! The very fact that such judgments will come is because people refuse to convert and continue to live in darkness.

Janie: Oh Beloved Savior, please continue to pour Your love and mercy into our souls so that we accept You as

Fire From Heaven

our Savior truly in our lives. I love You both.

Jesus: We love you, and all your prayers, your sacrifices and your little ways are pleasing to Us. We give you Our blessings. Until tomorrow, remain in the spirit of prayer as a family.

Janie: We will, we truly will.[26]

The Warning And Preparation For The Warning

On March 19, 1996 St. Joseph, appeared to Janie Garza and gave her a message on *The Illumination*

Janie: St. Joseph came with two big angels and many smaller angels. He was dressed with a golden tunic and an olive mantle that had golden designs on the edge of the hem. He blessed all the people with his presence. He had a beautiful, gentle smile. There was great light around him, and all the angels were in brilliant light. St. Joseph had two white roses in his hands. He knows that roses are my favorite flowers, because they have the fragrance of Our Lady....

Janie: Oh, we are so blessed to have you as Protector of the Family. Praised be God forever and ever.

St. Joseph: My little one, God's love for humanity is immense. He appeals to the world every second of the day to turn away from their sins. He gives them His love and mercy to help souls to convert. God will continue to appeal to His children to return back to His love and mercy.

116

The time is coming when God will allow all His children to look deep into their souls and see their sins as God sees their sinful hearts. God will send an illumination throughout the world. This will be a time of great grace and conversion to many souls. Shortly after this great illumination of souls, God will send a great miracle for the world to see.

After this great sign, the world will know peace. There will be great joy for all the faithful people of God. His children will be happy. There will be love in families everywhere. People will benefit from their labor, and they will build their homes and live to enjoy them. They will see their children's children, and all will live long lives.

Janie: Beloved St. Joseph, what should we do to prepare for this?

St. Joseph: Pray, my little one, pray. Remain faithful to all that the Holy Spirit directs you to do. Act in everything that Most Holy Mary is calling you to. Be a strong messenger of living her messages of peace, prayer, Holy Mass, fasting, conversion and reading Holy Scripture. Do this as a family. Do not reject God's Most Holy Name, so that He will not reject you. Decide to be a holy family, to pray together, to love, and to forgive one another. This is a time of decision for all of God's children.

Live as God's people, leading good, simple and just lives. Open your hearts to God's love and mercy.

117

Live each day as if it was your last.

Fire From Heaven

Every family must consecrate themselves to the Sacred Heart of Jesus, to the Immaculate Heart of Mary, and to my intercession and protection, that We may lead you closer to God. We will prepare you for the things to come. Live as children of the Lord, and you will live through all these troubled times.

Janie: Please help us, beloved St. Joseph, we need your help.

St. Joseph: My little one, be prepared by living all that I, St. Joseph, have shared with you on a daily basis, living each day as if it was your last day. This is God's Holy Will for His children. Do not fear anything, but abandon yourself to the Holy Spirit who will help you to do the Holy Will of God.

Janie: Thank you for this, most humble St. Joseph.

St. Joseph: I give you my blessing. Live in God's peace.

Janie: Later on this evening I was thanking God for St. Joseph, and my guardian angel said to me, "St. Joseph is the splendor of the interior life." I understood that both Our Lady and St. Joseph are the splendor of the interior life.[8]

Janie Garza's Vision Of The Warning

On March 19, 1997, Janie Garza had a vision and a message from St. Joseph. *This light pierced every heart at the same time*

St. Joseph: Greetings, my little one. God's peace to you and all who are present here.

Janie: Peace to you, beloved St. Joseph, on your feast day. I've waited for this time to spend with you.

St. Joseph: My little one, today will be a day of great joy for you, for on this day my foster Son, Jesus, will come to you as well.

Janie: Oh, beloved St. Joseph, I am so happy!

St. Joseph: My little one, today, I, St. Joseph, ask that you open your heart to what I share with you. It is important that you continue to pray and fast as a family. Offer your prayers and sacrifices to God in reparation for all the sins of the world. This is a time of great preparation. The call to conversion is urgent! There is no time for procrastination! Families must turn to God and abandon their sinful lives. The time for repentance is now, tomorrow may be too late! Know that God is already much offended, and His justice will come upon the world like a thief in the night!

Janie: Beloved St. Joseph, is God angry with us?

St. Joseph: No, my little one, God is not angry, but much offended for all the evilness that exists in many hearts. Know that God loves all His children, but many continue to reject His love. Behold, my little one, and see the love and mercy of God.

The Warning (Illumination)

Fire From Heaven

Janie: At this time I saw a bright light up in the sky. Then, this light was absorbed by yet a much brighter light, an immense light. My heart was pounding so fast. Then, I saw a huge Cross across the sky that covered every corner of the world. The Cross was like a neon light.

Then, Jesus, Our Lord, appeared on the Cross. I could see His wounds, His Sacred Heart. Then, before my eyes I saw rays of light that came from His wounds and His Heart down upon all the people in the world. These rays of light appeared to be like laser beams of light that pierced every heart. Then I heard horrible screams. I said to Our Lord, "Why are the people screaming?"

Jesus: Through divine grace all of humanity is absorbed with seeing all the sin which lies in the very core of their souls.

Janie: I understood that perhaps some souls would die from seeing their sinfulness. Then I saw people running in all different directions. I asked Our Lord, "Where are they going?"

Jesus: Behold the goodness of My Father.

Janie: I saw a multitude of angels all in the sky. Great light came from them. Their light was coming upon thousands of what appeared to be Cathedrals. These Cathedrals were beautiful. The people were racing to these beautiful Cathedrals. I understood that these

120

were the souls that had repented after seeing their sinful souls. They were seeking Reconciliation.

This great light that penetrated all souls happened all at once. Perhaps the duration was between five to ten minutes; I am not sure. It seemed to me like all time stood still. This great light from Jesus pierced every soul in the world at the very same time. I understood that this was truly a time of great grace. Before the vision ended, Our Lord said these words to me.

Jesus: The world must trust in the intercession of St. Joseph, for he has been chosen by My Father to help the world in these troubled times. Devotion to St. Joseph is most important. He will lead many to the Two United Hearts that are One with the Father.

Janie: Then the vision was gone.

St. Joseph: My little one, hold dear to your heart all that you saw today. Know that I, St. Joseph, will help all who seek my intercession. Peace, my little one, peace.

Janie: Thank you, beloved St. Joseph, and peace to you.[8]

Maria Esperanza - The Fourth Message Of Betania

There Is Coming The Great Moment Of A Great Day Of Light.

"Little children, today, healthful for your souls you must contribute to helping me build my house in this place. A refuge of a Mother with the title, 'Mary, Reconciler of People and Nations: Pray, meditate, and nourish yourselves with the bread of the Eucharist which gives you supernatural life. Be what you are: strong souls, healthy and strong, to combat with the weapons of love since it is love by which you are going to penetrate hearts and the consciences of all my children, dwellers of these lands, in a summons, an outcry shouting: 'Rise up, the hour has come for rebuilding the moral values of a People of God.'

"I want to be known, I repeat to you, under the name of Virgin and Mother, Reconciler for the People because man needs to find himself. He needs to see in each human being his or her own brother or sister. Ideologies may be respected because it is respect that is due to one's self, to each one, to recognize each one as a member of one same family, the family of God.

"Little children, all rise to a single ideal, struggle for the poorest and the most abandoned, struggle for the new generation that must grow and develop in a healthy environment.

Yes, my children, learn the value of each person in his or her own milieu where he or she lives and moves, with his or her way of thinking as well as in the negative side of their surroundings. Learn to value these people in or- der to help them to fight against the evil that surrounds them, drawing them forward to live in a healthy atmos- phere in spiritual peace as God, the Father, wishes to save you all by faith. It is man's answer in the midst of the structure of society, being sure that God has created you.

"**Little children, I am your Mother**, and I come to seek you so that you may prepare yourselves to be able to bring my message of reconciliation. **There is coming the great moment of a great day of light. The consciences of this beloved people must be violently shaken so that they may 'put their house in order' and offer to Jesus the just reparation for the daily infidelities that are committed on the part of sinners.**

"Little children, I want to take possession of your hearts! To give you in the Holy Spirit the gift of understanding that you may find the profound significance of my pres- ence among you. I am offering you the opportunity of the great promise that one day my Divine Son will make known to you. It is essentially important in these times: 'The Reconciliation of the Universe.' Oh may it be... people with God, and people with each other!

"Lo, this Mother who is pleading as the poorest of women, the littlest, the most humble, but the most pure; she wishes to transmit to you again the purity of heart, simplicity, loyalty, obedience to the service of your brothers and sisters, prudence, and still more, constant zeal for the works of our Mother, the Church. Today there is need of giving testimony with your life and your faith in God so that this Mother may be able to prepare you for the apostolate. Prepare you, yes, and the invitation is commendable and assuredly valid if you desire it. With a recommendation for perseverance, proceed and put it into practice."[31]

Christina Gallagher - The Warning

Everyone Will See Themselves As They Really Are In The Sight Of God

Christina said: "There will come a sign, which everyone in the world, in an interior way, will experience - - and it is not far away. Everyone will experience an inner awareness and they will know that this is from God, and they will see themselves as they really are in the sight of God. It is up to each one of us to help as many people as we can by our prayers, so that when this supernatural sign comes, they will change, and will be able to respond to that sign and be saved by God."[30]

The Coming Sign

Christina Gallagher on December 14, 1996 had a vision and message from Jesus, Our Lord.

Jesus said: "... Those who desire to live in the justice of the world, will receive the justice of My Hand.

"**Soon the world will receive a Sign to know of My Reign**, for all things are desired through My heart and the heart of My Father. **Know that Justice will be served.** So many shout of truth and that they know the truth. They neither know nor serve the truth..."

In reference to the coming Sign, Jesus said:

"**Soon the sign that will be given will be My Face. My Face will radiate in the skies and throughout the world more brilliantly than a thousand suns, to show the triumphant glory of the Son of God and the Immaculate Heart of My Mother. For She Is Immaculate** - ever honored in grace before My Father, for truly I tell you, the fruit of Her womb brought the Light of God into the world."

(Christina understood that this was Our Lord bringing His mother for the triumph of her Immaculate Heart).

When Christina asked when this Sign would come, Jesus responded: "Soon, child, soon, the world will recognize its Creator! Soon the heavens and earth will change in its seasons.

The birth pangs rage in the world, but will multiply – calamity after calamity, storm after storm."

Fire From Heaven

Light From Heaven

Christina is then shown the heavens open. As the sky opens, there is a huge outpouring of light. It comes down and goes out all over the world. She sees the Face of Jesus, luminous and yet transparent, in huge form, coming forth. Gradually, His hands form and then His feet. From the wounds In His hands and feet, brilliant light shines down, so that these stand out more than the rest of His Body, which can be seen in outline in the light.

Christina can see His Heart living and beating. Within His Sacred Heart can be seen Our Blessed Lady, with her own Immaculate Heart beating and angels are to be seen moving everywhere. As the Light radiates, it penetrates everything.

Christina could see billions of enormous, loathsome black 'lizards fleeing in all directions to escape, but in vain. No matter where they attempted to hide, in houses, under rocks, it is impossible to escape the Light, which seems to penetrate the very earth itself.

The world is saturated with the Light.

Christina is also aware that the darkness which will come before this heavenly Illumination will plunge everything into a dense obscurity. [From Christina Gallagher's official internet site.]

126

Joanne Kriva - The Warning

In An Instant You Will Have Revealed To You The Dark Secrets Of Your Unrepentant Hearts

On October 25, 1995 The Lord God told Joanne Kriva: "There is more I wish to say to you... In the profound moment of truth, in that moment of infinitely pure knowledge of its God, the soul is illuminated and what is hidden in its darkness is brought forth. Nothing can remain hidden in the light of truth. Make no mistake, I am the Light and the Truth. In an instant you will have revealed to you the dark secrets of your unrepentant hearts. My dear children, in that moment you shall see what I see, and the knowledge of the state of your soul will bring to each, in its own way, a depth of suffering heretofore unknown. Children, it is far better to be reconciled to me now, for so few can withstand the immensity of horror that sin is. This is why I call you to repentance. This is why I ask you to prepare now. Let this knowledge open your hearts to My mercy so that in the moment of truth you will stand pure in the light of that moment. I love you, That is all."[10]

Joseph DellaPuca and Denise Curtin - The Warning

Denise Curtin and Joseph DellaPuca receive monthly apparitions of Our Heavenly Mother while praying

127

together in a special prayer room inside Joseph's home in Southington, Connecticut. Our Heavenly Mother has declared the room Holy Ground. This room is filled with holy objects, pictures and statues. On numerous occasions the statues and pictures weep holy oils that have a light scent of roses. The apparition room is where both Denise and Joseph pray several times a week.

They have met with a Bishop, who has discerned the messages and has also confirmed that, so far, their writings and conversations do not contradict the teachings of the Catholic Church.

This Will Be A Time Of Much Confusion And Frustration

On January 13, 1996, Our Heavenly Mother told Joseph DellaPuca and Denise Curtin: "My dear children, soon you will see your hearts and souls as God sees them, and as I see them. This will be a time of much confusion and frustration. This is how Satan will try and deceive you into believing that a false peace has come to the world: he will try and convince my children that there is no need to pursue your conversion to God. This is where you, my chosen children, must be ready to do combat with the enemy and take control of my children's souls." [4]

Fire From Heaven

Before You See My Son's Glorious Return, Our Father Will Show His Merciful Justice

On June 13, 1996, Our Heavenly Mother said to Joseph DellaPuca and Denise Curtin: ".... Before you see my Son's glorious return, our Father will show His merciful Justice, because of His infinite Love for His children. His Love will give my children a chance to come into His arms where He will embrace and love you, my children, like never before. When the Father gives you the final opportunity of choosing Heaven or Hell, you will then, my children, choose your fate through your own free will, your free choice.

The Father and my Son, Jesus Christ, will invite you into the heavenly Kingdom. I, your mother, weep in much sorrow for many of my children have turned their backs to my Son, and He will turn His back on many of my children forever.

The time has come for you, my children, to make the most serious decisions in your lives, the decision of an eternity of happiness and love or an eternity filled with tears and regret. My children, my Triumph is here and is continuing in the hearts and souls of my children who acknowledge me. What joy, my children, you will feel and have when you see my Son, Jesus Christ, come into His glory! But only after the very turbulent times that must precede His Second Coming.

Be strong, my children. Trust in my Son, have faith in my Son and hope in my Son's Mercy for my children's sins. My children, all my teaching must be taken to heart, learned, studied and put into holy action, for you will be guided by the Holy Spirit at all times. Have a deep conviction of love, my little ones, a total confidence in my love and care for you. This will be your Peace.

Live in my Peace, my children, to see clearly the state of the sinfulness existing in each soul that will cause many of my children to panic. My children are not aware of the sinful lives they are living, for Satan has deceived many of my children. The revelation of this state of sinfulness will become a source of bitterness and great sorrow to many of my children who have fallen victim to Satan.

I have pleaded with the Father to allow me to gather my children under my Mantle, but I am in sorrow in knowing that the time has ended in delaying the Father's hand of Justice. Please ponder these words, my children, you must believe them completely. I am your Mother who loves you.

Hear my plea, my children!" [4]

Change Your Life Before It Is Too Late To Be Saved

On August 13, 1996, Our Heavenly Mother said to Joseph DellaPuca and Denise Curtin: ".... My children, your sins are scorching the Earth with evil, as the life-blood of your faith is being tested. Your chastisements on the land will force people to move to new lands.

Your current farms are suffering droughts and floods as never witnessed before. **Soon growing food will be difficult and it will be desperately needed.** My children, you have been turned into evil waters that are leading you away from my Son, Jesus Christ.

My children, you will soon perish in the hands of the Evil One. I keep sending you many messages to awaken the spirit. Without your Mother, you are nothing, and you will be swallowed up in your sins. In me, you will find the bounty of graces that will lead you to Eternal Salvation.

In order for my Son's Purification of the Earth to be effective, there must be dramatic changes. When you see these changes, brace yourselves, my children, for *my Son's Warning*, which will be a startling experience to see your entire life in judgment. My children, I bring you this message of hope, even amidst the adversity now around you. Heed the meaning of *this Warning* and change your life before it is too late to be saved. Believe me that I am with you always, ready to protect and help you prepare.

Whatever happens will be the direct result of the Father's Love and Mercy for all mankind. Do not worry about yourselves. Just remember, the King of Glory is returning to secure His victory for His people. Just as I have prepared myself and everything necessary to bring my Son, Jesus Christ, into the world, so now the Father is sending me to my children to prepare them to receive Him."[4]

Fire From Heaven

On February 13, 1998, Our Heavenly Mother said to Joseph DellaPuca and Denise Curtin: "... The Day of The Lord begins with a new dawn, for it is a time for salvation and co-redeeming each other, for there is little time left for conversion. Soon our Father will grant the graces for mankind to clearly see their sins, for then my children will not be deceived by the lies of the Prince of Darkness, whose powers and illusions confuse my children." [4]

On December 13, 1999 Joseph DellaPuca and Denise Curtin received the message: "O My dearest little Children of the world, come to me Your Heavenly Mother in Faith, Trust and Obedience, letting go all your pride and selfishness. The pride and selfishness, which exists in your hearts and souls, is a sign of My Adversary's presence. You must die to the flesh, and allow my Beloved Spouse the Most Holy Spirit to live within you. Completely abandon yourself to Our Lord and Savior Jesus Christ. Your protection lies within my Immaculate Heart. The hour has come when the love of your Heavenly Mother will shine forth, showing all of my Children the way to follow. During the New Year, the trials and sufferings which await you will become greater than ever before. My Dearest Little Children, as you journey along the road of holiness, it will lead you to an intimate relationship with Our Lord and Savior Jesus Christ and away from the sinful World in which you live. Pray, Pray, Pray my little ones -- for Peace, Love and God's endless Mercy. Much faith Will be needed in these the End Times. Your angels will surround you like never before. Fight my Dearest Little Children, for this is the hour of my battle, this is the hour of my great victory over My Adversary and the Triumph of my Immaculate Heart. Please LISTEN carefully to my Son's words, for they are the only way to Eternal Life. These times are filled with many gifts being showered down upon you from Our Father in Heaven. Seek his forgiveness through confession, cleansing your souls to receiving the Divine Will of Our Father in Heaven. The dawn of each New Day will bring a heightened awareness to consecrate yourselves to the Sacred Heart of Our Lord and Savior Jesus Christ, and the Immaculate Heart of your Heavenly Mother. To possess a strong faith, requires endless prayers and sacrifices. I am the dawn, preceding the Great Day of Our Lord and Savior Jesus Christ. Peace will come from the merciful love of my Son, who is about to pour forth torrents of fire and graces which will make all things new. When you live in the Divine Will, Our Father in Heaven will live completely and in total harmony with you. These are the times of the great chastisements. The Cup of Divine Justice is full and overflowing. Please trust in me your Heavenly Mother, that all will work out for the Glory of Our Lord and Savior Jesus Christ and the salvation of souls. Let your Faith, Trust and Obedience be the only light, which enlightens you in these times of great darkness. In the coming days when you will see the truth of your hearts and souls, you need to unconditionally surrender your lives to the Will of Our Heavenly Father. Prepare yourselves to now approach the throne of Endless Glory. Do not be frightened, my Dearest Little children, live immersed in my

Fire From Heaven

Motherly love. I love you my Dearest Little Children, I love you my Dearest Little Children, I will always love you my Dearest Little Children. I am the Mother of all virtues, helping all of my children to live in Divine holiness and love.

The Bright Cross In The Heavens During The Warning

Dozule, France – Madeleine

On May 3, 1974, the 16th apparition at Dozule, France Jesus said: "The Glorious Cross, or the Sign of the Son of Man, is the announcement of the imminent Return in Glory of Jesus, risen from the dead."

In the 33rd apparition, on July, 4, 1975, Jesus said: "But, fear nothing, for here will rise in the sky the sign of the Son of Man which Madeleine saw shining from east to west. I tell you, it is by this Cross set over the world that nations will be saved."

On April 1, 1994, in message # 516, Our Blessed mother told Father Gobbi: "The bloodied Cross, which you contemplate today in tears, will be the cause of your greatest happiness, because it will be transformed into a great bright Cross.

"The bright Cross, which will extend from east to west and will appear in the heavens, will be the sign of the return of Jesus in glory.

"The bright Cross will be transformed from a gibbet to a throne of his triumph, because Jesus will come upon it to establish his glorious reign in the world.

"The bright Cross, which will appear in the heavens at the end of the purification and the great tribulation, will be the door which opens the long dark sepulchre in which humanity is lying, to lead it into the new reign of life which Jesus will bring with his glorious return."[2]

Paola Albertini, Italy - A Great Cross In The Sky

It has been reported that The Blessed Mother has also said to Paola Albertini, Italy, the visionary instrumental in healing Mother Angelica, among others, during her recent trip to the United States, that "there will appear a great cross in the sky. All will see it. Some will be converted. Some will be so frightened that they will die. And others will be indifferent to it. There will be a test, and then there will come this sign... Jesus and Mary will help us. Let us not be afraid."

Fire From Heaven

Saint Sister Faustina Kowalska (1905-1938)

Before I Come As The Just Judge, I Am Coming First As The King Of Mercy

Jesus told Saint Sister Faustina Kowalska in Note-
book I, #83: "Write this: before I come as the just
Judge, I am coming first as the King of Mercy. Before
the day of justice arrives, there will be given to people
a sign in the heavens of this sort:

" All light in the heavens will be extinguished, and
there will be great darkness over the whole earth.
Then the sign of the cross will be seen in the sky, and
from the openings where the hands and feet of the
Savior were nailed will come forth great lights which
will light up the earth for a period of time. This will
take place shortly before the last day"[20]

The Heavenly Body of The Warning

Amparo Cuevas, the Spanish visionary at El Escorial,
during an ecstasy in 1982 received the message: "Soon
a Warning will be given which will affect all people
everywhere.

"Each and every person will see the Warning and will
understand its meaning. When the Warning comes
there will be those who will be so terrified that they
will die from sheer fright.

"A star, the Asteroid Eros, will illuminate the earth

causing it to appear to be surrounded by flames during a period of some twenty minutes, an event which will spread panic everywhere. All those who believe in God and the Holy Virgin will remain in a kind of ecstasy during this period. This will occur in the near future.

"When Eros lights up the earth making it appear that the whole world is in flames, many people will wish to die at that moment in that shower of fire, which will strike fear in everyone, a fear which will in fact cause the death of many people; those who are just and who believe, will not suffer."[45]

Father Gobbi - The Relationship Of The Second Pentecost, The Warning, The Triumph Of The Immaculate Heart Of Mary, And The Establishment Of The Glorious Reign Of Christ

On May 30, 1982 Our Lady told Father Gobbi: "By the fire of the Spirit of Love, the work of the great purification will be quickly accomplished... the Church will be led to its divine splendor... Through the power of fire and blood, the whole world will also be renewed. Humanity will return once again to the glorification of the Father, through Jesus, who will at last have established His reign in your midst... He will come to you in all his fullness, by means of the triumph of the Immaculate Heart of Mary, His most beloved spouse."[2]

Life Review

Fire From Heaven

In message of June 7, 1987 Our Blessed Mother told Father Gobbi: "The Spirit of the Lord will fill the earth and change the world. The Spirit of the Lord will renew, with His divine fire, all the Church and will lead her to the perfection of holiness and of her splendor. The Spirit of the Lord will transform the hearts and souls of men and make them courageous witnesses of His divine love. The Spirit of the Lord will prepare humanity to receive the glorious reign of Christ, that the Father may be loved and glorified by everyone." [2]

On May 22, 1988 Our Blessed Mother by locution told Father Gobbi that the Holy Spirit will come, to establish the glorious reign of Christ, and it will be a reign of grace, of holiness, of love, of justice and peace. With His divine love, He will open the doors of hearts and illuminate all consciences. Every person will see himself in the burning fire of divine Truth. It will be like a judgment in miniature. And then Jesus Christ will bring His glorious reign in the world. [2]

On October 2, 1992 Our Blessed Mother told Father Gobbi in locution: "Your liberation will coincide with the termination of iniquity, with the complete liberation of all creation from the slavery of sin and evil. What will come to pass is something so very great that it will exceed anything that has taken place since the beginning of the world. It will be like a judgment in miniature, and each one will see his own life and all he has done, in the very light of God." [2]

138

Fire From Heaven

A New Fire Will Come Down From Heaven And Will Purify All Humanity

On May 22, 1994 Our Blessed Mother told Father Gobbi: "My hour is the hour of the Holy Spirit. <u>The triumph of my Immaculate Heart will coincide with the great prodigy of the Second Pentecost.</u>

<u>"A new fire will come down from heaven and will purify all humanity, which has become pagan. It will be like a judgment in miniature and each will see himself in the light of the very Truth of God."</u> [2]

Tongues Of Fire - Illuminated By Divine Light

On June 4, 1995 Our Blessed Mother told Father Gobbi: that <u>tongues of fire will come down upon you all, my poor children,</u> so ensnared and seduced by Satan and all the evil spirits, who during these years, have attained their greatest triumph. <u>And thus you will be illuminated by the divine light, and you will see your own selves in the mirror of the truth and the holiness of God. It will be like a judgment in miniature, which will open the door of your hearts to receive the great gift of Divine Mercy.</u>

"Only then will you see how <u>the tongues of fire of the Spirit of Love will renew the whole world, which will become completely transformed by the greatest manifestation of Divine Mercy."</u> [2]

grace & fire

Fire From Heaven

The Greatest Prodigy Of Divine Mercy - The Second
Pentecost

On January 19, 1996 Our Blessed Mother told Father
Gobbi: "I am the Mother of Love and Mercy.

At the moment when the world will be set free from the
Evil One and the earth purified by the painful trial
which, in many ways, has already been foretold to you,
my Immaculate Heart will be the place where all will
see fulfilled the greatest prodigy of Divine Mercy.

Thus the Holy spirit will pour out upon the world his
Second Pentecost of grace and fire, to prepare the
Church and humanity for the return of Jesus in the
splendor of His divine glory, to make all things new."
2

In the May 26, 1996 message Our Blessed Mother told
Father Gobbi: "The Second Pentecost will come to
bring this humanity -- which has again become pagan
and which is living under the powerful influence of the
Evil One -- back to its full communion of life with its
Lord who has created, redeemed and saved it.

"Miraculous and spiritual tongues of fire will purify
the hearts and souls of all, who will see themselves in
the light of God and will be pierced by the keen
sword of His divine truth.

"The Second Pentecost will come to lead all the
Church to the summit of her greatest splendor....

140

"The Second Pentecost will descend into hearts to transform them and make them sensitive and open to love, humble and merciful, free of all egoism and of all wickedness...

"The Second Pentecost will burn away, with the fire of His divine love, the sins which obscure the beauty of your souls...

"The Second Pentecost will descend upon all nations which are so divided by egoism and particular interests, by antagonisms which often set them one against the other...

"And thus together let us implore the gift of the Holy Spirit and together let us await the descent of the Second Pentecost, which will renew the world and change the face of the earth."[2]

Chapter 8

The Warning - Day Of Thunder

On April 24, 1995 - 9:13 A.M. Our Blessed Mother told Sadie: "...I can only say now, and it is now, the whole world will feel the illuminating gaze of Him whom they reject. All things said and done in the darkness will be held in this light...." [6]

The Conversion of St. Paul Was A Precedent of The Illumination

On January 25, 1996, Jesus told Sadie Jaramillo: "The conversion of My Apostle Paul was a precedent set in My word. It was his experience of private revelation! As he was blinded by My light, he knew he could no longer deny the One whom he persecuted.

And now all will be caught in this moment of Mercy as My light reveals once again My persecution! For what is sin, no matter what kind, if not My persecution....

As you are illuminated in My light and this moment (that) will be just you and Me, you will see your persecution of Me, but even more you will see My great mercy and love. And this day, which will be to many as a night of terror, will pass and then many, for whom you and others have suffered, will be brought into the harvest... there yet remains the outpouring of Mercy before final justice..."[6]

The Warning Will Be The Most Awesome, Holy Fulfillment Of Calvary

On February 19, 1995, Our Blessed Mother told Sadie Jaramillo: "My little sorrowful rose, I request that you take down my words.... For the greatest moment of divine mercy will bring many to the foot of my Son's glorious Cross. It will also be a time of chaos and confusion. I clarify to you, to prepare for a shortage of food items upon the arrival of this moment. And then for the control of famine which will follow.

It is the illumination of man's heart and soul. The heaven will crack with God's thunder. It will be the most awesome, holy fulfillment of Calvary; a moment to choose the path to eternal life, or to be led to eternal damnation.

The moment which will lead my remnant to begin harvesting in God's vineyard. You will tire, but you will work ceaselessly..."[6]

The Warning Is Our Lord's Final Act Of Mercy

On July 5, 1996, Jesus told Sadie Jaramillo: "My Vicar will go into exile until his martyrdom. My final act of Mercy, that which My Faustina prepared the world for, through the image, will be fulfilled. But in the end, for My enemies, fire will rain down from heaven and the Mighty hand of God will seek you out and destroy you, every last one, and you will be no more.... I will see you through the storm, and you will increase in courage and strength, for it will be by the very power of God those destined to be My Remnant will go through these final dark moments."[6]

On August 10, 1996 - 10:00 A.M. Jesus told Sadie Jaramillo: "...I am the King of Mercy and mercy I desire to bestow. For the last moment before justice I call you and all to be apostles of divine mercy. The will of God the Father has called many, and few have responded. Yet for the sake of those few, their prayers of the heart have been heard and much has been mitigated, so great is God's love...."[6]

On November 20, 1996, Jesus told Sadie Jaramillo: "Soon you will behold the greatest prodigy in the heavens. You will behold this with your eyes and feel it in your soul. You will see Me on the Cross in the heavens and the weight of your sins will be revealed in your soul. By a means of your consecration to My Most Sacred Heart, I have truly placed you there in My Heart.

"You will behold this great manifestation of Mercy from within My Heart, and the flames of My purifying Love will raise and will consume all that is left, that keeps you from totally loving Me."[6]

Fire From Heaven

The Greatest Act Of Mercy Since The Beginning Of Creation

On January 31, 1997, **Jesus** told **Sadie Jaramillo**: "The rumblings within the Church are signs leading up to the revealing of this Man of Perdition, this Man of Destiny, this Man: the Antichrist....

"This I tell you now, child, <u>I have spoken once of a light that will brighten a night and will announce to you and to all, the greatest act of Mercy since the beginning of creation</u> You are going to live through this tremendous evidence of My love. Tangible, physical evidence of God's infinite love for every creature alive on the face of this earth. You will be pierced with the sword of truth when all is revealed....

"Very soon, as many events will follow another quickly, you will soon be in the midst of the chaos, confusion and turmoil....

"<u>Do not let yourselves be deluded into thinking nothing will happen. It should have happened long ago, but I have desired to show mercy and, through the great intercession of the Queen of Heaven, great acts of god's Justice have been averted.</u>

"But we are in the final hours...

"The economic ruin of this nation will come swiftly...
"I implore My priests: Return your hearts to Rome, the Chair of Peter, My Vicar John Paul II and all that he

145

Fire From Heaven

stands for. It is the Truth, the Life and the Way." [6]

Mercy Will Descend Amidst Fire And Turmoil

In her public message to Sadie Jaramillo on June 8,
1998, Our Blessed Mother said to Sadie: "... As the requests of My Heart have not been complied with, and as
humanity continues to close both heart and ears to the
Words of Heaven, I now announce to you that this
will be the last public message given by me to you.
This message will be given in its completed form by
June 14, 1998...

Now I tell you mercy will come from the heavens and
be revealed in the midst of great chaos and upheaval!
..."[3]

Sadie Jaramillo's Vision of the Warning

Vision Of A Large Flaming Ball With A Tail

Sadie Jaramillo was told about the three visions of a
large flaming ball with the tail, that she had on August
18, 1994. Jesus said: "This ball of light will explode in
the conscience of man and he will see the dread of his
soul. He will fall to his knees and My enemies will curse
Me to their perdition." [6]

Sadie Jaramillo had had a vision on August 18, 1994 of
A flaming object with a tail of flames hurling through
space downwards in total blackness; same object with

146

planet in the distance; object and the planet ready to collide. Jesus said: "I have just shown you what will cause Man to fall on his knees and know the dread of his soul." [6]

On August 14, 1996, Jesus revealed to Sadie Jaramillo: "As the darkness envelops totally this created world, your light will give light to others. When the light comes in the darkness, it will bring the darkness that will reveal the Light."

Sadie said: "While receiving these words, I had an interior vision: I saw first a dark night with stars in the sky, then a burst of light like a fireball with a tail, which I have been shown before; then I see daylight suddenly growing darker until there is nothing but total blackness; then appears the Cross with Jesus Crucified." [6]

On November 20, 1996, Jesus told Sadie Jaramillo: "Soon you will behold the greatest prodigy in the heavens. You will behold this with your eyes and feel it in your soul. You will see Me on the Cross in the heavens and the weight of your sins will be revealed in your soul. By a means of your consecration to My Most Sacred Heart, I have truly placed you there in My Heart.

"You will behold this great manifestation of Mercy from within My Heart, and the flames of My purifying Love will raise and will consume all that is left, that keeps you from totally loving Me." [6]

Fire From Heaven

"Concerning the three visions of the large flaming ball with a tail that Sadie had on August 18, 1994, Jesus told Sadie Jaramillo on January 5, 1997: "This ball of light will explode in the conscience of man and he will see the dread of his soul. He will fall to his knees and My enemies will curse Me to their perdition."[6]

Sadie Jaramillo's Visions During November 1998

What follows is an account of the visions that Sadie Jaramillo had during the month of November 1998, and her own personal commentary. Since she was told last Spring that she would receive no more public messages, what has been given to her since then has been visions, and later explanations of the visions by Our Lord and/or Our Lady. This month of November she did receive three visions, but no following explanation. Still, she believes that Our Lord wants her to get them out to you, his holy remnant. She believes that her not receiving an explanation of these three visions is, in itself, a sign for us.

Sadie stated she had three Visions in the month of November 1998:

"Early in the month of November, during prayer, I had the following vision over a period of time: "I am shown two balls of fire, or something that looks exactly like the picture on the book of messages given to me, "The Great Sign." But I see the two balls coming at each other from opposite directions, and then they meet in the center and collide. I see the illuminated cross in the heavens, then I see a man who is looking up into the heavens. As I have been shown before, I see the explosion of light, and then this man puts his forearm up to his forehead and reels back. He then falls to his knees and begins to cry, holding his hands up to his face.

"On November 29, 1998, during a Marian Movement of Priests cenacle, I am shown the following:

"I see Jesus, first pointing out to me something up in the heavens. I cannot see what it is. But then he holds up his arm and points for me to see a watch that He is wearing. I know Jesus does not need a watch. I look at the watch and both hands are pointing to the 12. He then says to me, "You will not get far into this new year without seeing a great catastrophic event, and many events that have been prophesied, fulfilled." Without my hearing words, but with a kind of infused knowing, I am given the understanding that just as the midnight hour indicates the new year, Jesus is talking about the new Church year that began on that day, which was the First Sunday of Advent.

"In the third vision, I am at the bottom of a very long, narrow shaft, or hole. As I am looking upwards, I can see a tiny bit of light at what would be the top. I then see someone falling towards me. It is a priest. As he passes different "levels," I see that other people come to

The Warning will be accompanied by 2 heavenly bodies colliding in the heavens.

Fire From Heaven

the edge, and watch him pass by. Clearly, I know he is going to the bottom of the hole, which would be the "lowest" level of purgatory.

"I believe that the Lord has clarified for me in the first vision that the Warning of the Soul or the Illumination of Conscience will be accompanied by a great cosmic event that will be 2 heavenly bodies colliding in the heavens.

"The vision about the priest gives me a very sad feeling, knowing that this is what is happening to many of our beloved priests who are passing away right now. It also makes me want to re-double my efforts to pray, sacrifice, and fast for them. I know that in the Warning, or Illumination of the Soul, if we continue to pray, many will return to the truth! **The priests hold the key for God's people! The more priests that convert and return to the Truth, the better it will be for us in the, what I call, "grand finale."**

Sadie's personal comment: "November has been the first month that neither Jesus nor Mary has explained the visions which were given to me. I believe this also is an indication of the impending events. I believe that the Lord has called me to be a sentinel in the watchtower, to alert His holy remnant. Even though it may seem to us that nothing is, or will happen, we must not be caught off guard! That is exactly what Our Lord says in Holy Scripture. "Watch ye, therefore, praying at all times, that you may be accounted worthy to escape all

150

these things that are to come, and to stand before the son of man." Luke 21:36

"Part of Our Lady's Triumph is that this time has been shortened! Again in Holy Scripture, "And unless those days had been shortened, no flesh should be saved: but for the sake of the elect those days shall be shortened." Matthew 24:22

"Pray my brothers and sisters, and give thanks to God and Our Lady. Every day that nothing happens is one day less that we have to be under the reign of the Anti-Christ, or in another term, the New World Order!....

"I remain united with you in prayer, and God's servant. Sadie..."[3]

The Illumination Will Set The Countdown To Christian Persecution

Our Blessed Mother said to Sadie Jaramillo on Feb. 24 1997: "For this reason I have asked you to have a supply of provisions. (Sadie: This is to say, water, food and blankets, etc..) The signs will bring the eclipse and great cosmic phenomena not able to be explained, though they will try. Jesus I trust in you. Fear is not of God. Trust In My Love and the ability to provide and protect, according to the permissive will surrendered to God. I need your permission children to protect you. Do not stop imploring God the Father for Mercy! ...Your an-

151

gels and the saints will make their presence shown in indisputable ways. This day of Love's illumination will set the countdown to Christian persecution. Remember you will see it, you will feel it! But, has it not all been foretold? *Jesus I trust in you*[6]

Day of Thunder – Cosmic Disturbance

On August 13, 1997, Jesus told Sadie Jaramillo: "…. There is quickly coming this day of thunder, this cosmic disturbance… For disturbance will come, plagues will come, famine will come, the sword will come…"[6]

Two Heavenly Bodies

Jesus said to Sadie Jaramillo on September 8, 1997: "The storms of God's justice brings to many the loss of your home, to many the loss of your means of employment and, at the height of tribulation, once the man of iniquity is revealed, you will lose your means of providing food and external provisions, for the mark of this man will be required. Therefore I ask you now to prepare as best as you are able. Heed well what I say, for then God will do the rest. Iniquity and his reign must abound for a short time more. But to you who hold fast and persevere, great is your reward. The nations will soon be one. Your money will be one. Man's religion will be one, but in My Own, the Truth of the Gospel will be the light that will dispel the darkness. My light will keep you secure in the Refuge of My

Heart. And soon, you will all know this by means of the two heavenly bodies which will cause such cosmic disturbance, then you will see what I have called in the past the dread of your soul..."[6]

The Whole Of Humanity Will Know There Is A God, And How God Sees Them

On December 8, 1997, Sadie Jaramillo was told by Our Blessed Mother: "This next year will, (because you have been in the tribulation), be the peak of suffering in the lives of all humanity!

"The Holy Father will be forced into exile (Editorial note: delayed or mitigated); More (people) will fall away from the Truth (of the Catholic faith); The underground church will be the only place The Holy Sacrifice of the Mass will be heard (Editorial note: delayed or mitigated). The abomination spoken of in Daniel Chapter 12: 10-11 will take his seat (Editorial note: delayed or mitigated). Much of the hidden preparations of the Antichrist will be revealed!

"To counter these:

"You will experience the greatest miraculous prodigy of all-time. The whole of humanity will know there is a God, and how God sees them. Your lives and this world will change dramatically. Some who now fight against you, will fight with you! The crosses as signs will rise and no force will be able to destroy them;

Thunder

Fire From Heaven

The signs in the heavens will cause many to tremble with fear, (but) for the children of Mary you will marvel at the power of God! You will be filled with the fearless love of Christ. The acts of charity and selfless love will abound. You will pray unceasingly in this time. Many will be brought together in many places and you will have clergy, protected by the Holy Angels, ministering to God's remnant.

"Until the last moment when all events begin, you must tell all to give themselves to the Love of the Two Hearts! Cease their doubts and come into the safety of the Ark of My Heart...."[6]

The Day Of Thunder
Is A Type Of
Second Pentecost

On March 24, 1994 - 9:00 A.M. Our Blessed Mother said to Sadie Jaramillo: "This day of thunder is upon My children! To My own (the children of light), it is an awesome and wonderful thing! To the godless, their hearts will be filled with terror!

"It is a type of second Pentecost. My Divine Spouse will descend and, in a swift but thorough sweep, convict those souls of the truth and those souls will be brought into the Mystical Body of Christ. Others will know also, this is of God and though they resist, it will be a type of warning for them...."[6]

154

On March 28, 1994 - 8:30 A.M. Our Blessed Mother said to Sadie Jaramillo: ".... You see once more a little, but a little, of the devastation and death that still awaits this humanity that refuses to see the call of God, the hand of God and the mercy of God. Very soon now, this day of thunder is upon you and will be the signal dispatched to the four corners of the world.

"The Holy Spirit of God will be, once again, the power which will renew the face of this earth; will cleanse, and will purify. The children of light will be filled with wondrous awe at this advent of His arrival, and the godless will know their dread and truth of their souls! Have I not requested of My children, 'Pray the Holy Spirit come?'"[6]

On September 1, 1994 Our Blessed Mother told Sadie Jaramillo: "I have made reference to this day before to you as the day of thunder. It will be a day of reckoning, everyone with their sins in clear view, just as they are seen by God. No longer will the darkness that has pervaded every inch of the world, be able to blind these souls." [6]

In this message of November 12, 1994, Our Lady told Sadie: "I come to reveal to you, little sorrowful rose, this day of thunder is upon you. Believe the words we speak are for the preparation of the faithful, for their encouragement. So that the time of stepping out in faith has come... By the very power of the Holy Spirit, My children will burn in the fire of His love, leading and guidance. These will be times of very great miracles. The days of distress will be lightened by this fact...."[6]

Second Outpouring Of God's Spirit – Permanent Signs

On April 25, 1997 -2:20 P.M. Our Blessed Mother told Sadie Jaramillo: "Oh this year of blood, sorrow and tears! The cries of the just have been heard. So very much has been mitigated. But in this second outpouring of God's Spirit, He will burn and purify the consciences of men. And the purification of this world by fire will come....

"For only Divine Intervention can save humanity from self destruction and enslavement.

"Woe to you who do not recognize the warnings and the signs, as humanity lives out the Book of Revelation!...

"There will be signs that are permanent soon!"[6]

On May 16, 1997 - 3:00 P.M. Jesus told Sadie: " The signs which are beheld in the heavens continue, and soon the thunder will crack and you will know the second Pentecost comes!"[6]

156

Chaos, Grief, Anguish and Repentance

On September 10, 1994 Sadie Jaramillo was told by Our Blessed Mother: "I tell you this grave moment arrives for all humanity, all My children. The serenity of this day will be replaced by chaos and great reconciling of My children to their God, the Father. That, His just and holy justice will pass by them swiftly!"[6]

On September 10, 1994 Sadie Jaramillo was told by Jesus: "Little daughter of My Heart, in a moment's flash, the reality of this world will pass away and great confusion come upon the world, though the world chooses ignorance to the warnings that have been given. The great illumination of men's souls will cause grief, anguish and repentance."[6]

The Warning Comes Amidst Great Confusion and Turmoil

September 21, 1995 - 1:41 A.M., Feast of St. Matthew, Sadie received a message from Our Blessed Mother.

(S.J., I heard a voice and commanded it to go in the name of Jesus, if not of God.)

Our Blessed Mother: My little sorrowful rose, I am the Virgin who keeps vigil with My Son. I, who bore the Incarnate Word in My womb, give praise to the endless omnipotence of God the Trinity in whose midst I dwell.

157

Fire From Heaven

I ask you to keep vigil with Me as great events are now upon this nation of yours. I ask you to console My Jesus once again, abandoned, left alone and betrayed.

Know that the greatest prodigy of the Holy Spirit is upon mankind. It will be the unveiling of one's soul, before the omnipotent light of Christ in whose light, perfect and true, all darkness of sin and guilt will be revealed! Many now are in that valley where the decision for or against God will be made!

I ask you to keep a continuous vigil with me, praying for souls. Souls that will receive grace to repent, to convert and to believe. Do not fear what man can do to you. Trust in the Divine Providence that you have surrendered to. He it is who will keep you. He it is who will sustain you. He it is who will defend you.

A storm of enormous portion, death and destruction, will strike. The storm revealed in your dreams. There will follow, as a continuous scourge, one disaster after another. Amid Great Confusion And Turmoil, Will The Great Warning Come.

Many of the faithful now will lose faith! The interior of the Church will go very dark. The enemies will rage and persecute truth and those who follow it...."[6]

The Great Prodigy Is The Warning

Jesus said to Sadie Jaramillo on May 16, 1997: "...The

events happen simultaneously

Fire From Heaven

Great Prodigy is the Warning ... Treasure will be given both before and after the Warning... The Great Harvest: shining and ready souls I thirsted for on Calvary will be brought in if you continue to fall on your face and implore My Father for Mercy... All circumstances are being used to lead My children, and soon many will know, as you know, and take refuge... **Many events will happen simultaneously."** [6]

The Thunder Of God's Justice Will Resound

On November 9, 1996 - 4:30 A.M. Jesus told Sadie Jaramillo: "Now. Nature will mirror the fury of God's anger and many will be brought to their knees. Great confusion and chaos will abound. This nation will soon be under martial law and many even now see the signs.

"But the persecution of ethnic groups will increase, but I will have My own in the eye of the storm and it will not overtake you!

"The stage is set for the fulfillment of great and wondrous things. The light that will break through the hardness of man's heart and conscience will suddenly break through, but their woes are yet to begin!

"But you, My Mother's faithful..., you are My own and these I will protect as My own. You will bring in a great harvest of souls for My Father's kingdom....

159

Fire From Heaven

"But you, oh enemies of God, tremble, for God will seek you out and destroy you! Repent before it is too late! Great mercy have I shown you for justice to be postponed so many times, but no longer will this be. Mercy will be fulfilled and justice will reign!..."[6]

The Heavens Will Shake, The Earth Will Tremble

Jesus told Sadie Jaramillo on September 29, 1994: "The heavens will shake, the earth will tremble, all of creation will resound with this knowledge. In the light of Mercy, all will see the darkness of their soul. The moment is here."[6]

In the message *The Final Times,* on November 13, 1994 - 8:00 P.M., Jesus told Sadie Jaramillo: "This illumination of men's souls is even now at the point of being. There will come mass confusion, chaos, darkness and despair."[6]

Our Blessed Mother in her message on February 19, 1995 told Sadie Jaramillo: "...For the greatest moment of divine mercy will bring many to the foot of My Son's glorious Cross. It will also be a time of chaos and confusion. I clarify to you, to prepare for a shortage of food items upon the arrival of this moment. And then, for the control of famine which will follow.

"It is the illumination of man's heart and soul. The heavens will crack with God's thunder. It will be the most awesome, holy fulfillment of Calvary; a moment to choose the path to eternal life, or to be led to eternal damnation.

160

Fire From Heaven

"The moment which will lead My remnant to begin harvesting in God's vineyard. You will tire, but you will work ceaselessly. Know that, as our chosen one, every word taken down in dictation has been a prayer for the soul of someone lost. And everything which has been required of you will be brought to fulfillment.

"Because My remnant have sacrificed and offered acts of reparation, the Father's holy anger has many, many times over, been appeased. But this time of all times has come. My children have entered into the ark of My Immaculate Heart. With Me are the angels and saints, to bring in the Triumph of the Two Hearts!...."[6]

Harvesting From The Vineyard

On March 7, 1995 - 7:13 A.M. Michael, Angel Guardian of God's People and Church told Sadie Jaramillo: "... Soon we will be doing hand-to-hand combat with the demons and those who serve them.

"But we will also be harvesting from the vineyard. And after this great day (warning), many souls will be taken from the kingdom of death and eternal damnation to the kingdom of light and everlasting life. Do not be surprised. God is doing the same as He did in the yesterdays of time. He is doing the same today and forever."[6]

You Will See New Hearts Replace Cold Stony Ones

January 2, 1996 - 2:27 P.M. Our Blessed Mother told Sadie: "... At the moment of the great outpouring of

Fire From Heaven

God's Spirit on all, so none will deny being given any chance to choose, you will see the beginning of the harvest. You will see new hearts replace cold stony ones, you will rejoice with Me, for the fruits of the labor will become visible and apparent...."[6]

With Free Will We Must Choose

On November 13, 1995 - 1:00 P.M. Sadie Jaramillo was told by Jesus: "My Mother's sorrowful rose and daughter of My Heart Jesus who is coming in glory! I, who became the Word Incarnate! I who am give praise to the Father for the moment of triumph arrives!

"And I speak these words to you:

"My people perish for lack of knowledge. It is not because the knowledge and the truth is not among them, but because they refuse to hear and to see the call I have given through many of My instruments.

"Now knowledge will be given to all. Knowledge of My triumph on Calvary. Knowledge of who I am. Knowledge of how I bore the sins of each and all. Knowledge of the Father's great love to send Me to mankind, that salvation might be made available to all. Each will know, to the tiniest speck, all that stains their souls!

"I am King, and I will return to take up My Scepter and rule with all who have enthroned Me in their

162

To Jew & to Gentile

hearts. I will give My mercy, which is limitless and boundless, to all who will receive it! For this you and many others have been praying. For this you, and many others, implore the Father to make His will known in the lives of all His children. For this, the petition to send forth the Holy Spirit, unceasingly ascends to My Father. For this, My Mother and yours, has been granted Her requests to make the hearts of Her smallest children the place where Her triumph begins.

"Those who have taken refuge within Her Immaculate Heart, those who have allowed Her to mold, those who have embraced and followed Her way of humility, Her way of holiness, Her way of love, know then, how to embrace the crosses of suffering, that through God's will, have come to them. The triumph is in the Cross!

"What I speak is not new but, it is truth, and the truth cannot be changed! All that has been spoken of will come to pass. In the next moment your life and the lives of all will change. I will come to all as the King of Mercy! To Jew and to Gentile. To all I will come. All will be able to see and hear and know the truth. Then, as their will is free and a gift from God, they must choose. Then I will take My seat as the just Judge and none will stand before Me and be able to say "I knew not."

"Through the impending events, My hand is on you and all who are Mine and My Mother's. This triumph of Her Heart is the peace that will see you through and lead you into the Era of Peace! Now know that clearer

Fire From Heaven

direction will be given to you. <u>Remain at peace and per-severe, child. You and others like you are strong for the weak</u>...."[6]

This Warning Will Be Man's Last Chance And Hope For Salvation

On December 30, 1994 -7:15 A.M. Jesus told Sadie: "....This time of My warning is My gift to this poor humanity that has chosen to live in disregard of their God and each other. <u>The laws of God are profaned and dissolved by your nation's courts.</u>

"Therefore, I will turn your nation over to captivity. This warning, this light into your soul that will penetrate the impenetrable, will be man's last chance and hope for salvation; and for you, daughter and others, the ceaseless work begins..."[6]

On December 2, 1995 - 5:30 A.M. Our Blessed Mother told Sadie Jaramillo: "....Peace will not come to this nation of many gods and idols, to this nation that has turned its back on God! Christ must reign in the hearts and in the governments.

God's laws cannot conform to the world, the world <u>must conform to God's laws. But it chooses instead, greed for power and wealth, and eternal damnation.</u> In this choice it brings down also the fulfillment of time, the living out the days of distress, the final and most painful and bloody of these days!

Once again, as at Calvary, I see the crucifixion of My Son, the crucifixion of His Body, the Church. At Calvary I was comforted by few. <u>Again, I am consoled and comforted by few, in proportion to the many.</u> At Calvary I stood by in silence and prayed for the forgiveness of those who had inflicted the most torturous and painful blows of My Son's passion. Retribution was reserved for the Father alone.

At My command, My faithful remnant, again prays for mercy. And <u>again, it will be the holy and just anger of God that begins the cleansing of profanation of His Temple, His Body, His Church!</u>

<u>The schism, split, has been foretold to you and many others.</u> The world wallows in mire and sin, exalts and revels in every kind of base perversion. Truly, as has been said, it is many times worse than Sodom and Gomorrah. I lead, I console, I guide, <u>I am Co-Redemptrix, I am Mediatrix of all Graces.</u> This is given to Me by the Triune God.

"The warning will come in the midst of upheaval.

"The chastisements continue and will increase, the blood will flow deep. For this United States, its downfall will begin in the West. But My faithful are given peace. Live every moment in this peace, for the Holy Spirit, the Spirit of the Living God, is being poured out in abundance, preceding the Second Pentecost, on those who have willingly surrendered, prepared and remained watchful.

Fire From Heaven
"The Bridegroom comes for His Church!"[6]

Priests Will Be Moved By The Very Power Of God

On June 5, 1996, Jesus told Sadie Jaramillo: "My priests, for whom you have prayed, will be moved by the very Power of God to do all that will confront them very soon. They will know, by the very events through which they will live, that these are the times for which humanity has been prepared.

(Sadie's note: "The events Our Lord refers to, which will bring many priests to believe are: Great calamities of nature; the exile and martyrdom of Pope John Paul II; the revelation of the Antichrist; the Warning; the extreme unrest coast to coast, racially and economically; the crash of the stock market. Sadie doesn't know in what order. Many will happen almost simultaneously.)[6]

Physical Preparation For The Warning

On February 24, 1997, Our Blessed Mother said to Sadie Jaramillo: "For this reason I have asked you to have a supply of provisions. (Sadie: This is to say, water, food and blankets, etc.) The signs will bring the eclipse and great cosmic phenomena not able to be explained; though they will try. JESUS I TRUST IN YOU.

"Fear is not of God. Trust in My Love and the ability to provide and protect, according to the permissive will surrendered to God. I need your permission children to protect you.

166

"Do not stop imploring God the Father for Mercy! ... Your angels and the saints will make their presence shown in indisputable ways.

"This day of love's illumination will set the countdown to Christian persecution. Remember you will see it, you will feel it! But, has it not all been foretold? JESUS I TRUST IN YOU."[6]

Preparations For The Warning Are Spiritual Ones

On June 14, 1998, in continuation of the message of June 8, 1998, Our Blessed Mother told Sadie: "...I tell you again, that Mercy will descend amidst fire and turmoil! The symbols shown to you on your trip indicate the Red Dragon will rear its ugly head and align itself with those of the race of the Orient! So too will the Freemasons make their move to accomplish their one-world order. Islam is a sleeping giant ready to awaken. Thus for many in the coming days they will pray for death, for these have not prepared for this battle of all battles! The preparations are spiritual ones and many have spent precious time in only cares of the world. They will find, as with many of the princes of the Church, that there is a God! A God of Love who only asked for their heart! All that has been foretold to you and many others is on the point of being fulfilled. Know that I your Mother and the Mother of God, ask now from you the total focus of your heart on My Son Jesus, for this apostasy which is eclipsing the Church will soon bring darkness and the fulfillment of Daniel's prophecy. (Daniel Chapter 12). The one who has prepared snares and traps for humanity prepares for his un-

167

short time from revelation of the antipope to revelation of the antichrist

Fire From Heaven

veiling to the world. Peace, security and wealth, he will promise, order to a world filled with disorder! *The message you proclaim is to awaken the dead souls of my children to the truth....*"

Chain Of Bondage Of The Slavery Of Sin Is Broken By The Warning

On March 20, 1997, Sadie Jaramillo had a vision. Sadie stated: "I see an interior vision of Jesus, as in the image of Divine Mercy, an illuminated cross above Him, a great chain, like the ones that anchor ships, and Our Lady standing on Satan's head. I see myriad and myriad of angels. I also see a capital <u>A</u> with another capital <u>A</u> upside down resting on the first <u>A</u>. I later learned that this is the Masonic Lodge symbol. Above this is a Pope's Miter in black." This means the defeat of Satan and the breakage of the bondage of the slavery of sin by Jesus' Victory of the Cross. Chain broken by the Warning. The Divine Mercy image represents the illumination of our souls. The Triumph of Our Lady is represented by Our Lady of Grace standing on the head of Satan. The Masonic symbol, with the black Pope's Miter above it, represents the Antipope who will reign with the Antichrist. The fact that these two visions are side-by-side represents the <u>short length of time from the warning to the revelation of the antipope and the antichrist</u>."[6]

168

After The Warning

Role Of Our Lord's Chosen Instruments After The Warning

On May 26, 1995 - 5:00 A.M. Sadie Jaramillo was told by Our Lady: "As you gather in cenacle to await this return and mighty outpouring of grace and love, you will be empowered by Him, the Holy Spirit, <u>to go forth and prepare the hearts of those open to be received back into the fold.</u>" (Sadie said: "Our Lady refers to those who through the illumination (Warning) will be ready to receive instruction on the faith.).["6]

On March 4, 1997, Jesus told Sadie Jaramillo: "Thus the importance of My promises for Mercy Sunday must be propagated far and wide!

<u>The time for souls to respond after the illumination will be quick to end and it is during this time that My chosen instruments and persons will and must work tirelessly and unceasingly,</u> for the one who opposes Me will swiftly be brought to the revealing and unveiling!"[6]

Prepare To Receive Priests Who Are Backed To The Wall After The Warning

On November 5, 1997, Sadie Jaramillo had a vision and its explanation: "I saw a block wall and to this

169

Fire From Heaven

wall priests are being backed up. The expressions of
these priests vary from extreme anger, confusion and
understanding. As these priests actually reach the wall,
a door, like a trap door, swings open and some go
through it. Then the door closes."

Sadie's understanding of this vision is: "The angry
priests are the ones who knowingly are trying to destroy the Church. The confused ones are good priests
that perhaps were not trained correctly and know
something is definitely wrong. The ones who actually
go through the doors in the wall are the priests, who
right now, know what is happening and know in their
hearts they cannot stay (in their particular parishes),
and will go to places being prepared for them right now.
For it is my belief that the laity are right now preparing to
receive many priests that will go underground. I also believe that many priests will have to make a decision one
way or the other. Whereas right now they may go along
with an abuse of the Liturgy because they are afraid, if they
take a stand, they will be let go and have no place to go."
Sadie's understanding is that this will begin to happen very
soon.

On October 30th and 31st, at prayer, Sadie was shown a
place that has some kind of fencing with barbed wire up at
the top, military-like vehicles, and "soldiers" (?) dressed in
black with black ski masks, holding automatic weapons.
Jesus said: "My Vicar readies himself to proclaim the
dogma of My Mother's that will come, despite the opposition. Before and after that time will be tremendous
testing for you, My Body. For those times will bring the
persecution of the Truth of the faith to those who know

170

and proclaim it... <u>I have told you once of a night that would bring a great light and be a sign of the forthcoming prodigy.</u> Therefore be yourself vigilant and prayerful. For what comes will bring the distress of the time of all times... Prepare to receive My brothers (priests) who will be backed up to this wall of decision, and those who, after the Light of Truth invades their souls, will see and reject the error they now embrace, promote and teach." [6]

Role Of The Priests After The Warning

On September 9, 1997, Our Blessed Mother said to Sadie Jaramillo: "I have asked you specifically to <u>pray for the Princes of the Church, for soon they will stand one against another, openly.</u> Whereas now, the division occurs where the heart of that shepherd is closed to the Vicar of Christ...I will tell you where you will find this Holiness: In the tabernacles...in the confessional of God's people... If you (priests) now are preparing to face oceans of people clamoring to be reconciled, to have their fears calmed, then you do well... The dawn of many storms is upon you and in the midst of turmoil, again I tell you *the cosmic disturbance brings forth your judgment in miniature...* Prepare to assist My priest sons, My children, for they will soon be at the crossroads of decision." [6]

March 1, 1998, at 5:30 P.M. in a message to Sadie Jaramillo, Our Blessed Mother said: "Pray the exorcism prayer of St. Michael, for the enemy knows no rest!....

Hold fast & persevere.

Fire From Heaven

My priest sons, prepare to reconcile My children to their God! My priest sons, prepare to receive your brothers now embracing error, soon accepting truth!

My child, prepare to receive many who will come for counsel and teaching, instruction and Love! My children, prepare to take in My priest sons. Darkness falls upon the Church!"[6]

Status Of The People After The Warning

On September 9, 1997, Jesus then said to Sadie Jaramillo: "The storms of God's justice brings to many the loss of your home, to many the loss of your means of employment and, at the height of tribulation, once the man of iniquity is revealed, you will lose your means of providing food and external provisions, for the mark of this man will be required.

Therefore I ask you now to prepare as best as you are able. Heed well what I say, for then God will do the rest. Iniquity and his reign must abound for a short time more. But to you who hold fast and persevere, grace is your reward.

The nations will soon be one. Your money will be one. Man's religion will be one, but in My Own, the Truth of the Gospel will be the light that will dispel the darkness. My light will keep you secure in the Refuge of My Heart.

172

And soon, you will all know this by means of the two heavenly bodies which will cause such cosmic disturbance, and then you will see what I have called in the past the dread of your soul."[6]

In a message to Sadie Jaramillo on January 30, 1998 at 7:00 a.m., Our Blessed Mother said: "The warning of God's Love will be upon you and the whole world! In the crucible of Truth and His Love the lost will be found; the lukewarm will be fanned into flame; the fervent will rise to the degree of the heroics needed for the Truth of the Church to flourish once again!"[6]

Sadie's Vision Of And Her Own Experience Of The Warning

On December 30, 1997, at 1:45 A.M., Sadie Jaramillo received a message. Sadie was awakened an asked by Our Lord to write of her recent visions... Sadie stated: "On Sunday, December 28, the feast of the Holy Innocents, I'm making my thanksgiving after receiving Holy Communion, when I see a brilliantly illuminated cross against a very dark sky. It seems as if this cross is beaming rays of light down towards the earth. There is some light and I see people prostrate in adoration, like the kneeling Magi in my nativity scene. This is very intense and seems to be occurring for each person individually. It seems that this cross is close enough that I could reach out and embrace the foot of it.

Fire From Heaven

Even where there is no light, I can see silhouettes of people, cowering back in intense fear, almost to the point of despair, hands up to their faces, crying, and then some falling to their knees. I have been shown this before.

At this point, I begin to see scenes of my own life from early childhood, beginning around seven years of age. It seems as if I am seeing a series of still photos of many scenes that lead to the time of my conversion. I feel intense shame and I begin to cry uncontrollably (yet silently for I am still in Mass). Through all of these scenes I did not see Our Lord, but I felt His Presence of Love. Though I did not hear these words, this understanding was given: 'I beheld all these things of your life and I still love you. For I do not remember them ever. I reveal them to you, for I place you in the crucible of My Love."

Jesus told Sadie: "Yes child, it is I, Jesus. Born as a child to walk among men, to be crucified and die, so that many could live and experience the Glory of My Resurrection!

"The hour is late and I have told you, 'I am going to place you in the crucible of My Love,' to experience, if you will, a mini-judgment.

The illuminated cross all will see, and if it seems you could embrace the foot, it is because on Calvary I saw each and all and it is a personal experience for those who finally surrender unto Me in their heart.".... [6]

fire of the Holy Spirit AND physical fire.

Fire From Heaven

Vision of Sadie Jaramillo on May 10, 2000

In a message on June 11, 2000 Sadie states regarding her vision on May 10, 2000: "I refer here to a vision of the world exploding in fire, given to me almost one year ago on June 10, 1999, which included the Blessed Trinity and the Blessed Mother. (The Great Sign, Volume II, page 92)

"Today I was shown a similar vision, with this difference. This time I only saw the world. Very simply, while in prayer, I saw a vision of the world, and then it exploded into fire. The fire I saw this time indicated to me that it would be the "fire of the Holy Spirit" (as in the Warning) and also the element of physical fire that would purify the world. This will be from natural causes that could include human acts, storms, earth movements and even a collision with an object from deep space.

Chapter 9

The Co-Rulers Of Evil

The False Prophet And The Antichrist

The Evil Head Of The Anti-Christ Will Now Rise In Conjunction With The Antipope

On November 13, 1997 Our heavenly mother said to Denise Curtin and Joseph DellaPuca: "My beloved daughter and son, the End Times have now come upon us, and as I have prepared you, you must now prepare

my children. And you shall see the unfolding of
events, which shall take place in rapid succession.
The evil head of the Antichrist will now rise in conjunction with the Antipope. My Son's Church prostrates, caused by the schisms within the Church,
which is causing the division of the Catholic religion,
and soon your daily Mass will be held underground,
as the cohorts of the Anti-Christ seek to destroy those
who follow my Son, our Lord and Savior, Jesus Christ.
Prepare your souls, for the final battle is about to begin."[4]

Exile and Martyrdom of Pope John Paul II Followed By The False Pope

Ida Peerdeman, Holland, during her tenth vision on
June 9, 1946, saw stars everywhere in the air, then suddenly in front of her, a cardinal's hat. A sign in the
form of an X appeared and covered it over. Rome was
shown to her. There was a dispute over the pope. She
saw numerous bishops who were not Roman Catholics. A voice rang out: *"What A Pity!"*[1]

Julia [Julka] of Yugoslavia on February 28, 1976, in a
conversation with Our Lord Jesus Christ about Pope
Paul VI and the false Pope. who according to the
prophecies will come, was told: "The false Pope has
not yet come! One day, when the false shepherd rules
he will spread a false doctrine and will persecute the
Church. You will recognize him by the persecution of

the Church. He will not have much time at his disposal. His rule will be short but strong. The good Christians and My true servants will have to hide themselves... The safest is to be with one's relatives... Once the false Peter is in, he will persecute My Church and My Flock will be dispersed..." [33]

On March 3, 1976 Julia had a vision of the Antipope. Julia said, "In Rome, in the Square of Saint Peter's, very many people were crowded. Over their heads flew a great white flag, with four red bands, lengthwise. From the entrance of the Basilica of Saint Peter a priest appeared with a tall cylinder on his head and a strange coat over his shoulders. His robust face and the cylinder were surrounded for some moments by a white mist. But on the top of the cylinder the mist was not joined. This priest radiated no mildness and goodness. He watched the gathered crowd with a gloomy face. Above the priest a Voice was heard: "This will be the false Pope." He did not remain for long; after a short time he disappeared." [33]

Joanne Kriva on June 25, 1992, received a message from Our Lord which noted that one cardinal, who works seditiously to destroy what Pope John Paul II, his chosen vicar, seeks to affirm as the revealed truth of His Word is a son of Satan. This son of Satan, whose plotting and scheming will usher in the apostate church, and his cohorts, who stands poised to step into the shoes of the Fisherman, [who] is not

Our Lord's successor, but a usurper and not the legitimate heir to the throne of Peter. In this apostate church every aberration will be condoned, every blasphemy permitted. This abomination is the church of Satan. The desecration of Our Lord's holy temple will be complete. Our Lord said prepare well for his hour of infamy is upon you. The true sacrifice and the living Eucharistic Presence will disappear from His Churches." [10]

Jesus told Sadie Jaramillo on July 5, 1996: "My Vicar will go into exile until his martyrdom. My final act of Mercy, that which My Faustina prepared the world for, through that image, will be fulfilled.... all you who will accept My Teachings and Words of everlasting life, who still look towards the Chair of Peter, My Vicar, as your true representative of Me, you are anchored safely in My Heart and the Heart of My Mother, two yet one, and the storm will not prevail.... I have never left My Church, though in many churches I have been put out. I will see you through the storm, and you will increase in courage and in strength, for it will be by the very power of God those destined to be My Remnant will go through these final dark moments. Just as I opened the way, in many other times of persecution, so it will be again." [6]

On August 12, 1996, Jesus told Sadie Jaramillo, "There will be intense changes in the weather soon. Prepare! The wolves who hide in sheep's clothing are known to Me as they prepare to remove My True Vicar from the Chair of Peter. Prepare for the priests who will flee." [6]

Our Lady spoke to Sadie on October 7, 1996: "And the intentions [nine hour novena] today must be for the Pope of My Heart. How he suffers. I will receive him soon to be clothed in his heavenly garments and martyr's crown." [6]

On December 9, 1996, Our Blessed Mother told Sadie: "For the souls of my priests lie perilously in danger. Some have not the courage to fight and stand against the errors of disobedience. The darkness that comes will reveal the True Light. It will separate My faithful from those who will gleefully embrace the great Apostasy of the Church. Up to now changes have been through rebellious acts of disobedience, but very soon the cry will resound from East to West - No to Rome! (No to the Holy Father!)" [6]

Blessed Anna-Maria Taigi (d. 1837), who for forty-seven years saw past and future events throughout the world, through a gift from God, stated: "Religion shall be persecuted, and priests massacred. Churches shall be closed, but only for a short time. The Holy Father shall be obliged to leave Rome." [18]

St. Pius X (d. 1914): "I saw one of my successors taking flight over the bodies of his brethren. He will take refuge in disguise somewhere; and after a short retirement he will die a cruel death. The present wickedness of the world is only the beginning of the sorrows which must take place before the end of the world."[18]

A Masonic Pope - The Black Pope

Sadie Jaramillo, on June 16, 1996, had a vision during Mass, after communion, as she was giving her thanksgiving. She states, "I saw something very strange. There was this man, dressed in black, in black pontifical robes, with a black miter, the type the Pope wears. I felt nothing but evil looking at this man who will be the next Pope, the false Pope."[6]

At 7:00 P.M., June 16, 1996, Sadie was told by Our Blessed Mother, "This man exists and awaits his moment to take the seat of Vicar of Christ, though he, along with many, are the wolves in sheep clothing. This day is near. This storm will break, not only in the Body of Christ, but then onto the world."[6]

On March 20, 1997, Sadie had an interior vision of Jesus, as in the Image of Divine Mercy, an illuminated cross above Him, a great chain, like the ones that anchor ships, and Our Lady standing on Satan's head. Sadie said: "I see myriads and myriads of angels. I also see a capital A with another A upside down resting on the first A. I later learn that this is a Masonic lodge symbol. Above this a Pope's Miter in black."

Sadie, writing about her understanding of this vision, said: "The Masonic symbol, with the black Pope's Miter above it, represents the Antipope who will reign with the Antichrist. The fact that these two visions are side by side represents the short length of time from the Warning to the revelation of the antipope and Antichrist."[6]

The Black Pope's Reign Will Be Shortened

On March 31, 1997, Jesus told Sadie: "... The black Pope will soon be seated and reign with the one who opposes Me. From the time of the illumination of your souls to the time of the revelation of this man of perdition will be short. (I hear the Number 6). And he will reign 6 and 6 and 6 more. Of this be assured: The Queen of Mercy has obtained the shortening of his reign. Scripture says 'if this time had not been shortened, not one would survive.'"[6]

The Antichrist

On November 26, 1990, Our Lord told Joanne Kriva, a midwestern housewife and mother: "The day of destruction is at hand... The Pope (John Paul II) will die. His death will signal the reign of Antichrist.[10]

Satan, Antichrist And The New World Order

On August 11, 1991, Our Lord said to Joanne Kriva: "Do not doubt that I, the Lord God, act with justice in a world

Fire From Heaven

suffering its final assault permitted to the Evil One. His days are numbered... I, the Lord God, speak now in warning. Be alert, my people to the dangers that surround you. Do not be deceived by those who seek a new world order. This is the plan of the Evil One. The promise of a new order created by the hands of man is doomed to fail. It is an illusion of minds seduced once again by the Serpent -- 'You will be as gods'." [10]

On September 20, 1991, Our Lord said to Joanne Kriva: "The Evil One now embarks upon his plan to subjugate all the nations of the earth. Be thou warned of his plan to make himself emperor of all nations and all peoples. His peace is a false peace. His minions create havoc and turmoil, doubt and confusion. The leaders of the world are puppets in his scheme of world domination. His name is Anathema. His presence is death.. Know that his hour is at hand. He begins now his final assault. From the holy place does he begin the final conflagration. Keep alive the faith. He desecrates My holy tabernacles. He spills the blood of My holy ones. He sustains himself on the blood of the martyrs. He violates what is pure and chaste; he ravishes the maiden; he crucifies without mercy the undefiled. He is the carnivorous beast who feeds on the flesh of his enemies. He is the beast of the Apocalypse." [10]

On March 5, 1992, Our Lord told Joanne Kriva: "Say in My name, say to My people: Mankind now enters a most critical period of its history. Nations form alliances, but I tell you there shall be no alliances when the Son of Evil announces his dominion. All nations shall be as one, and he will rule with an iron fist. He does not offer mercy as your Father in heaven offers mercy. He shall call himself

183

the Messiah. My children on earth will pay him homage and raise him up upon the throne of infamy. My children of My Spirit will he raise up upon the cross of persecution. These are of the kingdom of the Father..."[10]

On April 28, 1993, Joanne Kriva was told by the Lord God: "I am Jesus the Lord who comes to bring you the good news of your deliverance from this age of Satan. The diabolical plans of the Son of Corruption slowly unfold and soon he will claim his place as undisputed leader of the world. His scheme for world domination has long been evolving, and the time for its fulfillment is at hand."[10]

On September 19, 1993, Our Lord said to Joanne Kriva: "I wish to speak, little child of My heart. Today begins the rapid unfolding of events which will usher in the final holocaust of the end times. My people are lulled by a false security. My people must understand that the agreements of peace between peoples and nations are but a prelude to great deceptions by those who seek to rule the world. I solemnly tell you that the stage is being set for the one who will step forth as the great deceiver of all mankind. He orchestrates this masterpiece of deception, and those open to My Spirit understand the meaning of the events that are about to befall mankind..."[10]

On October 3, 1993, the Lord God, Prince of Peace, told Joanne Kriva: "In My name say: "...Stop your evil. I warn you solemnly that the world now stands on the brink of disaster. Beware of those who plot to secure a world federation of nations. Beware, for these agents of Satan will succeed in destroying all of creation. Beware of the one who beguiles you with the promise of world peace. This is a peace forged out of lies, deceptions, brutal inhumanity, and ruthless enforcement of lethal laws and policies. I solemnly tell you that this peace is a delusion which is the prelude to the annihilation of the world. Therefore, My people, you must keep vigilant and seek your peace in Me. If you know Me, you will not be seduced by the promises of the false prophet of the Apocalypse (Rev. 16:13-15)..."[10]

Rome Will Lose The Faith And Become The Seat Of The Antichrist

On September 19, 1846, at La Salette, Our Blessed Mother, in an apparition approved by the Church, stated: "Rome will lose the Faith and become the seat of the Antichrist".[7]

The Person Who Is The Antichrist

In message #362, September 15, 1987, at Akita (Japan), Our Blessed Mother told Fr. Gobbi: "Even now, that which I predicted at Fatima and that which I have revealed here in the third message confided to a little daughter of mine is in the process of being accomplished. And so, even for the Church the moment of its great trial has come, because the man of iniquity will establish himself within it and the abomination of desolation will enter into the holy temple of God."[2]

In message #425, May 13, 1990, at Fatima (Portugal),

Our Blessed Mother told Father Gobbi: "*My third secret*, which I revealed here to three little children to whom I appeared and which up to the present has not yet been revealed to you, will be made manifest to all by the **very** occurrence of the events. The Church will know the hour of its greatest apostasy. The man of iniquity will penetrate into its interior and will sit in the very Temple of God, while the little remnant which will remain faithful will be subjected to the greatest trials and persecutions. Humanity will live through the moment of its great chastisement and thus will be ready to receive the Lord Jesus who will return to you in glory." [2]

In message #450, May 19, 1991, Berlin (Germany), Our Blessed Mother told Father Gobbi in locution: "You have now entered the times of the Second Pentecost... The Holy Spirit will make you understand the signs of your time. They are the times foretold by Holy Scripture as those of the great apostasy and of the coming of the Antichrist." [2]

In message #489, at Fatima, on March 15, 1993, Our Blessed Mother told Father Gobbi in locution: "... as of now - as of this year, - you have entered into the events of which I foretold you, and which are contained in the third part of the secret, which has not yet been revealed to you. This will now be made evident by the very events themselves which are about to take place in the Church and in the world. My Church will be shaken by the violent wind of apostasy and unbelief, as he who sets

3½ years of abomination
Mass not sacrifice, but meal
Fire From Heaven

himself against Christ will enter into its interior, thus bringing to fulfillment the horrible abomination which has been prophesied to you in Holy Scripture. Humanity will know the bloody hour of its chastisement; it will be stricken with the scourge of epidemics, of hunger and fire; much blood will be spilt upon your roads; war will spread everywhere, bringing down upon the world incommensurable devastation."[2]

On Dec 31, 1992, Our Blessed Mother told Father Gobbi that the Antichrist "will enter into the holy temple of God and will sit on his throne and have himself adored as God." When he does this, he will begin the 1290 days, the three and a half years of the horrible abomination predicted by Daniel in the Old Testament, during which the Holy Sacrifice of the Mass will be abolished, with the Mass being considered only as a sacred meal and not a sacrifice, a remembrance of that which Jesus did at his last supper; the protestant doctrine."[2]

The False Church As The Antichrist

In message # 407, on June 17, 1989, Our Blessed Mother by locution told Father Gobbi: "Join with me in battle, little children, against the beast like a lamb, Masonry, infiltrated into the interior of ecclesial life in order to destroy Christ and his Church. To attain this end, it seeks to build a new idol, namely a false christ and a false church....

Fire From Heaven

"Ecclesiastical Masonry goes as far as even building a statue in honor of the beast and forces all to adore this statue....

"And so they substitute for God a strong, powerful and dominating idol. An idol so powerful that it puts to death all who do not adore the statue of the beast. An idol so strong and dominating as to cause all, small and great, rich and poor, freeman and slaves, to receive a mark on the right hand and on the forehead, and that no one can buy or sell without having this mark, that is to say, the name of the beast or the number of its name. This great idol, built to be served and adored by all, as I have already revealed to you in the preceding message, is a false christ and a false church.

Lucifer, the ancient serpent, the devil or Satan, the Red Dragon, becomes, in these last times, the Antichrist... The statue or idol, built in honor of the Beast to be adored by all men, is the Antichrist. You have thus arrived at the peak of the purification, of the great tribulation and of the apostasy. The apostasy will be, as of then, generalized because almost all will follow the false christ and the false church. Then the door will be open for the appearance of the man or the very person *of the Antichrist!*" [2]

In message # 449, *The Pope of My Secret*, May 13, 1991, Our Lady told Father Gobbi: "When this Pope will have completed the task which Jesus has entrusted to him and I will come down from heaven to receive his sacrifice, all of you will be cloaked in a dense darkness of apostasy, which will then become general.

There will remain faithful only that little remnant which, in these years, by accepting my motherly invitation, has let itself be enfolded in the secure refuge of my Immaculate Heart...."[2]

In message # 528, September 29, 1994, "The Angels of Your Time", Father Gobbi was told by Our Blessed Mother: "Saint Michael will above all intervene to fight against the ancient enemy, Lucifer, who in the final hour will appear with all the dark power of the Antichrist."[2]

From these messages we have the identities of Antichrist discussed below by St. Augustine: a.) a church, the mass of people, the whole body of Satan, the false church and false christ, and b.) the real person, the Antichrist possessed by Satan, as Lucifer in these end times becomes the Antichrist.

The Antichrist And The Temple Of God

Is the temple in which the Antichrist sits to be adored as God the rebuilt Temple of God in Israel (as some of the Fathers of the Church such as St. Irenaeus and St. Cyril believed), or is it a Church, a question raised by St. Augustine?

St. Augustine held: "It is not certain what temple the

Fire From Heaven

Antichrist will use to accept divine worship, whether the ruined and restored temple of Solomon or a Church. Yet the Apostle, it would seem, would not call a temple of an idol or demon the temple of God. Some think therefore, that the Antichrist in this passage refers not specifically to the prince of evil himself, but to his whole body, the mass of people who adhere to him as their prince. Others think that the Antichrist will act as if he were the temple of God himself, as if he were the Church itself."

St. Thomas said: "that others maintain that never will Jerusalem or the temple be rebuilt and that he (Antichrist) will sit in the Church in the sense that many from the Church will receive him. St. Augustine says that he (the Antichrist) with his adherents will form a church just as Christ and his followers are a Church."

Except for an underground Church, subject to intense bloody persecution, worse by far than any prior persecution of the Church, there will be no valid public Mass, no valid public sacrifice for 1290 days, until the fall of Antichrist, when he will be cast into Hell with his false prophet for all eternity.

The Church At The Time Of Antichrist

Jeanne Le Royer, Sister Mary of the Nativity, born 1731, died 1798, a visionary, said that she saw that "when the Second Coming of Christ approaches, a bad priest will do much to harm the Church... When the time of the reign of Antichrist is near, a false religion will appear which will be opposed to the unity of God and His Church. This will cause the greatest schism the world has ever known. [32]

On Sunday, September 13, 1992, Marmora, Ontario, about 4 p.m., Our Blessed Mother appeared to Josyp Terelya and said: "... My child, I tell you the final times are near. My children. You are on the threshold of the day of judgment... Remember that Satan has infiltrated the very womb of the Church, and is spreading the idea of ecumenical Christianity, of his new interpretations of the faith. This has led to today's indifference and neglect in the religious education of children and the youth. There is a loss of the awareness of the true Catholic faith. The dangerous ideology of a modern ecumenical Christianity is spreading. Satanists are seeking to destroy Holy Sunday, so that modern Christians cannot discern between good and evil. Sunday is the greatest day in the Church of Christ. Defend if against Satan." [28]

Joanne Kriva related the message from the Lord God on April 20, 1994: "The powers of the Anti-Christ grow bold in their efforts to dismantle my Church. Slowly but surely the foundation upon which my Church was founded is subjected to the chisel of false teachers and the heresy of modernism. These shepherds listen to the dissonant voices and seek to please these faithless apostates rather than affirming the statutes and precepts which are the foundation of

My truth. They betray My faithful ones in the name
of progress and persecute, by their indifference, those
who remain firmly committed to the Church of Peter.
I am displaced. My people, you have forgotten the first
commandment --'I am the Lord thy God, thou shalt not
have strange gods before thee.' I will not permit these
strange ideologies and diverse egoism to be placed above
Me. No! I shall not permit this. However strong this
new church may seem, it will collapse upon itself for
it is founded upon lies, deceptions, false doctrines,
and the egos of those who seek only their own importance and power. I ask you, my faithful ones, to pray
unceasingly lest you fall victim to these strange gods
promoted under the guise of renewal. True renewal
does not destroy the foundation and the structure
thus, when the dismantling of the Church seems
complete, the seeds of truth and faith being nour-
ished by the care of the Mother, the Woman, will
flower in the New Era of Peace. Remain steadfast, My
people, and remember that I am God, and the gates of
hell will not prevail. Mine is the triumph. Thus say I the
Lord God." [10]

Modern Revelations About The Appearance
Of The Antichrist

Eileen George, a housewife and mother from Massachusetts, who has the support of her diocesan bishop, several cardinals and bishops, and many priests, is reported
as receiving visions and messages from God the Father
and Jesus.

Moslem

Fire From Heaven

On February 20, 1982, God the Father told Eileen George: "There will be a World War III and it will be started by a man who wears the turban of the faith, a Moslem. He will be an anti-Christ put on earth by Lucifer. Yet there is a more powerful one to rise in Syria, when this one has accomplished his work. He will cause destruction and pain. He will cause heartbreak and tears, and a great persecution of Christians. The earth will tremble with earthquakes. He will be a great ruler of Satan."

Eileen states Jesus showed him to her: "he has a mustache, black hair and wears a turban."

Eileen George has also said that the anti-Christ is going to arise from the Mohammedan race, a Moslem. He is going to have a turban. The people will call it "the eye of Satan." He is young.

Eileen stated that the antichrist wore a long robe. [29]

Christina Gallagher states she has seen visions of the Antichrist. She relates: "I was seeing this man time and time again. I had no idea who he was at first. I just saw his face and his head. I saw him a number of times and I didn't think there was anything wrong with him, but I used to feel from him a sort of horror. There was something different about his eyes. His eyes were so piercing. I could feel his eyes penetrate me and I didn't like it. Now, I didn't know what to make of this so I asked God one day, talking in prayer. I said: 'Dear

193

God, who is this?' much like the way I had asked Catherine of Siena who she was. The next thing I knew I heard an echo of the Virgin Mary's voice saying: 'Antichrist.' I got the shock of my life. I've seen this man a number of times since then, but I just ask the Precious Blood of Jesus to cover me.

"He's a man in his fifties. But he has a round face and he's bald on top with very short black hair, in a fine haircut. He would remind me of somebody like a bishop. There's something very strange and very peculiar about his eyes. They were dark brown or black. I'd say he was not a bad looking man. From what I can understand of what Our Blessed Mother has said about antichrist, there will be a number of them; a number in the world right now who are 'anti-christs' or 'anti' of Christ.

"If he's not the Antichrist, I wonder why the Lord permitted me to see him and hear the words 'antichrist'. Because I didn't know anything about the antichrist at that particular stage in my life. I don't think it would be given to me otherwise. The Virgin Mary said to me: 'Few realize how soon the Antichrist will raise himself up.' There are many antichrists now, but one, as time goes on, will be elected at the top. I have recently been told by the Heavenly Father, in the course of a message, 'He who is anti of Me is now in the flesh'..."

In another description of this antichrist Christina stated: "His face has a sallow complexion. His hair was cut short and it was very black. He had a roundish bold-looking face with very dark eyes. He was broad-shouldered. His looks were piercing and penetrating. They were unusual. He did not smile. He seemed to be a priest or a bishop, I'm not saying he was. I've seen him twenty, twenty-five times, always the same. I would know him instantly if I saw him on television or in reality. I would know him instantly." She says she was shown this man and during each apparition, she heard Our Blessed Mother's voice repeat the word "**Antichrist**."

Christina in late 1991 was given three dates and told to observe what would happen on those dates. "The three dates are all linked with the power of the antichrist to get control of the governments of the world, and so the money of the world, and to render it almost impossible for people to exercise their own rights and freedom." Christina added: "I know it is linked up to the Maastricht Treaty and the uniting of the currencies. This is through the Maastricht Referendum."[36]

Don't Take The Mark Of The Beast - The Mark Of Antichrist

Sadie Jaramillo, on August 13, 1997, received a message from Jesus after He told her to write Jeremiah Chapter 25, verse 4 - 7 and 29 -35, which she did from Douay - Rheims Bible.

Jesus said: "It is so! I have sent My prophets to proclaim the impending events and many refuse to hearken to My plea, to My requests, the request to return one and all to the Lord Your God that you would know salvation, peace and joy!

"My Mother, assumed into the Glory of Paradise, has left countless signs among all God's children from one corner of this earth to the other. And they still have not believed! Amidst great confusion, amidst great turmoil, amidst great signs shown forth in the heavens, many will come to believe.

"And those who refuse will not believe those whom I have sent, but will believe he who comes to say he is Christ. His signs they will believe and accept. But woe to them who receive his mark. You shall seek death, but death will not come. And when you die, you will condemn yourself to the eternal fires of hell...."[6]

On the same day, August 13, 1997, Mary, Queen of Heaven said to Sadie Jaramillo: "... I have ceaselessly and tirelessly worked to this end: To prevent as long as possible this justice, and the reign of the Antichrist.... Tell all to trust in Jesus because of His Mercy: Protection is afforded My remnant. 'For you have not seen, but believed,' Do not fear in the coming days for what you will see. The decree of God is against His enemies, not His children. There is Triumph soon and in the midst of great difficulties, Triumph reigns!..."[6]

The Fall Of Antichrist

Our Blessed Mother at La Salette, France on September 19, 1846, in a vision and message approved by the Church, told Melanie about bloody wars, famines, plagues and infectious diseases, rain with a fearful rain of animals, thunderstorms which will shake cities, earthquakes which will swallow up countries, that the Church will be in eclipse, the world will be in dismay. Our Blessed Mother told Melanie that Enoch and Eli will come and preach with the might of God, and are put to death, pagan Rome will disappear. "At that time the Beast will rise proudly in the air to go to Heaven. He will be smothered by the breath of the Archangel St. Michael, fall and the earth which will have been in a continuous series of evolutions for three days, will open up its fiery bowels; and he will be plunged for eternity with all his followers into the everlasting chasms of hell. And then water and fire will purge the earth and consume the work's of men's pride and all will be renewed. God will be served and glorified."[7]

These events surrounding the reign of Antichrist and the great chastisement which destroys evil in the world usher in the New Times.

Jeanne Le Royer, Sister Mary of the Nativity, stated: "With the fall of Antichrist will come severe earth-quakes, thick darkness will cover the Earth, the ground will open in thousands of places under the feet of the inhabitants and cities, towns, castles and an immense number of people will be swallowed up. One-half of that immense crowd on Mt. Olivet will be cast in the abyss with Antichrist. The ocean will move frightfully and waves arise heavenward overflowing the coast and inundate the earth. All these calamities are only to frighten the remaining into accepting the Grace and Mercy of God. Fifteen days after the ascension of Henoch and Elias into heaven, terrible catastrophes will come upon the earth: most severe earthquakes, tidal waves inundating much of the earth's surface, culminating in a thick darkness over the entire earth."[44]

On March 25, 1998, Our Blessed Mother told Sadie Jaramillo: My little sorrowful rose, ... "The time left now is nearly expired. My children do you not understand? Though the warning of man's conscience was to have come long ago, this would certainly have meant that the length of the Antichrist's reign would have been longer! As it is now, I have shortened the length of his reign... "[3]

Chapter 10

The Triumph of Mary's Immaculate Heart

Excerpts From An Interview with Father Stefano Gobbi, Rubbio, Italy, August 4-5, 1999

6 In her messages, Our Lady speaks often about the "Triumph of her Immaculate Heart" What is this triumph? How is it going to happen? And what are the signs that her triumph has come?

Fr.G. [...] "When will it occur?" I have always said in all America that it will happen by the Great Jubilee of the Year 2000. I have said this also in an interview with Mother Angelica.

I repeat it now. One must understand, however, what this triumph is about. Our Lady does not build this triumph of God all at once from one evening to the following morning, almost like a magical trick -- like a magician who shows his hat and says: "See, there is nothing in it," then lifts it again, and a dove emerges. It does not happen this way. Our Lady builds the triumph of her Immaculate Heart during these times, in these years in which Satan has built his own.

In order to build his triumph, Satan has formed the cohort of the most powerful at every level of diabolical and masonic forces, especially of masonry. And he managed to build an atheistic, pagan society, which has made for itself a law which is contrary to the commandments of God. Our Lady, being the little servant of the Lord, builds her cohort in silence, and she hides it for now in every part of the world. It is formed by the littlest ones, by the poorest — those who say "yes" and who live for the glory of God

Our Lady is gathering her cohort with the littlest from every part of the world. In these years, she builds her triumph because she makes them live for God, in the observance of his law, in the grace of God, in the practice of the Christian virtues. Our Lady impresses her spirit within her little children. This is where her Immaculate Heart triumphs. For now, she keeps it hidden.

When the time will come -and for me it is the Great Jubilee of the Year 2000 -- she will lift her mantle, and a cohort formed in every part of the world will be seen: her Marian Movement of Priests formed by the bishops, the priests and the faithful. At that moment she will say: "This is the triumph of my Immaculate Heart in the world."

7   In message #532 given in Mexico City on Decem-

ber 5, 1994, Our Lady says: "I confirm to you that by the great jubilee of the year 2000, there will take place the triumph of my Immaculate Heart, which I foretold to you at Fatima, and this will come to pass with the return of Jesus in glory, to establish his reign in the world. Thus you will at last be able to see with your own eyes the new heavens and the new earth."

How are we to understand the expression: "...by the great jubilee of the year 2000?"

Fr. G. By the following year -- by the Great Jubilee of the Year 2000.[1] I said many times, not only in Mexico but also in the United States — every time I came -- that it would take place by the Great Jubilee of the Year 2000.

However, I have explained before in which sense this triumph takes place. At the moment of the greatest crisis, Our Lady will show the cohort of her little children, formed in every part of the world, to whom she has given her spirit and who will remain faithful to Christ.

This faithfulness will bring the reign of Christ into these people, and through them, it will bring it every-where. And this will coincide also with the triumph of the divine mercy, because for this humanity, in the state in which it is, the Lord will work the prodigy of his merciful love which will lead all those who are far away, the sinners, to an act of conversion and of re-turn to Him.

Fire From Heaven

This is what the triumph of the Immaculate Heart of Mary is about.

Many interpreted Message # 532 to mean that the triumph would occur before January 1, 2000 The Italian text reads, "Ti confirmo che per il grande giubileo...' The Italian word per can be translated into English as any one of the following, "for, by, through, in, during..."

8 How are we to understand the "return of Jesus in glory?"

Fr. G. -- We are to understand it according to the interpretation given by the Scriptures and by the Church.

The triumph of Jesus in glory will occur when He will give a glorious manifestation of Himself which will be visible to all.

This will coincide — listen well — with the great triumph of the divine mercy: a second Pentecost, when the Holy Spirit will transform the hearts and souls of all, who will see themselves in the light of divine truth, bringing them to convert and return to God.

It will coincide with the fulfillment of what we say in the *Our Father:* the Father being glorified by all creation; the reign of God coming into our midst - a reign which will be above all a reign of grace, of sanctity, of love, of peace and of communion.

And then [it will coincide] with the fulfillment of the divine Will upon this earth, and above all with the triumph of the Eucharistic reign of Jesus.

From Interview with Fr. Gobbi, Rubbio, Italy, August 4-5, 1999, The Marian Movement of Priests, pages 6-9

The Triumph Of Mary's Immaculate Heart

At La Salette on September 19, 1846 Melanie was told by Our Lady at the end of the long message: "... and the earth, which will have been in a continuous series of evolutions for three days, will open up its fiery bowels; and he [Antichrist] will have plunged for eternity with all his followers into the everlasting chasms of hell. And then water and fire will purge the earth and consume all the works of men's pride and <u>all will be renewed. God will be served and glorified.</u>"[7]

On October 27, 1988, in message #392, *This Is Your Hour*, Our Lady told Fr. Gobbi: "The miracle of the merciful love of Jesus is about to be accomplished in your time. <u>In this consists the triumph of My Immaculate Heart</u>: in the greatest triumph of the merciful love of Jesus, which will change the whole world and bring you to a new era of love, of holiness and of peace...."[2]

Fire From Heaven

The Triumph Is Not A Sudden Event

Fr. Gobbi, responding to many questions put to him, in a video made in 1999 and released in the beginning of the year 2000, has related that the triumph of Mary's Immaculate Heart is not a sudden event.

This video of questions and answers and a Cenacle of Rubbio, Italy on August 5, 1999 and a 40 page transcription of this video are available, while they last, from The Marian Movement of Priests National Headquarters, P. O. Box 8, Saint Francis, Maine 04774-0008. Tel. 207 398-3375. Fax: 207 398-2252. There is a suggested donation for this.

Messages To Father Gobbi About The Triumph of Mary's Immaculate Heart

On February 2, 1990, in message # 418, *Only In the Hearts of Little Ones,* Our Lady told Fr. Gobbi: "Today, as you are venerating me at the moment when I am carrying in my arms the Child Jesus to the temple of Jerusalem, <u>I announce to you that here my triumph has already begun.</u> Each day, only in the hearts of my little ones, am I forging the greatest triumph of my Immaculate Heart."[2]

On June 26, 1991, in message #452, Our Lady through Fr. Gobbi told her beloved sons in cenacle: "In you I manifest myself as Queen, because it is by means of you

204

that each day I am bringing about the triumph of my Immaculate Heart in the world. Open the doors of your lives, so that I can reign in you and prepare the way for the glorious reign of Christ." [2]

On May 13, 1992, in message #473, Our Lady told Fr. Gobbi: ".... Indeed, through my Marian Movement of Priests, I am calling all my children to consecrate themselves to my Heart, and to spread everywhere cenacles of prayer: among priests, the faithful, children, youth, and in families.

"In this way I am able to obtain a great force of intercession and reparation, and I am able to intervene in order to change the hearts of my poor sinful children; in this way I am bringing about each day the triumph of my Immaculate Heart...."[2]

On December 8, 1993, in message #507, *The Years of My Triumph*, Our Lady told Fr. Gobbi: "Thus in the very years when Satan is triumphing, by leading humanity along the road of its own destruction, my motherly Heart is also triumphing, as I bring my little children along the way of salvation and peace....

"These are the years when Satan is ruling as a sure victor; these are also *the years of my triumph....*"[2]

The Great Prodigy

In message # 553 *The Times Will Be Shortened*, September 29, 1995, Our Lady said to Fr. Gobbi: "Thus you are being prepared for <u>the great prodigy</u> which will take place when, with the triumph of my Immaculate Heart, the heavenly dew of divine mercy will descend upon the world."[2]

Jesus Returning On The Clouds In His Divine Glory

In message # 576 on August 15, 1996 Our Lady told Fr. Gobbi: "Look up to heaven. From heaven, you will see my Son Jesus returning on the clouds in the splendor of his divine glory. Then finally the triumph of my Immaculate Heart will be accomplished.

"To prepare for <u>this divine prodigy</u>, I want to establish my motherly triumph in the hearts and souls of all my children....."[2]

In message #428, *The Second Pentecost*, on June 28, 1990, Our Lady told Fr. Gobbi: "*The second Pentecost* will come like a dew upon the world and will transform the desert into a garden, in which all humanity will run, like a spouse, to meet her Lord, in a renewed covenant of love with Him. Thus the Most Holy trinity will receive its great glory, and Jesus will restore his glorious reign of love among you....."[2]

In message #521, on May 22, 1994, Our Lady told Fr. Gobbi: "My hour is the Hour of the Holy Spirit. The triumph of my Immaculate Heart will coincide with <u>the great prodigy of the second Pentecost</u>....

"Then my motherly Heart will have its triumph over all humanity, which will return to a new marriage of love and of life with its Heavenly Father." [2]

In message # 595 Our Lady said to Fr. Gobbi on May 18, 1997: "The hour has come when my Son Jesus must be glorified by all. <u>With the prodigy of the second Pentecost</u>, humanity will acknowledge Jesus Christ as its Redeemer and as its only Savior.

"Then the Holy Spirit will open hearts and souls to welcome Christ, who will return to you in the splendor of his divine glory.

"Thus my Immaculate Heart will finally attain its great triumph." [2]

His Glorious Return When He Will Initiate The New Time

In message #534, December 24, 1994, Our Blessed Mother told Father Gobbi: "In the mystery of this Night, understand also how the fullness of time is accomplished in the new time which awaits you, because <u>this first coming of Jesus in the frailty of his human nature is directed toward his second coming</u>, when He will appear in the splendor of his divine glory... Then, <u>his glorious return will bring to fulfillment the fullness of time, when He will initiate the new time of the new heavens and the new earth</u>."[2]

Fire From Heaven

Peace Will Come To The World
After The Promulgation Of
The Last Dogma
Of The Marian Mystery

Ida Peerdeman, a visionary from the Netherlands on
May 31, 1954 was told by Our Lady of All Nations:
"My prophecy, 'From henceforth all generations shall
call me blessed', will be fulfilled more than ever before, once the dogma (Mary is Co-Redemptrix, Mediatrix and Advocate) has been proclaimed..."

"On that day all nations shall call me blessed..."

"When the dogma, the last dogma of the Marian mystery, will have been promulgated, it will be then that
the Lady of All Peoples (Nations) will give peace to
the world, true peace..."[1]

The Pope and The Final Marian Dogma

On August 15, 1951, the Lady said to Ida, "Holland is
on the brink of total degeneration... Rome, do you
know, how completely everything is being under-
mined? The years will speed by unheeded, but the
longer you wait, the more the Faith will decline; the
greater the number of years, the greater the apostasy... The Church will be attacked greatly over the

Fire From Heaven

new dogma." [Co-Redemptrix, Mediatrix and Advocate].[1]

On May 31, 1979, Ida Peerdeman heard the Voice say: "The Netherlands will be revived through Her whom I have sent. Implore the Spirit of Truth... The Holy Father will proclaim Her Co-Redemptrix, Mediatrix and Advocate. Tell him this."[17]

Co-Redemptrix

Sister Maria Natalia of Hungary (20th Century), had a vision of Jesus and Mary holding back the hand of the Father from punishing the world for its sin, which was crying out for vengeance. The Heavenly Father lifted up his hand and said: "My Son! Mercy has prevailed. The sinful world has gained mercy on account of the supplication of the Immaculate Mother of God. We will entrust the saving work of the world to her. To save the world, she needs power. Therefore we endow the Immaculate Mother of God with the powers of Queen. Her title will be: the Victorious Queen of the World. As Co-Redemptrix of the world, mankind, which is condemned to die because of its sins, will receive grace and salvation through her. We place under her command the host of angels."

In the vision God in Three persons worked in the Immaculate Mother, as if the Holy Spirit had overshadowed her again, that she might give Jesus to the world again. The Heavenly Father showered her with a flood of graces. From the Son, unspeakable happiness and love radiated toward her, as if He would congratu-late her while He said: "My Immaculate Mother, the Vic-torious Queen of the World, show your power! This time you will be the savior of humanity. As you were part of My saving work as <u>Co-Redemptrix</u> according to My will, so I want to share with you My power as King. With this I entrust you with the saving work of sinful humanity. You can do it with your power as Queen. It is necessary that I share with you everything, that you be-come comparable to Me. <u>**You are the Co-Redemptrix of humanity.**</u>

Sister Natalia states: "Then I saw that her mantle was saturated with the blood of Jesus, and this gave it a scar-let color... The Virgin Mother stood on the globe as the Victorious Queen. Her first act as Queen was to cover it with her mantle, saturated with the blood of Jesus. Then she blessed the world, and I saw that at the same time the Holy Trinity also blessed the world. The satanic ser-pent attacked her... (she) quietly stepped on the ser-pent's neck. The serpent did not cease to spew forth flames, the symbol of hatred and revenge, but he was not able to do any more damage, while the crown of thorns, made of sin, had disappeared from around the world, and from the center a lily came forth and started to bloom..."

Jesus explained to Sister Natalia: "My Immaculate Mother will be victorious over sin with her power as Queen. The lily represents the cleansing of the world, the coming Age of Paradise, when humanity will live as if without sin. This will be a new world and a new age. This will be the age when mankind will get back what it lost in Paradise. When My Immaculate Mother will step on the neck of the serpent, the gates of hell will be closed. The hosts of angels will be part of this fight. I have sealed My own with My seal that they shall not be lost in this fight."

Sister Natalia asked: "What can we do to hasten the victory of the Queen of the World?"

Jesus said: "My Immaculate Mother will be the Co-Redemptrix of this coming age."

Jesus also said: "Ask her often: 'Our Immaculate Mother, show us your power!'"

Sister Natalia said this prayer and asked Our Mother: "What do you wish us to do till the glorious new age of yours arrives?" She folded her hands and begged the world, seemingly calling everybody: "Come my dear children, and together with me console the Heavenly Father Who is deeply offended!" [33]

Mary Is Coredemptrix, Mediatrix and Advocate

On July 26, 1976, Jesus said to Pierina Gilli, Montichiari, Italy: "We are one God in three Persons. God the Father, God the Son, and God the Holy Spirit. Everything comes from Us. My Mother is the Mediatrix of all graces. I gave you My Mother, and you have all been placed in Her hands. I am the source of all grace.

211

I give you grace through My Mother."

On October 13, 1999 Jesus told Sadie Jaramillo: „,
"The time arrives for all humanity to undergo the greatest of all trials. You will see my True Church broken
in two! You will see them try to stamp out belief in
My True Presence! This will happen as a result of the
crowning title given to My Mother, Mary: <u>Co-
redemptrix, Mediatrix and Advocate of all Graces!</u>

"Behold the doors open and you will see great destruction, chaos, and devastation. But you will also
behold great wonders of God and the greatest prodigy of Grace and Divine Mercy to transform those
who will accept this grace!...."[3]

The Triumph and the Jubilee Of The Year 2000

Our Blessed Mother has told Father Gobbi that The
Times Have Been Shortened [message # 553], and
twice [messages # 532 and # 586] that by the Jubilee of
the Year 2000 we will have the Triumph of her Immaculate Heart in the world."[2]

In message #532, December 5, 1994, Blessed Mother
told Father Gobbi: "I confirm to you that, <u>by the great
Jubilee of the year two thousand, there will take
place the triumph of my Immaculate Heart, of which
I foretold you at Fatima,</u> and this will come to pass
with <u>the return of Jesus in glory, to establish his</u>

212

<u>Reign in the world</u>. Thus you will at last be able to <u>see</u> <u>with your own eyes the new heavens and the new</u> <u>earth.</u>"[2] (Editor's Note: The Italian word per which has been translated as by also has the meanings of during, by means of.)

In her message # 586 to Father Gobbi, on December 31, 1996, Our Blessed Mother again confirmed this date. Our Blessed Mother stated: "With this coming year, enter into the time of immediate preparation for the great jubilee of the year 2000. This special preparation which the Pope is urging of you through his apostolic letter, 'Tertio Millennio Adveniente,' is to make you understand that this date is important and significant for the Church and for all humanity. <u>This date should be</u> <u>particularly significant for you, because I have previously announced to you, for that date, the triumph of my Immaculate Heart in the world.</u>"[2] (Editor's note: This leads to the interpretation of the word (per) by, as *during*, since date rather than causation is stated.)

Our Lady, appearing as Our Lady of Fatima, on December 8, 1997 said to El Salvadoran visionary Nelly Hurtado: "My children, we are in times of Grace, in times of Conversion and at the same time in times of Purification, and I am here to prepare you for the Great Jubilee of the year 2000, for the Second Coming of My Son Jesus Christ, to show you the way to my Son Jesus Christ."[25]

On February 11, 1999 Our Lady said to Nelly Hurtado: "<u>These, my children, are the end times</u>. I have come to

213

prepare you for the upcoming events that have been foretold. My prophecies are about to come to be....
"The Triumph is near.

"The Great Sign that will happen before the events will be at 7:30 am, the sky will be orange and it will be very cold. Everyone will be able to see the orange sky. I will not tell you the day because I love you....

" I am hidden because of the Purification. The comet you will see has a yellow tail and is approaching very fast....

"A great Cross of light will appear in the sky in the west. But before this, all will see a great light. I prom-ise you I will warn you right here, at this place, before the first event, because this is a place of intercession, a refuge....

"The change from day to night and from night to day is something only God can bring about. Do not fear then, because I, the Mother of Consolation, am here....

"I do not come to announce the end of the world, but the end times; I come to warn that the comet is near the Earth. Prepare yourselves with prayer.

"I tell you, the family that prays together stays together. Organize prayer chains from north to south. This whole country is a place of intercession, as is this special place.

"This is a message of warning, like the one I have

given in Yugoslavia. Everything I said there happened, and the world took a different turn....

"These are times of peace and mercy, but know that soon the great events will take place, and be prepared for them....

"Thank you for responding to my call..."[25]

What The Triumph of the Immaculate Heart of Mary Is

From Messages To Joanne Kriva
- Jesus is the Triumph of Mary
- Brings His people to the safety of His Sacred Heart

From Messages Sr. Natalia To Hungary
- Peace will be here before the next century

From Messages To Fr. Gobbi:
- Is won in the souls and the lives of her faithful children
- Consists in the greatest triumph of the merciful love of Jesus, which will change the whole world and bring us to a new era of love, of holiness and of peace.
- Return of humanity, like a prodigal son, into the arms of the Heavenly Father
- The triumph coincides with the triumph of divine mercy upon the world
- The miracle of the second Pentecost will come with

the triumph of my Immaculate Heart in the world
- The new heart of the new Church will be born with the triumph
- With the triumph enter into the New Era of Peace: for the Church, for humanity, for all of you
- Then the miracle of divine mercy, in the power of the Holy Spirit, will renew the face of the earth
- The Coming Together Of All The Christian Confessions In The Catholic Church
- You will see my Son Jesus returning on the clouds in the splendor of His Divine Glory
- You will be completely liberated from every form of practical atheism
- Will come about in the greatest triumph of Jesus: who will bring into the world His glorious reign of love, of justice and peace, and will make all things new

From Messages To Joanne Kriva

I Am the Triumph of Mary

Joanne Kriva on October 29, 1994 received the message from Jesus Christ: "But I tell you this day that the Son of Glory, God Incarnate, and ascended from whence He came, returns in power and glory as the Triumph of the Immaculate Heart of Mary. I am the Triumph of Mary. From the moment of My conception in her virgin womb, she has been the instrument by which mankind has come to receive its Lord of Lords and King of Kings. Now I wish you to know that My

Second Coming, which is imminent, is the fulfillment of the Word of God spoken in Genesis -- 'I will put enmity between you and the Woman and between your seed and her seed" 9 Genesis: 15).... **I who am Love have conquered My adversary, and the reign of peace commences...**"[10]

She Has Brought My People To The Safety Of My Sacred Heart.

On November 20, 1990 The Lord Your God told Joanne Kriva regarding Our Blessed Mother, the glorious queen: "When you love her, your love fills the heavens. When you honor her, you honor Me. My Mother is My gift to you. Receive My gift. She is your loving Mother. My loving Mother intercedes for you. Whatever you ask through her I grant...

"Now say: Rejoice My people, for **the triumph of our Holy Mother is at hand**... Her role in My plan for your salvation is at an end. <u>She has brought My people to the safety of My Sacred Heart</u>. She enfolds you within her motherly embrace. You are under her special protection. Rejoice! Let your whole being rejoice...."[10]

From the Messages To Sr. Natalia of Hungary

The Peace Will Be Here Before The Next Century

Sr. Natalia of Hungary in 1985 was told by the Holy

Fire From Heaven

Virgin: "Do not be afraid! The peace, the gift of my Son for those who believe in Him, won't take long to come. It will come through me, and it is very near to you. The peace - what my Son brought at His birth, and the world has not yet enjoyed - will be here before the next century. Trust me! I solemnly tell you, this generation shall not pass till all these things happen!" [24]

From the Messages To Father Gobbi

The Triumph Is Won In The Souls And The Lives Of Her Faithful Children

In message # 116, January 1, 1977 Our Lady said to Fr. Gobbi in interior locution: "The triumph of the Heart of the Mother is won in the souls and the lives of her faithful children." [2]

Consists In The Greatest Triumph Of The Merciful Love Of Jesus

In message # 392, October 27, 1988, Our Lady told Fr. Gobbi: "The miracle of the merciful love of Jesus is about to be accomplished in your time. In this consists the triumph of my Immaculate Heart: in the greatest triumph of the merciful love of Jesus, which will change the whole world and bring you to a new era of love, of holiness and of peace..." [2]

Fire From Heaven

Return Of Humanity, Like A Prodigal Son, Into The Arms Of The Heavenly Father

In message # 523, June 30, 1994, Our Lady told Fr. Gobbi: "My Immaculate Heart will triumph over this ailing and materialistic humanity... Let this humanity return, like a prodigal son, into the arms of the Heavenly Father, who awaits it with love, so that a new, profound and universal reconciliation may be thus achieved between God and humanity." [2]

The Triumph Coincides With The Triumph Of Divine Mercy Upon The World

In message # 536 on January 1, 1995 Fr. Gobbi was told by Our Lady: "... the divine mercy of Jesus, in order to reach you, must pass through the motherly way of my Immaculate Heart. For this reason, the triumph of my Immaculate Heart coincides with the triumph of divine mercy upon the world." [2]

The Miracle Of The Second Pentecost Will Take Place with The Triumph

In message # 546, June 4, 1995, Our Lady told Fr. Gobbi: "Tongues of fire will come down on you.... And thus, you will be illuminated by this divine light, and you will see your own selves in the mirror of the truth and the holiness of God. It will be like a judgment in miniature, which will open the door of your heart to receive the great gift of divine mercy. And then the Holy Spirit will work the new miracle of universal transformation in the heart and life of all: <u>sinners will be converted</u>; the weak will find support; <u>the sick will receive healing</u>; <u>those far away will return to the house of the Father; those separated and divided will attain full unity.</u> In this way, the miracle of the second Pentecost will take place. It will come with the triumph of my Immaculate Heart in the world. Only then will you see how the tongues of fire of the Spirit of Love will renew the whole world, which will become completely transformed by the greatest manifestation of divine mercy...."[2]

The New Heart Of The New Church, Which Will Be Born

In message # 547 on June 28, 1995 Our Lady told Fr. Gobbi: "And thus you will form the <u>new heart of the new Church, which will be born with the triumph of my Immaculate Heart.</u>"[2]

New Era Of Peace, Which Will Come For The Church, For Humanity And For All Of You

On August 15, 1995 in message # 549, Our Lady told Fr. Gobbi: "At the conclusive moment of the great trial, you will feel my motherly presence, which assists you to cross the threshold of hope, in order to <u>enter into the new era of peace, which will come for the Church, for</u>

220

humanity and for all of you, with the triumph of my
Immaculate Heart in the world." [2]

The Miracle Of Divine Mercy, In The Power Of The
Holy Spirit, Will Renew The Face Of The Earth

In message # 554 on October 7, 1995 Fr. Gobbi was
told by Our Lady: "My complete victory will come
about with the triumph of my Immaculate Heart in
the World. Then the miracle of divine mercy, in the
power of the Holy Spirit, will renew the face of the
earth, and it will again become a fragrant and precious
garden in which the Most Holy Trinity will be pleased
to be reflected and will receive from the whole created
universe its greatest glory." [2]

The Coming Together Of All The Christian
Confessions In The Catholic Church

In message # 565, on February 22, 1996 Our Lady told
Fr. Gobbi: "However, the coming together of all the
Christian confessions in the Catholic Church will
take place with the triumph of my Immaculate Heart
in the world." [2]

You Will See My Son Jesus Returning On The Clouds
In The Splendor Of His Divine Glory

In message # 576, on August 15, 1996 Our Lady told

Fire From Heaven

Fr. Gobbi: "Look up to heaven. From heaven, you will see my Son Jesus returning on the clouds in the splendor of his divine glory. Then finally the triumph of my Immaculate Heart in the world will be accomplished." [2]

You Will Be Completely Liberated From Every Form Of Practical Atheism

In message # 577, on September 2, 1996 in Prague, Our Lady told Fr. Gobbi: "And this will be done when, with the triumph of My Immaculate Heart in the world, you will be completely liberated from every form of practical atheism, which has been *the greatest evil of your century.*" [2]

Will Come About In The Greatest Triumph Of Jesus: Who Will Bring His Glorious Reign Of Love, Of Justice And Peace, And Will Make All Things New

On December 31, 1997, in message # 604, her final public message to Fr. Gobbi, Our Lady said: "I have announced to you the triumph of my Immaculate Heart in the world. *In the End my Immaculate Heart will triumph.* This will come about in the greatest triumph of Jesus, who will bring into the world his glorious reign of love, of justice and peace, and will make all things new...." [2]

The Glorious Reign of Christ

Christ's Eucharistic Reign Among Us

In message # 421, April 12, 1990 Our Lady told Fr. Gobbi: "In fact, the coming of the glorious reign of Christ will coincide with the greatest splendor of his Eucharistic reign among you. The Eucharistic Jesus will release all his power of love, which will transform souls, the Church and all humanity.

"Thus the Eucharist becomes a sign of Jesus who, still today, loves you to the end, because He is leading you to the end of these times of yours, to introduce you into the new era of holiness and of grace, toward which you are all journeying and which will begin at the moment when Jesus will have restored his glorious reign in your midst." [2]

In message # 505, on November 21, 1993 Our Lady told Fr. Gobbi: "The glorious reign of Christ will be above all established in hearts and souls..."

"The glorious reign of Christ will also be reflected in a new form of life in everyone, because you will be drawn to live only for the glory of the Lord. And the Lord will be glorified when his divine Will will be perfectly accomplished by each one of you. The glorious reign of Christ will coincide, then, with the perfect accomplishment of the Will of God on the part of every one of his creatures, in such a way that, as it is in heaven, so it will also be on this earth.

"The glorious reign of Christ will be established after the completed defeat of Satan and all the spirits of evil, and the destruction of Satan's diabolical power. Thus he will be bound and cast into hell, and the gates of the abyss will be shut so that he can no longer get out to harm the world. And Christ will reign in the world.

"The glorious reign of Christ will coincide with the triumph of the eucharistic reign of Jesus, because in a purified and sanctified world, completely renewed by love, Jesus will be made manifest, above all, in the mystery of his Eucharistic presence.

"<u>The Eucharist will be the source from which will burst forth all his divine power</u>, and it will become a new sun, which will shed its bright rays in hearts and souls and then in the life of individuals, families, and nations, <u>making of all one single flock</u>, docile and meek, <u>whose sole shepherd will be Jesus</u>.

"Your heavenly Mother is leading you on toward these new heavens and this new earth, the Mother who is gathering you today from every part of the world to <u>prepare you to receive the Lord who is coming</u>."[2]

Heaven's Intervention Is Needed

On June 16, 1996, at 7:00 P.M., Sadie Jaramillo was told by Our Blessed Mother: "There is hope if you trust, <u>trust in the Mercy of God. Only Heaven's intervention can defeat and cleanse the stain of man's sins</u>

<u>in the body, in the world</u>. Then you will see Heaven and Earth meet and transformed into that which was taken away through the fall of man, <u>the paradise of the era of peace</u>."[6]

Chapter 11

The Great Chastisement

Prior to the great chastisement humanity will have experienced:

- The Warning or Illumination of Conscience, followed within the year by the Miracle, and a Sign left at all Apparition sites where Our Blessed Mother had appeared.
- The Second Pentecost.
- The bright Cross in the sky at the time of the Warning
- A short period of time for people to get their house in order.
- The Final Marian Dogma of Mary as Co-Redemptrix, Mediatrix and Advocate will have been proclaimed resulting in the formal Schism then being openly declared by dissidents, as a new, false pope replaces Pope John Paul II in a Vatican coup. Pope John Paul II who has been climbing Calvary is killed at its summit [Third part of the secret of Fatima revealed June 2000.]
- The Antichrist coming on the scene and ac-

complishing the fulfillment of Daniel's prophecy.

- The persecution of the Church and then the faithful remnant. [The Third part of the secret of Fatima revealed June 2000 describes the persecution and martyrdom.]

La Salette 1846

At La Salette on September 19, 1846 Our Lady gave Melanie a secret which she revealed later. In the November 21, 1878 written message revealing this secret Melanie wrote concerning part of the revealed secret: ".... The seasons will be altered, the earth will produce nothing but bad fruit. The stars will lose their regular motion. The moon will only reflect a faint reddish glow. Water and fire will give the earth's globe convulsions and terrible earthquakes which will swallow up mountains, cities, etc..."

" Rome will lose the faith and become the seat of the Antichrist.

" The demons of the air together with the Antichrist will perform great wonders on earth and in the atmosphere, and men will become more and more perverted. God will take care of his faithful servants and men of good will. The Gospel will be preached everywhere, and all peoples of all nations will get to know the truth.

Fire From Heaven

" I make an urgent appeal to the earth. I call on the true disciples of the living God who reigns in Heaven; I call on the true followers of Christ made man, the only true Savior of men; I call on my children, the true faithful, those who have given themselves to me so that I may lead them to my Divine Son, those whom I carry in my arms, so to speak, those who have lived according to my spirit. Finally, I call on the Apostles of the Last Days, the faithful disciples of Jesus Christ who have lived in scorn for the world and for themselves, in poverty and in humility, in scorn and in silence, in prayer and in mortification, in chastity and in union with God, in suffering and unknown to the world. It is time they came out and filled the world with light. Go and reveal yourselves as my cherished children. I am at your side and within you, provided that your faith is the light which shines upon you in these unhappy days. May your zeal make you hunger for the glory and the honor of Jesus Christ. Fight, children of Light, you, the few who can see. For now is the time of all times, the end of all ends.

"The Church will be in eclipse, the world will be in dismay. But now Enoch and Eli will come, filled with the Spirit of God. They will preach with the Might of God, and men of good will will believe in God, and many souls will be comforted. They will make great steps forward through the virtue of the Holy Spirit and will condemn the devilish lapses of the Antichrist. Woe to the inhabitants of the earth! There will be bloody wars and famines, plagues and infectious diseases. It will rain with a fearful hail of animals. There will be thunderstorms which will shake cities, earthquakes which will swallow up countries. Voices will be heard in the air. Men will beat their heads against walls, call for their death, and on another side death will be their torment. Blood will flow on all sides. Who will be the victor if God does not shorten the length of the test? At the blood, the tears and the prayers of the righteous, God will relent. Enoch and Eli will be put to death. Pagan Rome will disappear. The fire of Heaven will fall and consume three cities. All the universe will be struck with terror and many will let themselves be led astray because they have not worshipped the true Christ who lives among them. It is time; the sun is darkening; only faith will survive.

"Now is the time; the abyss is opening. Here is the king of kings of darkness, here is the Beast with his subjects, calling himself the savior of the world. He will rise proudly into the air to go to Heaven. He will be smothered by the breath of the Archangel Saint Michael. He will fall, and the earth, which will have been in a continuous series of evolutions for three days, will open up its fiery bowels; and he will have plunged for eternity with all his followers into the everlasting chasms of hell. And then water and fire will purge the earth and consume all the works of men's pride and all will be renewed. God will be served and glorified."
7

Punishment Worse Than The Flood

In message # 328 on July 30, 1986 in locution Our Lady

told Fr. Gobbi: " At the time of Noah, immediately before the flood, those whom the Lord had destined to survive this terrible chastisement entered into the ark. In these your times, I am inviting all my beloved children to enter into the Ark of the New Covenant which I have built in my Immaculate Heart for you, that they may be assisted by me to carry out the bloody burden of the great trial, which precedes the coming of the day of the Lord.

"Do not look anywhere else. There is happening today what happened in the days of the flood, and no one is giving a thought to what is awaiting them. Everyone is much occupied in thinking only of themselves, of their own earthly interests, of pleasures and of satisfying in every sort of way, their own disordinate passions...."[2]

On September 15, 1987 Our Lady told Fr. Gobbi: "... A chastisement worse than the flood is about to come upon this poor and perverted humanity. Fire will descend from heaven, and this will be the sign that the justice of God has as of now fixed the hour of his greatest manifestation...."[2]

In message # 489 Our Lady on March 15, 1993 at Fatima told Fr. Gobbi in locution: "I have wanted you here, to tell you that you must now all enter right away into the safe refuge of my Immaculate Heart. Just as Noah, in the name of the Lord, called into the ark those who would be saved from the flood, so now must you, my littlest child, in the name of your heavenly Mother, call into the refuge of my Immaculate Heart those who must be protected, defended and saved from the great trial which has now come for the Church and for all humanity.

"I have wanted you here, because you must communicate to all as of now - as of this year - you have entered into the events which I foretold to you, and which are contained in the third part of the secret, which has not yet been revealed to you. <u>This will now be made evident by the very events themselves which are about to take place in the Church and in the world.</u>

"<u>My Church will be shaken by the violent wind of apostasy and unbelief, as he who sets himself against Christ will enter into its interior, thus bringing to fulfillment the horrible abomination which has been prophesied to you in Holy Scripture.</u>

"Humanity will know the bloody hour of its chastisement; it will be stricken with the scourge of epidemics, of hunger and of fire; much blood will be spilt upon your roads; war will spread everywhere, bringing down upon the world incommensurable devastation...."[2]

In message # 507 on December 8, 1993 Our Blessed Mother told Fr. Gobbi: "... During these years, you will see the great chastisement, with which the justice of God will purify this world, which has become a thousand times worse than at the time of the flood and so possessed by evil spirits...."[2]

At Akita Japan, on September 15, 1987, the Feast of Our

Fire From Heaven

Lady of Sorrows, Fr. Gobbi, received the interior locution from Our Blessed Mother: "<u>A chastisement worse than the flood is about to come upon this poor and perverted humanity.</u> Fire will descend from heaven and this will be the sign that the justice of God has as of now fixed the hour of his great manifestation. I am weeping because the Church is continuing along the road of division, of loss of the true faith, of apostasy and of errors which are being spread more and more without anyone offering opposition to them. <u>Even now, that which I predicted at Fatima and that which I have revealed here in the third message confided to a little daughter of mine is in the process of being accomplished.</u> And so, even for the church the moment of it's great trial has come, because the man of iniquity will establish himself within it and the abomination of desolation will enter into the holy temple of God."[2]

On October 13, 1973, at Akita, Japan, an apparition approved by the Church, the Holy Mother gave this message to Sister Agnes Sasagawa: "If men do not repent and better themselves, the Heavenly Father will inflict a great punishment on all humanity. It will definitely be a punishment greater than the Deluge, such as has never been seen before. Fire will plunge from the sky and <u>a large part of humanity will perish... The good as well as the bad will perish, sparing neither priests nor the faithful.</u> The survivors will find themselves plunged into such terrible hardships that they will envy the dead. The only arms which will remain for you will be the Rosary and the sign left by My Son (Eucharist)."[21]

232

Physical Chastisements

Blessed Anna Maria Taigi (d. 1837) said: "God will send two punishments: "One will be in the form of wars, revolutions and other evils; it shall originate on earth.

"<u>The other will be sent from Heaven.</u> There shall come over the whole earth an intense darkness lasting three days and three nights. Nothing can be seen, and the air will be laden with pestilence which will claim mainly, but not only, the enemies of religion. It will be impossible to use any man-made lighting during this darkness, except blessed candles. He, who out of curiosity, opens his window to look out, or leaves his home, will fall dead on the spot. During these three days, people should remain in their homes, pray the Rosary and beg God for mercy.

"All the enemies of the Church, whether known or unknown, will perish over the whole earth during that universal darkness, with the exception of a few whom God will soon convert. The air shall be infected by demons who will appear under all sorts of hideous forms.

"Religion shall be persecuted, and priests massacred. Churches shall be closed, but only for a short time. The Holy Father shall be obliged to leave Rome...."[18]

Mother Elena Patriarca Leonardi

Mother Elena Patriarca Leonardi was told by Bl. Padre Pio on February 4, 1947 that the Virgin would entrust her with a great Mission. Mother Elena Leonardi was born on November 4, 1910. She was married at age 20. Her husband died in 1934. She had a son and grandson. On April 22, 1968 she was run over by a car. Since then her life was completely devoted to the realization of the Work, pronounced by Bl. Padre Pio in the Confession of February 4, 1947 in San Giovanni Rotondo. From March 21, 1953 to October 9, 1983 she received many messages.

Mother Elena Patriarca Leonardi was, it appears, actually given the Third Secret by Our Blessed Mother, although Our Lady didn't tell her it is the Third Secret; the messages given to Mother Elena have both the Apostasy and the Great Chastisement for Mankind spelled out in some detail.

On March 26, 1978, Our Blessed Mother told Mother Elena Leonardi: "Because of the great sins of all kinds, a great punishment will befall mankind: flames and fire will fall from heaven; ocean waters will turn into vapor and their foam will rise up to overthrow humanity; a great war will break out, sowing death and hunger; diseases of all kinds. If penance is not done, and they do not pray, the punishments will be ghastly!

"... The time of the great trial will come also for the Church: cardinals will oppose cardinals, bishops against bishops. Satan marches triumphantly in the midst of their ranks due to their hubris and lack of charity! My daughter, there will be death everywhere because of the errors committed by the obstinate followers of Satan! Awareness of the terrible reality is urgent. Everyone must pray, do penance with the Holy Rosary, Holy Masses and Confessions. No sacrilegious Communions!"[16]

In the message of March 26, 1978, the Virgin also told Mother Elena Leonardi: "The Vatican knows how urgent it is to make men pray, but it does not want to alarm the people. Nevertheless, the whole world is living a terrible reality, the true Apocalypse. These are the dark days... Scandals, divorce, free abortion laws, have all accelerated the punishments."[16]

On February 12, 1979, Our Lady as the Mother of all Peoples said to Mother Elena Leonardi: "You, my daughter, must atone and make others atone for the sins which are committed: these evil mothers kill their own children in their wombs.., so many human lives thrown down the drains that cry for vengeance before God! My daughter, many diseases sent from heaven will befall and hurt mankind... God the Father has repeated many times that many nations will disappear off the face of the earth. Godless nations will be the scourge chosen by God Himself to punish the disrespectful and unscrupulous humanity. My daughter, a great punishment will befall mankind, a great war will break out, fire will fall from heaven, the ocean waters will be converted into vapor, and the foam will rise to sweep all humanity, wherever you look, there will be anguish, misery and ruin. Communism will triumph because of the godless rulers; many magistrates will perish; freemasonry in the churches, prelates without dignity... My daughter, the time has run out; this is the Apocalyptic hour; if they do not return to my Heart, they will know only desolation. Cardinals and bishops will confront the Pope who will be accused and mistreated, since the days of suffering are being prepared for the Holy Father. Speak to him and tell him to be prudent and strong; I protect and watch over him."[16]

Other Visionaries And Locutionists

Shortly after March 1988, Christina Gallagher, County Mayo in Ireland, had a vision in which she saw a very large figure of Christ in the sky with hand outstretched, looking down on the earth and saying "Woe," and she then saw balls of fire in countless numbers falling from the sky, and people on a road, running in every direction, some falling, and all looking up fearfully. She found the vision very frightening."[30]

Sadie Jaramillo had a vision on April 8, 1997. Sadie said: "During the rosary I see flashes of light and like balls of fire falling from the sky. I also see a man running like he is trying to avoid being hit. I hear 'the time of conflagration is here.'"[6]

On April 19, 1994 Janie Garza received seven visions from Jesus. Janie said: "In the sixth vision I saw the sky and it became as if at night time only I knew it was still day time, about noon time. Yet, the day became like night. Then I saw the stars in the Heavens turn into balls of fire and they began to fall on the earth. The fire began burning the areas where it was falling. People had begun screaming in fear as the day had turned into night. People were running and trying to find safety but there was no safety. Although it was dark I was given the ability to see them."[26]

Jesus told Janie: "... Only prayer can lessen the severity of these events.... It is not important that dates or times are revealed to you. What you have seen is for you to plead for My Father's mercy through your prayers."[26]

On September 29, 1995 Janie Garza was told by St. Michael: "Behold, beloved one of the Almighty God, and embrace what the Almighty has willed for you to see - this vision of evilness in the world, for this is what God sees every day. See the many souls that are infected with sin and who choose to remain in darkness. See the poison in their hearts and souls. Know, beloved daughter of the Most High God, that God is much offended by all the evil that exists in the hearts of many souls. Behold! And see the wrath of the Almighty One if souls do not repent!"[8]

Janie said: "I saw the world become dark and then the sky turned an orange color, and I saw <u>balls of fire falling from the sky</u>, destroying the areas where they hit. This caused great fear in me, and I begged St. Michael not to show me anymore, but he said that God wanted me to see all this, so that I would understand the evil which exists in many, many souls. I was sick and scared with pain, but St. Michael asked me to bless myself with the sign of the Cross. I immediately did this, and I felt God's peace. Praised be God and His goodness." [8]

Chastisements for our world, according to Patricia of Ecuador, a visionary who received Apparitions and Messages from the Holy Virgin as the Guardian of the Faith during the period August 24, 1988 until March 3, 1990:

- Natural disasters
- Man-made disasters
- Possibility of a third world war. [22]

On Tuesday, May 13, 1997 Our Heavenly Mother said to Joseph DellaPuca and Denise Curtin: "My dear children, time is short! There is soon to come much of what has been foretold you in scripture. The Earth will be punished with all kinds of plagues and wars. The Ten Kings will be allied to the Anti-Christ and be the only ruler of the world.

The Earth is at the beginning of it's pain and will die, -- a prey of terror and anguish caused by Satan. There will be famine and contagious diseases, rain of hail storms that will destroy cities, earthquakes, and <u>fire from Heaven will fall</u>. The whole world will be struck with terror, for many of my children have been seduced by Satan and his pleasures, and do not adore my Son, Jesus Christ, Who lived among them.

You must prepare by spiritually focusing on the condition of your souls and my Son's Second Coming. You will then see the Reign of Two Hearts, the Triumph of my Immaculate Heart and the Reign of the Sacred Heart of Jesus."[4]

On August 13, 2000, in the World Message from Our Heavenly Mother to Denise Curtin and Joseph DellaPuca Our Blessed Mother said: "**These Final Hours in which you are living** are truly difficult and painful... In these very serious times, you must consecrate yourselves daily to the Sacred Heart of Our Lord and Savior Jesus christ and the Immaculate heart of your Heavenly Mother.. **You must live each hour in greater Trust, Faith and Obedience for the glorious return of our Lord and Savior Jesus Christ...The greatest trial has arrived, and the chastisement foretold to you at Fatima which has been revealed, is about to take place in the world. Our Heavenly Father will strike the heels of wickedness.** You must remain in constant prayer to receive the abundant graces being poured forth unto you..."

239

Fire From The Sky – Heaven Continues To Warn Us

The Great Chastisement could come from either a Nuclear World War III or from a comet or asteroid of sufficient size grazing or striking the earth. Catholic Prophecy deals with both possibilities.

At Cojutepeque, El Salvador, on February 11, 1999, El Salvadoran visionary Nelly Hurtado received this message from Our blessed Mother: "... I am the Immaculate Conception, the Virgin Mary. I am the Woman dressed with the sun. I am the Queen of Love, and I come to this place as the Virgin of Fatima. ...

"I am the Bride of the Holy Spirit. I am the Mother of the Jubilee. I am the Mother of the Council. I am the Mother of Jesus. I am the Mother of All.

"The gates of Heaven have opened right now. I am surrounded by profound silence because my messages are not heard, they are not meditated upon, (even though) I am the Immaculate Conception!

"These, my children, are the End Times. I have come to prepare you for the upcoming events that have been foretold. My prophecies are about to come to be.

"You don't know when the first event will take place. I have announced three. I have spoken about:
- A comet that will be visible this year.

- <u>Of the Third World War.</u>
- <u>And of the Miracle of Garabandal.</u> "[25]

Possibility of A Third World War

Our Blessed Mother in October 1988 gave to Patricia of Ecuador a secret with three parts. Our Lady spoke several times about <u>the possibility of a Third World War</u>, of natural disasters and man-made disasters. Our Lady said: "Little children, know that all you do benefits the world. *Your prayers, penances, and fasts are helping to deter the determination of the Third World War...* <u>Great catastrophes are coming upon humanity; the Third World War threatens the world. Natural catastrophes created by man are coming.</u>"[22]

Our Blessed Mother told Patricia some details of the war that she was allowed to share with us: "The war is near. It will be started wit<u>h false peace treaties, treaties in which we should not place our trust. Many countries would be involved, among them China, Romania, Russia, and the United States. Initially Poland will be involved also,</u> but when the Holy Father leaves Rome, going first to France and then to Poland, Poland would be protected."[22]

Our Blessed Mother stated to Patricia: "You know, my daughter, that <u>the third nuclear war is near.</u> Pray, my children, for China, Russia, Czechoslovakia. Pray for the countries from the South. Catastrophes come there. Pray for Panama, Nicaragua, El Salvador. Repent, fast, make penance. The Third World War is near, natural catastrophes, earthquakes, floods such as humanity has never seen before, <u>because of so much sin in the world</u>... Pray much for the countries of Latin America. Pray very much for the countries of Central America. Pray for the Soviet Union, Russia, United States, Czechoslovakia, and China." [22]

In Chapter 12 of the book *Witness, Russia in Flames*, Josyp Terelya had an apparition from Our Blessed Mother in which he "saw a map." He stated: "I saw a map and parts of it were burning. There were fires erupting all over Russia. Surrounding countries were also involved. There were flames in various parts of the world. It was what could happen if mankind does not comeback to her Son. I saw entire landscapes. I saw a river. I recognized, the Amur. I don't know how I knew it was that river. I saw many islands there. I saw tanks on the Soviet side -- but not the Soviet type -- and a city in flames. Siberia was on fire to the Ural Mountains. I saw Moscow, and the people there had faces that were twisted and deformed. Moscow was sinking, and throughout the city were strange creatures running down the streets. Their faces were those of rats and their tails were long and fat with scaly skin and hairs sticking out like spikes. They were as big as a dog and whoever the creatures spat at would fall to the ground, as if by venom. There was a tremendous fear that filled Moscow, and the city was falling into the earth. I saw hills, forests, cities, walls. The whole countryside was aflame. And all these explosions were taking place..."

Josyp said "prophecies are difficult to interpret, and they are not always set in concrete. Was it civil war, or solely war with a foreign power? All I understood was that this was war and saw one country against whom this war was waged -- China! The tanks were Chinese. This war is inevitable and I got the sense it might come before the year 2000. If it does, the war will be a warning to all God's people...." [page 144]

On September 18, 1992, Our Blessed Mother in an apparition told Josyp Terelya that: "The word 'Beast' is that sign which you understand as symbolizing the visible organization of Satan on earth, which today dominates many nations on earth and is composed of the three evil spirits of: false religions, politics and commerce.... It is Satan himself [who] speaks through the false prophet of the Organization of the United Nations using the corpse of the organization of the United Nations to deceive mankind ... Now understand that the Devil uses invisible evil spirits, who act upon visible servants throughout the world, who are mustering the nations of the world for a world war that has never been witnessed before, which the Lord calls the Battle of the great day." Personal Communication that was subsequently published in the book *In The Kingdom of The Spirit* [28]

On September 18, 1992, Our Blessed Mother appeared

to Josyp Terelya and said: "I have come because there are terrible events that will befall a godless humanity, that does not want to receive my Son... But there is an event coming that will shake the entire world. A great war, the greatest that has ever been until now is imminent. So many will not survive it; only those who accept Christ the King and obeys God's commandments. All this has been written in the Holy Book in the Gospel of Christ. Everywhere are the servants of the Antichrist, the sons of Satan, who will come proclaiming peace and quiet, but Satan is preparing a great war, such as has never been seen until now. His power is invisible, this power will drive people to arm themselves." Personal Communication that was subsequently published in the book *In The Kingdom of The Spirit* [28]

On September 18, 1992, Our Blessed Mother in an apparition told Josyp Terelya: "We are in those times, when the end is near... In the end times Satan will be punished and all his forces will be destroyed. The devil knows well his time is short, the time to prepare for the great battle and his purpose is to destroy all mankind rather than seeing all men serve God.... This is why the devil is into such a frenzy to drag all the nations of the world into a great War, in order that he might destroy God's creation.... This is why the invisible evil servants of the devil, the evil spirits, and also his visible evil forces who represent all the godless rulers of the earth, are being used by Satan to prepare the great war with only one purpose, to obliterate God's human creatures..." Personal Communication that was subsequently published in the book *In The Kingdom of The Spirit* [28]

On May 13, 1993, Father Gobbi received in locution from Our Blessed Mother in message No. 495: "... Wars have multiplied in every part of the world, and <u>you are now living in the danger of the new terrible world war which will bring destruction to peoples and nations, a war from which no one will emerge victorious.</u>" [2]

On April 19, 1994 Janie Garza received seven visions from Jesus. The first five were of wars, the fourth of war in the Church, the fifth of war in the Family. Janie said of the first three visions of war:

"In the first vision I saw Red China in total chaos. There were loud noises that sounded like guns all over. People were lying in puddles of blood in the streets. Houses were destroyed. I could hear screams of people, and I could see men with weapons killing people. The vision was graphic in the sense of the numerous bodies that lay in the streets and that were burning in cars. Their body parts were dismembered from the fire and the weapons. The area was filled with smoke and fire.

"In the second vision I found myself in the Holy City of Jerusalem. I could hear screams of men, women and children who were being killed by men. This city was also filled with fear. The buildings were destroyed, the churches were places of refuge for the people. This was a terrible place to be at this time. No safety, no safety only fear and death.

"In the third vision I saw South Africa in total chaos. People were being killed by men with hate in their hearts. These men had weapons and were running all over the city killing whoever crossed their paths. Buildings were destroyed as well as houses. Cars and trucks were all over the streets, burning, and some had people burning in them. This seems to be a war for political power."[26]

Nuclear War

A nuclear war could be brought on by the errors committed by the financial and political leaders, the non-believers, the followers of Satan, who worship the gods of power and money in their steadfast drive for a One World Government that ends up in Antichrist's hands.

It appears there will be at least two events that cause fire to fall from heaven, each destroying a substantial part of mankind: the chastisement from man -- nuclear war, and the chastisement from God -- the Comet with the Three Days of Darkness. This will fulfill Blessed Anna-Maria Taigi's prophecy: "God will send two punishments; one will be in the form of wars, revolutions and other evils; it shall originate on earth. The other will be sent from heaven."

With a nuclear world war fire will fall from heaven, both the good and the bad will die, the great and the small, the princes of the church with the faithful, the rulers with their people. With nuclear warfare in the oceans, the waters of the oceans will turn to steam and overflow everything. The waters will become a mist. Millions and millions will die from hour to hour. This will cause anguish and misery and ruins in every country.

Those who survive will experience hunger and famine. The Antichrist, who will survive the nuclear holocaust, will offer food to those who take the mark of the beast to buy and sell and who will worship him. Those who will not do this will be persecuted and killed.

Then God will send the second punishment -- the punishment from heaven: There is a possibility that one comet will just miss the Earth causing fire to fall from heaven, then later the Comet of Chastisement -- the Comet of Darkness will strike the earth.

In Apocalypse chapter 8 we are told about a great mountain, burning with fire being cast into the sea, and a great star falling from the heavens burning like a torch falling on the rivers. In Apocalypse Chapter 9 we are told about a star falling from heaven upon the earth opening the bottomless pit with the smoke of the pit arising as smoke from a great furnace, with the sun and the air darkened by the smoke. This describes literally a comet or asteroid falling upon the earth and into the ocean, bursting through the earth's crust and opening into the fiery magma beneath, darkening the skies with smoke and causing volcanism adding to the darkness of the skies.

Fire From Heaven

This Comet of Chastisement causes the period of darkness which we call the Three Days of Darkness during which prophecy tells us that the demons will roam the earth rounding up Satan's followers who will be cast into Hell with them, the Antichrist and the false prophet and Satan himself. Satan will be bound with the chain of the Rosary.

We then will enter into the Era of Peace.

Prophecies About A Comet And The Earth

Nuclear War Could Be In Progress At The Time The Comet Hits Earth

On April 2, 1976 there was a vision of the Heavenly Mother and Padre Pio to Mother Elena Leonardi in which Our Lady said: "My daughter,.... Men live in the obstinacy of sin, but God's wrath is near, and the world will be tormented by great calamities; bloody revolutions, strong earthquakes, famines, epidemics, and terrible hurricanes which will force the seas and rivers to overflow. The world will be entirely transformed by a terrible war! The most deadly weapons will destroy peoples and nations and those things which are most cherished. In this sacrilegious struggle, much of which has been created by Man will be demolished due to both savage impulse and enraged resistance. Finally, incandescent clouds will appear in the sky, and a flaming tempest will fall over the whole world. The terrible calamity never before seen in

Man's history, will last for seventy hours; the impious will be pulverized, and many will be lost in the obstinacy of their sins. Then, the power of light over the power of darkness will be seen. Do not be silent, my daughter, because the terrible forsaken hour is near! Bending over the world, I have suspended Divine Justice. If this were not the case, these things would have already happened.".... [16]

There may be two different comets involved in the chastisement. The first of these would not strike the Earth, but just graze it causing fire to fall from heaven and the oceans to overflow their boundaries. Fragments landing in water could cause steam and mist. The Antichrist could possibly then come on the scene after this event only to perish in a short time when the Comet of Chastisement, also called the Comet of Darkness strikes the Earth.

A Comet Skims Across the Surface of the Earth

Josyp Terelya, in interviews given in May and June 1993 stated: "There is a large comet that is approaching the earth. It will not hit the earth, but it will cause many cataclysms on the planet. Land today in America will be under water. Because of the tremendous flooding, crops won't grow, the animals then will have nothing to feed on, and this will contribute to the great famine. Sooner or later there will be a tremendous struggle for products. We will survive, but we will all witness major catastrophes. Do not be afraid or worried; pray and the Holy Spirit will lead you."

The Comet Of Darkness

Julka (Julia) of Yugoslavia during period 1960-1966 had a vision of darkness over the earth.

The Lord Jesus, Our Saviour, and his suffering Holy Mother, weep over the fate of sinful humanity, which is unwilling to be converted. Our Lord Jesus Christ says: *"A small Last Judgment is approaching!"*

Julka said: "The God-fearing Christians, Mary's true admirers, will be specially protected by their Heavenly Mother when the Great tribulation comes."

"God will punish the sins of earth very severely." [33]

The Comet of Chastisement

During The Great Trial A Comet Strikes Earth With Resulting Darkness

Julka (Julia) of Yugoslavia in the period 1960 to 1966 had a vision in which she states: "I found myself in a garden, looking after the flowers. Suddenly something so gigantic fell to the earth, that the whole world shook and reared itself as though it was going to break in pieces. All the air is in flames. The whole

Fire From Heaven

atmosphere of the earth from the ground to the sky, was a gigantic sheet of flame..."[33] Vol.1 pg. 220

Julka (Julia) of Yugoslavia in messages from 1974 through 1976 reported visions of the comet of the Chastisement striking the earth. Julka named it the Comet of Darkness.

Julka (Julia) of Yugoslavia, (1974 visions and messages). October 21, 1974. The Great Purification, "The Earth's crust began to contract like the surface of the ocean during a tremendous storm. The surface rose and sank, writhed and folded as if it would break apart. In the East a great fire fell on the Earth..." [33]

Julka: In 1975 the Heavenly Father agreed: "The whole Earth will be covered by a great fire and will be infertile for some time for those who survive it." [33]

Julka (Julia) of Yugoslavia (1975-1976: visions and messages). "Then the great calamity, together with all the demons, plunged to the Earth. After this began an indescribable horror. The people struck and killed each other mercilessly. The air was filled with screams, lamentations and cries of help. The mountains were raised, fell over and disappeared into the abyss. It appeared as if they were smashed and thrown about by the demons... After a certain amount of time, Our Lord Jesus commanded the Great Trial to cease. Thereupon the great darkness receded from the Earth and, along with all the demons, disappeared into the horrible abyss. The Earth's surface was rent asunder and filled with craters. It was as if it had

251

Fire From Heaven

experienced a dreadful bombardment. Only here and there some small areas were preserved... Our Lord said: "I have removed the living earth from the dead earth. To the living earth I have given the Grace of My Wisdom that it may live in My Spirit. God the Father and the Holy Spirit commanded the sun should shine with renewed strength upon the Earth. The air became crystal clear and the Earth appeared new-born."[33]

On June 20, 1976, the Lord Jesus appeared in front of the Tabernacle. He glanced at all present there and commanded Julka, the seeress: "Come with Me!" And they ascended. Several Angels joined them. After a while the Lord said to Julia: "Look at the Earth!" From that height it seemed as small as a full moon. When Julia looked carefully, she saw huge craters everywhere. Only a few areas remained without holes. The whole Earth was stained with blood. Our Lord Jesus explained: "This is how the face of the Earth will look during the Catastrophe!"[33]

On June 21, 1976, The Comet of Darkness, the Heavenly Mother said to Julka of Yugoslavia: "My dear children":... Julia, in ecstasy, observed something strange. 'Dear Mother, what is this?'... The Comet of darkness... I am afraid!" Julka the seeress said: "Something long and black came towards the Earth. It looked like a comet. Our dear Mother rushed past it to help us. Whilst She spoke, the comet stood still in space."[33]

Part Of World Destroyed

Our Lady gave message #1,377, on March 21, 1988 to Gladys Quiroga de Motta, in San Nicholas, Argentina after Gladys had a vision.

Gladys said: "I have a vision: I see the earth divided in two parts. One part represents two-thirds and the other one-third, in which I see the Blessed Virgin. She is with the Child and from her breast rays of light go towards the part that represents two-thirds of the earth. Immediately, she says to me:

'Gladys, you are seeing the world half destroyed. These rays of light are sent from my heart that wants to save as many hearts as it can.

'My Heart is all powerful, but it can do nothing if hearts are unwilling. The means to save souls are prayer and conversion. Every soul must prepare so as not to be imprisoned eternally by darkness. Amen, Amen.'" page 293 Messages of Our Lady At San Nicolas, 1991

Marie-Julie Jahenny, the Breton stigmatist, born 1850, died 1941, announced that three quarters of the population of the globe will disappear in the last crisis; terrible earthquakes, epidemics of unknown diseases whose ravages would be frightful, terrible famines, inclement weather, cyclones, rising seas that would cause terrifying tidal waves.

The last crisis will be divided in three parts: the first long and painful when divine vengeance will be manifested, during which the most guilty will be destroyed. "This blow of justice will only irritate them."

The second will be shorter but more formidable, more sinister: "My Divine Son, seeing all these blows cannot bring back His people to pardon and mercy – lost souls – will strike again more fearfully..."

The third: "Everything must be lost from top to bottom. That, my dear children, is when St. Michael, the Archangel, who is awaiting orders from Heaven, will descend with his armies to fight with my good children, the true and good children of victory... Justice will pass everywhere. During this time you will not have the bread of the strong... No apostles, you will have only your faith as food, my Divine Son, as Sovereign Priest, to forgive you..."

"My dear children, all the souls living in His Divine Heart will run no danger; they will only have a faint knowledge of His anger.

"They will be enclosed in this immense sea of prodigies and power, during these great blows of divine justice." (August 17, 1905). [42]

The Good As Well As The Bad Will Perish During This Great Chastisement

On October 13, 1973, at Akita, Japan, an apparition which was twice approved by the Bishop, Bishop Ito, and twice approved by the Bishops of the Church in Japan, the Holy Mother gave this message to Sister Agnes Sasagawa: "If men do not repent and better themselves, the Heavenly Father will inflict a great punishment on all humanity. It will definitely be a punishment greater than the Deluge, such as has never been seen before. Fire will plunge from the sky and a large part of humanity will perish... The good as well as the bad will perish, sparing neither priests nor the faithful. The survivors will find themselves plunged into such terrible hardships that they will envy the dead. The only arms which will remain for you will be the Rosary and the sign left by My Son (Eucharist)." [21]

In Tokyo, Japan, on September 15, 1993 Our Lady in message # 501 told Father Gobbi: "In this very country I have given you an extraordinary sign, causing copious tears to fall more than one hundred times from the eyes of one of my statues, in which I am represented as the Sorrowful Mother beneath the Cross of my Son Jesus. And I have given you three messages to warn you of the great dangers into which you are running. [at Akita]

"I now announce to you that the time of the great trial has come, because during these years all that I have foretold to you will come to pass The apostasy and the great schism in the Church is on the point of taking place, and the great chastisement, about which I foretold you in this place, is now at the very doors. Fire will come down from heaven, and a great part of humanity will be destroyed. <u>Those who survive will envy the dead, because everywhere there will be desolation, death and ruin."[2]</u>

Our Lady Has Succeeded In Postponing The Time Of Chastisement

On August 15, 1996, Our Lady said to Father Gobbi, in message number 576: "....I gather in the chalice of my Immaculate Heart all your sufferings, the great sorrows of all humanity in the time of its great tribulation and I present them to Jesus, as a sign of reparation for all the sins which are committed each day in the world.

"And thus I have again succeeded in postponing the time of chastisement decreed by Divine Justice, for a humanity which has become worse than at the time of the flood.

"Look up to heaven. From heaven, you will see my Son Jesus returning on the clouds, in the splendor of his divine glory. Then finally the triumph of my Immaculate Heart in the world will be accomplished.

"To prepare for this divine prodigy, I want to establish my motherly triumph in the hearts and the souls of all my children." [2]

The Times Will Be Shortened

On November 23, 1976, Our Lord Jesus Christ told Julka (Julia), Yugoslavia: "The True Roman-Catholic Faith is being put to a great test because of My Most Holy Mother and My Words from Her mouth.* It will be even more difficult when the hour comes which I have decided upon for Earth.

"Then the face of the Earth will be renewed and all Sanctuaries will become holy. These are My chosen Places in every country, on every Continent, wherever I Myself appear or My Mother, or My Servants of Heaven.

"In the young Church of My Little Flock My Teaching is being confirmed. My pious faithful who will survive the Great Tribulation will visit such Places and Shrines wherever they will be. My pious servants, priests whom I shall let live on Earth, will carefully explore all Areas and Places where My Holy Words and those of My Mother, have been preached. All this must be because of the far too heavy sins of the world; but I shall shorten everything and sincere, Christian hearts will inhabit the Earth, My Spirit will be above them. We Ourselves shall approach Earth, and Earth will come close to Us - thus speaks the Most Holy Trinity." [33]

On September 29, 1995, Father Gobbi was told by Our Lady: "My plan is now being accomplished everywhere. My little son, you see how the triumph of my Immaculate Heart is taking place in the world... **The times** will be shortened, because I am Mother of Mercy and each day I offer, at the throne of Divine Justice, my prayer united to that of the children who are responding to me with a yes and consecrating themselves to my Immaculate Heart... How many times have I already intervened in order to set back further and further in time the beginning of the great trial, for the purification of this poor humanity, now possessed and dominated by the Spirits of Evil."[2]

The Great Chastisement Is Conditional

At Garabandal We Were Told It Is Conditional

According to the messages at Garabandal The (Great) Chastisement can be avoided.

June 19, 1962 Maria Dolores Mazon (Mary Loli) and Jacinta Gonzalez said: "The Virgin told us:
That we do not expect the Chastisement. That without expecting it, it will come, since the world has not changed.

And she has already told us twice; and we do not pay attention to her, since the world is getting worse. And it should change very much. And it has not changed at all. Prepare yourself. Confess, because the Chastisement will come soon. And the world continues the same...

I tell you this: That the world continues the same. How unfortunate that it does not change! Soon will come a very great Chastisement, if it does not change." Page 193 *She Went In Haste To The Mountain. Book Two*

On March 25, 1965 Mary Loli wrote: "For my good believer in Christ, William A. Nolan!.... I also tell you this, that in order to avoid the Chastisement, we have to make many sacrifices and penances, to pray the family rosary every day; this is what Our Most Holy Mother requests of us. Also, that we should love one another, as Our Lord loves us. We have to love; the whites must love the blacks; and the blacks, the whites, since we are all brothers." Page 159 *She Went In Haste to The Mountain, Book Three*

Conchita said: "The chastisement, if we do not change, will be horrible." Page 159 *She went In Haste To The Mountain. Book Three*

On June 19, 1965 this was read at Garabandal:

The message that the Most Holy Virgin has given to the world through the intercession of [by means of] St. Michael.

The Angel said: "As my message of October 18 has not been fulfilled, and as little has been done to make it known, I tell you that this is the last.
- Before the cup was filling up; now it is overflowing.
- The Priests: Many are on the road to perdition, and with them they are taking many more souls.

Fire From Heaven

- The Eucharist: It is being given less and less importance.
- With your own efforts, you should avoid the wrath of the Good God.
- If you ask pardon with a sincere heart, He will forgive you
- I, your Mother, through the intercession [by means of] the Archangel Michael, want you to amend your lives.
- You are in the last warnings!
- I love you very much, and do not want your condemnation.
- Ask us sincerely, and we will give you what you ask.
- You should sacrifice yourself more.
- Think of the passion of Jesus." ^{Page 176 She Went In Haste} To The Mountain, Book Three

On September 19, 1965 Conchita said: "The miracle of Fatima is nothing in comparison to what will happen here. This will he much, much greater."

"The Miracle here will be much greater, more tremendous than Fatima. It will cause such an impression that none of those who see it will be able to leave with doubts. It would be well if all the world were here, since that way there surely would be no chastisement, since everyone would believe." ^{Page 189 She Went In} Haste To The Mountain, Book Three

Fire From Heaven

At Akita We Were Told The Great Chastisement Is Conditional

On October 13, 1973, at Akita, Japan, an apparition approved by the Church, the Holy Mother gave this message to Sister Agnes Sasagawa: <u>"If men do not repent and better themselves</u>, the Heavenly Father will inflict a great punishment on all humanity. It will definitely be a punishment greater than the Deluge, such as has never been seen before, <u>Fire will plunge from the sky and a large part of</u> humanity will perish... <u>The good as well as the bad will perish, sparing neither priests nor the faithful.</u> The survivors will find themselves plunged into such terrible hardships that they will envy the dead. The only arms which will remain for you will be the Rosary and the sign left by My Son (Eucharist)."[21]

The Triumph Of The Immaculate Heart Without The Great Chastisement

In his concluding remarks in his interview of August 4-5, 1999 at Rubbio, Italy Father Gobbi stated: "Observe how many chastisements have already been removed by means of these cenacles!

<u>"Our Lady was able to move everything up to the year 1999. If in the Great Jubilee, rather than by means of a chastisement, the triumph of the Immaculate Heart, the glorious triumph of Christi. should come about as an explosion of the merciful love</u> of Jesus and 'as a gift of the Holy Spirit whose second Pentecost we

261

await – who leads the hearts to change, the souls to free themselves from sin, the people to return to God who is waiting for us like a Father to welcome us in his arms – I would think that this is truly the greatest triumph of the Heart of the Mother, who so much loves her children, who never abandons them, and who leads them by the hand along the path of good, of love and of sanctity." [37]

Chapter 12

The Three Days Of Darkness

The Earth Going Out Of Orbit, And The Three Days Of Darkness

At the end of the message of La Salette, given to Melanie Calvat, Sister Mary of the Cross, in an apparition of Our Weeping Blessed Mother on September 19, 1846, we are told: "Now is the time; the abyss is opening. Here is the King of Kings of darkness, here is the Beast with his subjects, calling himself the savior of the world. He will rise proudly into the air to go to Heaven. He will be smothered by the breath of the Archangel Saint Michael. He will fall, and the earth, which will have been in a continuous series of evolutions for three days, will open up its fiery bowels; and he will have plunged for eternity with all his followers into the everlasting chasms of hell. And then water and fire will purge the earth and consume all the works of men's pride and all will be renewed. God will be served and glorified." [7]

Our Blessed Mother, Guardian of the Faith, (during

the period 1988 to 1990) told Patricia Talbott of Cuenca, Ecuador that "the earth would go out of its orbit for three days. At that time the Second Coming of Jesus will be near, the devil will take over the world. During those days, families should be in continuous prayer. Because of false prophets, who will falsify the Words of Christ, we have to be in the state of grace so that we can discern the good from evil. We have to have the flame of Jesus Christ in our soul. We should not open the door of our homes to anybody. We are simply to keep on praying. The Virgin said it would be better not even to look through the window because we will see the justice of God over the people. It will be so terrible, that we will not want to see it."[22]

The Three Days Of Darkness

Julka (Julia), Zagreb, Yugoslavia in the period of years from 1960 to 1966 had a vision about which she stated:

Julka (Julia), Zagreb, Yugoslavia: "A little more about the Great distress. To begin with, a strong wind will come from the south. It will seize upon the whole globe and cause dreadful storms. After this about ten claps of thunder at once will strike the earth with such force that it will shudder throughout. This is a sign that the Great Tribulation and the Black Darkness are beginning. These will last three days and three nights. On this account people should go into their houses, close them up well, darken the win-

dows, bless themselves and the house with holy water, and light blessed candles. Outside such dreadful
things will be happening, that those who venture to
look out will die. All the devils will be let loose on
earth, so that they can destroy their prey themselves.

"The demons will howl upon the earth and call many,
in order to destroy them. What? They will imitate
the voices of relations and acquaintances, who have
not reached a safer place. Once the horror commences, do not open your door to anyone at all!"[33]

Some People Will Fall Into A Deep Sleep

Julka of Yugoslavia said: "In many places several people
will gather together in fear. From the same group, some
will perish, others remain alive for this Day and moment, and for that darkness many will have prepared
the blessed candles, but they will not burn, if the
people have not lived in accordance with My Commandment, others will even be unable to light them
for fear. But, for those who believe, although they
have but a stub of the blessed candle, it will burn for
three days and nights without going out. Some people will fall into a deep sleep granted by Me, so as not
to see what is happening on the earth. All the buildings on earth will collapse, and only here and there
will remain a simple, modest, little house, in which
the light of a candle will glimmer. In many places, the
heaps of corpses will be so great, that no one will be
able to make a passage through them on account of
these bodies, there will not be anyone to bury them."

3 Vol. 1 pp. 223-224

Fire From Heaven

The Followers Of Evil Cause Will Be Annihilated

Sister Marie of Jesus Crucified (19th century): "All the nations will be shaken by war and revolution.

"During the three days of darkness, the followers of evil cause will be annihilated, so that only one-fourth of mankind will survive." [18]

Blessed Gaspar Del Bufalo (19th Century): "The death of the impenitent persecutors of the Church will take place during the three days of darkness. He who out-lives the darkness and the fear of these three days will think that he is alone on earth because the whole world will be covered by carcasses." [18]

Blessed Anna-Maria Taigi, (19th century): "There shall come over the whole earth an intense darkness last-ing three days and three nights. Nothing can be seen, and the air will be laden with pestilence which will claim mainly, but not only, the enemies of religion. It will be impossible to use any man-made lighting dur-ing this darkness, except blessed candles. He, who out of curiosity, opens his window to look out, or leaves his home, will fall dead on the spot. During these three days, people should remain in their homes, pray the Rosary and beg God for mercy.

"All the enemies of the Church, whether known or unknown, will perish over the whole earth during that universal darkness, with the exception of a few whom God will soon convert. The air shall be infected

266

by demons who will appear under all sorts of hideous forms."[18]

Marie-Julie Jahenny, born 1850, died 1941, announced the three days of darkness during which <u>the infernal powers will be loosed and will execute all the enemies of God</u>. "The earth will become like a vast cemetery. The bodies of the wicked and the just will cover the ground."

The famine will be great... Everything will be thrown into confusion... The crisis will explode suddenly; the punishments will be shared by all and will succeed one another without interruption... (January 4, 1884).

The three days of darkness "<u>will he on a Thursday, Friday and Saturday.</u> Days of the Most Holy Sacrament, of the Cross, and Our Lady..." three days less one night.

Our Lady on the 20th of September 1882 said: "The earth will be covered in darkness, and hell will be loosed on earth. <u>The thunder and lightning</u> will cause those who have no faith or trust in my power to die of fear."

"During these three days of terrifying darkness, <u>no windows must be opened,</u> because no one will he able to see the earth and the terrible color it will have in those days of punishment, without dying at once...

"The sky will be on fire, the earth will split... During

Fire From Heaven

these three days of darkness let the blessed candle be lighted every where, no other light will shine...

earthquake 1989. Arriving home just minutes before

"No one outside a shelter.., will survive, The earth will shake as at the judgment and fear will be great. Yes, We will listen to the prayers of your friends; not one will perish..." December 8, 1882.

On the 24th of March 1881, Our Lady added: "Those who have served me well and invoked me, who have my blessed picture in their house, who carry my Rosary on them and say it often, I will keep intact all that belongs to them... The heat from Heaven will be unbearably hot, even in the closed homes. The whole sky will be on fire, but the lightning will not penetrate into the houses where there will be the light of the blessed candle. This light will be the only thing that will protect you."

"The candles of blessed wax alone will give light during this horrible darkness. One candle alone will be enough for the duration of this night of hell... In the homes of the wicked and blasphemers these candles will give no light."

"Everything will shake except the piece of furniture on which the blessed candle is burning. This will not shake. You will all gather around the crucifix and my blessed picture. This is what will keep away this terror."

"During this darkness the devils and the wicked will take on the most hideous shapes... red clouds like blood will move across the sky. The crash of the thunder will shake the earth and sinister lightning will streak the heavens out of season, The earth will be shaken to its foundations. The sea will rise, its roaring waves will spread over the continent

"The wicked will commit all kinds of horrors. The Holy Hosts will he dispersed on the roads. They will be discovered in the mud. The priests as well as the faithful will pick them up and will carry them on their breasts" (October 17, 1883).

"I understood that the angels would carry away many tabernacles from the churches to shield the Holy Sacrament."[42]

The Seven Seals

Jesus told Christina Gallagher, Ireland, on January 30, 1991: "Tell all humanity to prepare themselves: the time has come for the cleansing of all humanity. A great darkness will come upon the world. The heavens will shake. The only light will be through the Son of God and Man..... My hand will come over the world more swiftly than the wind... the demons rage upon the earth. They are loosed from their pit. Tell all humanity of the Seven Seals of God... Seek only the Kingdom of God."[30]

Fire From Heaven

Signs That Great Chastisement And The Three Days Of Darkness Are Beginning

Brother David Lopez, a Franciscan brother, on the Texas-Mexican border, in a hamlet called El Ranchilo, in a hermitage known as Our Lady of Tenderness, received a message from the Blessed Virgin, while in Medjugorje on August 15, 1987: "Do not be afraid of the Three Days of Darkness that will come over the earth, because those who are living my messages and have a life of interior prayer will be alerted by an interior voice three days to one week before their occurrence."

Brother David Lopez said: "During these three days of darkness there is not going to be one demon left in hell. All are going to be on earth. Those three days are going to be so dark that we will not be able to see our own hands before our faces. In those days, the ones who are not in the state of grace are going to die of fright because of the horrible demons that they will see. The Virgin told me to close all the doors and windows and not to respond to anyone who calls from the outside. The biggest temptation we will have is the devil is going to, imitate the voices of our loved ones. She told me: 'Please do not pay attention because these are not your loved ones; those are demons trying to lure you out of the house.'... She told me that the hours of darkness will be exactly 72, and the only way to count them is with mechanical clocks, because there won't be any electricity...

270

Devastation Of A Large Area Of The Earth

Our Lord God told Joanne Kriva, a mid-western housewife and mother, on July 29, 1991: "I will permit the devastation of a large area of the earth. I will permit the winds of the air, the waters of the sea, the fires below the earth to converge upon the face of the earth. One country will cease to exist. Its inhabitants will be swallowed in the roaring seas and raging fires. A mountain will be leveled to a flat plain. No sign of life will remain. The peoples of the earth will tremble in fear and bewilderment before the awesome might of the forces of nature which obey the commands of their Creator. The winds will move over the whole earth. The rain shall fall in torrents until the seas move over the land. Black clouds will move through the air and large areas of the earth will be in darkness. Buildings will fall and many will perish beneath them... When the furies of nature have subsided, the numbers of dead will be countless; the landscape of the earth will be forever changed... Believers will be sustained by the mighty power of God Almighty. Carry with you at all times your blessed candles and the armor of the rosary. Keep with you the water of baptism. Provide food and drink for yourself and your families. Protect your homes with My image. Bless your homes with holy water. Support your neighbors in need. Pray!"[10]

Fire Falls To The Earth

Julka (Julia) of Yugoslavia, (1974 visions and messages): October 21, 1974, The Great Purification, "The Earth's crust began to contract like the surface of the ocean during a tremendous storm. The surface rose and sank, writhed and folded as if it would break apart. <u>In the East a great fire fell on the Earth...</u>" [33]

Julka: In 1975 the Heavenly Father agreed: "The whole Earth will be covered by a great fire and will be infertile for some time for those who survive it." [33]

Flames In The Sky, Earthquakes, Tidal Waves

On May 9, 1973, Mother Elena Leonardi was told: "Listen well and listen to what I tell you: "For some days, darkness will cover the Earth. The sky will be clouded with flames. The earth will tremble. Torrential storms will be unchained. Men will perish. Nations will be stricken, and much blood will shed..." [16]

December 28, 1975, Our Heavenly Mother told Mother Elena Leonardi that Divine Justice is prepared to act, that she is "the Lady of Sorrows because of the great cataclysm which will simultaneously convulse the earth. It will be terrible, frightful as if it were the end of the world! But the end of the world has not yet arrived, however, it is not far away... This is a dangerous hour. Five nations will be completely razed.... The rigors of God's Justice are awful! Blood will be shed for mortal sins; disease, earthquakes, scourgings, <u>flames from heaven</u>, tidal waves, family-- devastating thieves..." [16]

Fire From Heaven

The Earth's Surface Rent Asunder And Filled With Craters

Julka (Julia) of Yugoslavia (1975-1976: visions and messages). "Then the great calamity, together with all the demons, plunged to the Earth. After this began an indescribable horror. The people struck and killed each other mercilessly. The air was filled with screams, lamentations and cries of help. The mountains were raised, fell over and disappeared into the abyss. It appeared as if they were smashed and thrown about by the demons...

"After a certain amount of time, Our Lord Jesus commanded the Great Trial to cease. Thereupon the great darkness receded from the Earth and, along with all the demons, disappeared into the horrible abyss. The Earth's surface was rent asunder and filled with craters. It was as if it had experienced a dreadful bombardment. Only here and there some small areas were preserved... Our Lord said: "I have removed the living earth from the dead earth. To the living earth I have given the Grace of My Wisdom that it may live in My Spirit. God the Father and the Holy Spirit commanded the sun should shine with renewed strength upon the Earth. The air became crystal clear and the Earth appeared new-born."[33]

Julka of Hungary said: "But after the darkness the earth remained waste. The beautiful warm sun rose to shine upon the earth and all living things upon it, but only here and there was any human being still alive. Nature created by God, remained empty - without human beings. The Lord Jesus counseled the visionary, and left her in the little flock...All My creatures who survive the great tribulation, will see Me. No one will then be able to say that I do not exist, because I shall be near the earth; and all the creatures of the earth will hear My voice. They will see Me present then, and, for the second time, at the Final Judgment."[33]

Mitigation

We have been able by our free will response in accepting the remedies given by Heaven in these last days of the End of the Times to mitigate, i.e., decrease and/or shorten the duration of the chastisements during the purification. Fr. Gobbi in his recent video (1999 - released in 2000) tells us that the prophesied events had all been moved forward from earlier dates.

On March 25, 1998, Mary told Sadie Jaramillo: My little sorrowful rose, ... "The time left now is nearly expired. My children do you not understand? Though the warning of man's conscience was to have come long ago, this would certainly have meant that the length of the Antichrist's reign would have been longer! As it is now, I have shortened the length of his reign... "[3]

There is hope

If humanity freely responds to the Warning by penance, penance, penance as proclaimed by the angel
with the flaming sword in the third part of the secret
of Fatima, God's wrath may be appeased and He may
totally mitigate the Great Chastisement and Three
Days of Darkness. Our Blessed Mother has been appearing frequently all over the world to bring us back to
God the Father, her Divine Son and her Spouse the Holy
Spirit.

With humanity's proper response to Heaven's intervention by means of the great act of God's mercy, the Warning, also called the Illumination, God may allow us to
enter directly into the Era of Peace with the Triumph of
the Two Hearts, The Sacred Heart of Jesus and the Immaculate Heart of Mary without the necessity of the
cleansing of humanity by the Great Chastisement. If
we respond, the remainder of the vision of the third
secret of Fatima will be of events in the past up to the
present; otherwise these events are in our immediate
future.

Cardinal Ratzinger characterized the vision of the
third part of the secret of Fatima as a prophetic vision of the 20th century in which the world is seen
under "the threat of judgment" unless there is a conversion of hearts to Christ.

Fire From Heaven

Interview Of Father Gobbi On August 4-5, 1999
At Rubbio, Italy

In his concluding remarks in his interview of August 4-5, 1999 at Rubbio, Italy Father Gobbi stated: "Observe how many chastisements have already been removed by means of these cenacles!

"Our Lady was able to move everything up to the year 1999. If in the Great Jubilee, rather than by means of a chastisement, the triumph of the Immaculate Heart, the glorious triumph of Christ, should come about as an explosion of the merciful love of Jesus and 'as a gift of the Holy Spirit whose second Pentecost we await —who leads the hearts to change, the souls to free themselves from sin, the people to return to God who is waiting for us like a Father to welcome us in his arms — I would think that this is truly the greatest triumph of the Heart of the Mother, who so much loves her children, who never abandons them, and who leads them by the hand along the path of good, of love and of sanctity."[37]

The Heart of the Mother

Chapter 13

THE ERA OF PEACE

After The Three Days Of Darkness

Blessed Anna Maria Taigi (d. 1837) said: "After the three days of darkness, St. Peter and St. Paul, having come down from Heaven, will preach in the whole world and designate a new Pope... **Christianity will then spread throughout the world...**

"Whole nations will come back to the Church and the face of the earth will be renewed. **Russia, England, and China will come back to the Church.**"[18]

Julka (Julia), of Yugoslavia said of her vision of the three days of darkness: "But after the darkness the earth remained waste. The beautiful warm sun rose to shine upon the earth and all living things upon it, but only here and there was any human being still alive. Nature created by God, remained empty - without human beings. The Lord Jesus counseled the visionary, and left her in the little flock...All my creatures who survive the great tribulation, will see Me. No one will then be able to say that I do not exist, because I shall be near the earth; and all the creatures of the earth will hear My voice. They will see Me present then, and, for the second time, at the Final Judgment.[33]

The Era of Peace and The Year 2004

When Maria Esperanza was in Canada in early 1998 she spoke at a conference of Native Americans (the descendants of Sitting Bull) and told them that after the year 2004 the world would enter into a beautiful time of peace.

Josyp Terelya in a personal communication related that there are 3 periods of 10 years, 1985 to 1995, 1995 to 2005, and 2005 to 2015. We are now in the second of these 10 year periods. 2005 is the beginning of the third period of 10 years.

What Might Happen Between The Years 2000 and 2005

The problem of the apparent discrepancy between Fr. Gobbi's Jubilee of the year 2000 date and Maria Esperanza's and Joseph Terelya's and Patricia of Ecuador's dates of 2004-2005.

Catholic Prophets of this century tell us that after the Warning there will be a short period of time for people to be ministered to regarding what they had experienced and what the Faith is about and what they are now to do for salvation. Then those who are not converted by this experience and the Miracle to follow, after a period of persecution by the Antichrist and the False Prophet (the Antipope of these end times), will be lost for all eternity. During the Three Days of Darkness that results from the Great Chastisement these followers of Antichrist and the False Prophet will be cast into Hell for all eternity along with Antichrist and the False Prophet. The faithful remnant will live on into the wonderful Era of Peace that has been foretold by the Old Testament Prophets, The New Testament, The Apostolic Fathers, and the Prophets of these End Times.

Sadie Jaramillo on November 13, 1995 was told by Jesus: "Through the impending events, My hand is on you and all who are Mine and My Mother's. This triumph of Her Heart is the peace that will see you through and lead you into the Era of Peace!..."[6]

Between the beginning of the year 2000 and the real beginning of the start of the Third Millennium January 1, 2001, it definitely appears that there will not be enough time for all the prophesied events of the Warning, the Miracle and the Great Sign, the schism in the Church with the False Prophet as Antipope, the reign of Antichrist, the abomination of desolation prophesied by Daniel and the Great Chastisement to have occurred;

Purer, more humble, more enlightened, stronger

Fire From Heaven

even if the reign of Antichrist is shortened for the sake of the elect.

Because of this apparent lack of sufficient time for all the above events to occur, and the revelations from Maria Esperanza and Josyp Terelya and Patricia of Ecuador, it is probable that, after the triumph of the Immaculate Heart of Mary - by, during the great Jubilee of the year 2000 - there will be a short period of time, from the year 2000 through the year 2004 during which these other necessary events will occur.

These events will be necessary for us to fully enter into the Era of Peace with the Second Coming of Jesus in glory, the Era of the Eucharistic Reign of Jesus, <u>and the Era when we will learn to live in the Divine Will and will live in the Divine Will.</u>

These events which must occur are the renewal of the earth so that we have The New Earth that is promised, the fulfillment of evangelization so that all who survive the Great Chastisement will become one, as members of the renewed Church, which Our Lady in message # 171 to Fr. Gobbi tells us will be purer, more humble, more enlightened, stronger.

The Era Of Peace As Revealed To Sr. Natalia of Hungary

Sr. Natalia of Hungary, b 1901,was told by Jesus that

the Church, cleansed and renewed by the great sufferings, will dress again in humility and simpleness,
and will be poor as at her beginning.... They will live
by the spirit of the Sermon on the Mount. Sr. Natalia
said that she saw that when the glorious peace arrives
and love reigns, there will be only "one fold and one
shepherd."[24]

Jesus told Sr. Natalia: "I brought peace when I was
born, but the world has not yet enjoyed it. The world
is entitled to that peace. Men are the children of God.
God breathes His own souls into them. God cannot let
Himself be put to shame, and that is why the children
of God are entitled to enjoy the peace that I promised."[24]

Sr. Natalia was told by Jesus about the cleansing of
the world, "the coming age of paradise, when humanity will live as if without sin. This will be a new world
and a new age. This will be the age when mankind
will get back what it lost in paradise. When My Immaculate mother will step on the neck of the serpent,
the gates of hell will be closed. The host of angels will be
part of this fight. I have sealed with My seal My own
that they shall not be lost in this fight."[24]

Jesus told Sr. Natalia that all those who will not convert before or during the period of grace will receive
eternal death. "The right hand of my Father will anni-
hilate all those sinners who, despite the warnings and
the period of grace and the tireless effort of the
Church, will not convert."[24]

Blue color of peace

Fire From Heaven

Sr. Natalia states: "I saw God's Holy Spirit -- as a dev-astating fire -- inundate the world. This fire did not bring peace, nor mercy, but devastating punishment. Wherever the flame of the Holy Spirit swept through, the evil spirits by the thousands fell back to hell." In this vision of Sr. Natalia: "The Holy Virgin took off from her shoulder the mantle of peace and sud-denly covered the world with it. All those parts of the world covered with the mantle escaped the punishment and shone in the blue color of peace. But where the man-tle did not cover the surface, the red color of anger could be seen radiating as embers." Sr. Natalia said: "I under-stood that we can escape from the just punishment of God only if we seek refuge under the mantle of our Blessed Virgin Mother, and supplicate mercy through her."[24]

The Era Of Peace As Revealed To Joanne Kriva

On September 23, 1991 the Lord God in locution said to Joanne Kriva: "All is in readiness for the coming of the Lord God in power and majesty. When there seems no hope, will I come. When all seems lost, will I come in power and glory to lift you out of the earthly hell. What a glorious people you are who persevere; what a glorious triumph awaits you."[10]

On December 24, 1991 the Father said to Joanne Kriva: "I, the Father, announce to My creation the end of your days as you know them. I announce to you the reign of peace and justice. I tell you -- the reign of God is at hand." [10]

The Lord God on February 3, 1991 spoke to Joanne Kriva in locution and said: "When the power of Almighty God descends upon the earth the foundation of the universe will be shaken to its core. I bring My Mighty power to re-form My creation. A new heaven and a new earth... All shall be restored as I intended from the beginning. The sin of the original ones is expiated. The power of the most high is upon the face of the earth. The forces of the universe move at My command. What was destroyed will be restored. Peace shall reign supreme and all creation will exist in harmony with its Creator.... In My heavens the bodies that give light will be no more. All that exists will live in the light of My presence. There will be no darkness; in My light will they have their being. What man has destroyed I will make new.

"Now say: The power of the Almighty God will move and the new earth will be formed out of the old. Springs of living water will flow through the land. New growth will spring forth out of the soil. All will flourish, and the face of God will look with favor upon what He has brought forth. I, the Lord God, have spoken. Go in peace. Thanks be to the Almighty Trinity from whom we are ransomed into a new life. Bow down, oh holy people of God, to the saving power of the Three-In-One. Thus says the Lord God..." [10]

Fire From Heaven

The Lord God on July 26, 1991 spoke to Joanne Kriva: "When the power of evil runs rampant throughout the earth, I, the Lord God, seek out the remnant and shelter it within the power of My Divine Love. Those of you who remain to the end I protect in a special way. From this remnant I call forth the Spirit of rebirth to bring forth a new creation of purity and peace. You are given the task of renewing the earth by the power of the Spirit. Your seed will repopulate the kingdom of the Son. You are worthy stewards of the new creation. Your suffering in the trial prepares you for the glorious reign of the triumphant King. You will serve well He who calls you into the restored Eden. Your generations will be holy and upright. You shall see the face of God. You shall live in peace all the days of your life. No memory of the trial will remain, and you shall know the loving presence of your King and Savior in your midst. You shall walk hand-in-hand with the saints, and all your days will be serene. Your hearts will be filled with the fullness of My love, and all creation will live in harmony with its mighty King. Your days will know no strife. All is ordered by My hand. When the days allotted to you are ended, you will enter into the kingdom of the Father -- into the special place He has prepared for you alone, for you the most faithful of all His faithful ones. Know that what I tell you through My instrument is truth. Thus says the Lord God..."[10]

The Lord God on October 26, 1993 said to Joanne Kriva: "What has been foretold now comes to pass in these last days before the power in the hand of God refashions the new heavens and a new earth. What has been since the beginning of time, ushered in under the power in the hand of the Evil One, will cease to exist.... And thus must the old order of sin and evil give way to the New Age of Grace, the New Jerusalem...["10]

The Lord God on January 18, 1994 said to Joanne Kriva: "I come now through the triumph of Mary -- virgin undefiled -- in bringing salvation history to its culmination, to establish the history of the Era of Peace.

"Oh My dear ones, if you would but believe that beyond the strife is the sublime union of mind and spirit in perfect harmony with the harmony that is the inheritance given by the hand of the Creator -- the one bread, one body, one Spirit in the Lord Jesus Christ. A house united is a house built upon the foundations of truth and faith whose members are one in body, spirit, and soul in the unity of the one God. Come, My children, come to the reunion which marks the beginning of the New Age of Grace that awaits you following the tribulation of the end time. Thus say I the Lord God...["10]

On February 18, 1994 the Lord God said to Joanne Kriva: "In My name speak and tell My beloved children that what dawns upon the horizon of human history is the coming of the Era of Peace in which all will be united in truth and faith and love. Speak joyfully of the era for My people must keep hope in their hearts during the dark hours of their purification... find comfort in the promise of the restoration of the kingdom of God in

285

the affairs of human creatures... There is but one Word; there is but one Church; and where there are now many there shall be but one as I intended from the beginning."[10]

The Era Of Peace As Revealed To Janie Garza

On September 5, 1996 Janie Garza had a vision of the new earth. Janie said: St. Michael showed me a vision of the world as it is in these evil times. Then he <u>showed me a vision of the new earth</u>. It was beautiful. There was no pollution, and the earth was impregnated with much life. The ocean was so beautiful and abundant with sea life. There was no poverty, no suffering, no violence, only true peace from Heaven. This was a vision of hope for all of God's children who keep their focus on God in these evil times."[8]

On April 19, 1994 Janie Garza received from Jesus a vision of the New Jerusalem. Janie said: "In the seventh vision I saw new life. I saw a garden full of life. The trees were beautiful and very green. I saw flowers of all kinds. I saw beautiful springs of water in different areas of the garden. This is the most beautiful garden I have ever seen, and I knew it was like no garden on this earth. Then I heard Jesus speak Scripture to me. Jesus said: "This is the New Jerusalem. This is the new house of the people of My Father. Here there will be no more weeping, no more calling for help. Babies will no longer die in infancy and all people will live out their life span. Those who live to be a hundred will be considered young and to die before that time will be a sign that My Father had punished them.

"Like trees, people will live long lives. They will build their homes and get to live in them. Their homes will not be used by someone else. The work they do will be successful and their children will not meet with disaster."[26] [cf. Isaias 65:19-21]

The Era Of Peace As Revealed To Fr. Gobbi

In message # 236, November 12, 1981 Our Lady told Fr. Gobbi: "By your prayer, your suffering and your personal immolation, I will bring my plan to completion. I will hasten the time of the triumph of my Immaculate Heart in the reign of Jesus, who will come to you in glory. <u>Thus a new era of peace will begin, and you will at last see new heavens and a new earth</u>."[2]

In message # 324, March 30, 1986 Our Lady told Fr. Gobbi: "I am the Mother who is calling you from all sides to bring you all to Jesus and thus prepare for you <u>a new era of peace</u>..."[2]

In message # 379, April 2, 1988 Our Lady told Fr. Gobbi: "To make amends for these offenses which are being committed against the Immaculate Heart of your

heavenly Mother, I am asking you to propagate again today the devotion of the five first Saturdays of the
month. I had asked for this during the first part of this
century of yours; I am returning today to ask for it as
this century turns towards its most painful close.

"If you do what I ask of you, devotion to me will spread
more and more, and then I will be able to exercise the
great power which the Most Holy Trinity has granted
to me. Thus I will be able to prepare for all humanity
the new era of its complete renovation, in the glorious
triumph of my Son Jesus." [2]

The Duration Of The Era Of Peace

La Salette And The Duration Of The Era Of Peace

At La Salette, in the message to Melanie Calvat, we are
told that the period of peace will be twenty-five years:
"The righteous will suffer greatly. Their prayers, their penances, and their tears will rise up to Heaven. And all of
God's people will beg for forgiveness and mercy, and will
plead for my help and intercession. And then Jesus
Christ, in an act of His justice and His great mercy, will
command His Angels to have all His enemies put to
death. Suddenly, the persecutors of the Church of Jesus Christ and all those given over to sin will perish

and the earth will become desert-like. And then peace will be made, and man will be reconciled with God. Jesus Christ will be served, worshiped and glorified. Charity will flourish everywhere. The new kings will be the right arm of the holy Church, which will be strong, humble, pious in its poor but fervent imitation of the virtues of Jesus Christ. The Gospel will be preached everywhere and mankind will make great progress in its faith, for there will be unity among the workers of Jesus Christ and man will live in fear of God.

" <u>This peace among men will be short-lived. Twenty-five years of plentiful harvests will make them forget that the sins of men are the cause of all the troubles on this earth."</u> [7]

Julka Of Hungary (Period 1960-1966) Messages On The Duration Of The Era Of Peace

Jesus said to Julka: "As you have seen, so it will be. I shall come quickly and in splendour. <u>All My creatures who survive the Great tribulation, will see Me.</u> No-one will then be able to say that I do not exist, because I shall be near the earth; and all the creatures of the earth will hear My Voice. They will see Me present then, and, for the second time, at the Final Judgment.

This will be the Little Flock and I shall hover over it. In those days there will be one Shepherd and one Faith, that of the Roman Catholic Church, which I established when I walked visibly on earth. After the distresses, which I am now permitting to come upon My obstinate people on earth, there will arise a fair and pure Race and the earth will abound with My Gifts. My Sons and My daughters will keep My Commandments. Thus everything will live and grow with My Blessing for thirty years."

Our Lord said also: "<u>If I should protract the years of the Little Flock, it will live at the most for 34 years in peace; 30 years is the destined time.</u>" [5]

The Exact Length Of Time Of This New Era Of Peace Is A Mystery

The exact length of time of this New Era of Peace is a mystery. The Church has ruled that we cannot hold that it must be a thousand years, however it could be. In interpreting the thousand years St Augustine, in City of God, Book XX, Chapter 7 tells us 1000 is a number of perfection, 10^3 meaning totality, marking the fullness of time.

The Number 1,000 Is Used To Mean Totality, Marking The Fullness of Time

In City of God, Book XX, Chapter 7, St. Augustine writes: " Now the thousand years may be understood in two ways, so far as occurs to me: either because these things happen in the sixth thousand of years or

sixth millennium (the latter part of which is now passing), as if during the sixth day, which is to be followed
by a Sabbath which has no evening, the endless rest of
the saints, so that, speaking of a part under the name of
the whole, he calls the last part of the millennium-the
part, that is, which had yet to expire before the end of
the world-a thousand years; **or he used the thousand
years as an equivalent for the whole duration of this
world, employing** the number of perfection to mark
the fullness of time. For a thousand is the cube of ten.
For ten times ten makes a hundred, that is; the square on
a plane superficies. But to give this superficies height,
and make it a cube, the hundred is again multiplied by
ten, which gives a thousand. **Besides, if a hundred is
sometimes used for totality,** as when the Lord said by
way of promise to him that left all and followed Him "He
shall receive in this world an hundredfold;" of which the
apostle gives, as it were, an explanation when he says,
"As having nothing, yet possessing all things," -for even
of old it had been said, The whole world is the wealth of
a believer,-with **how much greater reason is a thousand put for totality since it is the cube, while the
other is only the square?**

Conclusion About The Era Of Peace

We will soon enter into an Era of Peace. The duration
of this Era of Peace before the final judgment occurs
is not determinable, it is a mystery; it could be a thousand years or more, or it could be a much shorter period
of time, such as only 25 years, we don't know. We can-

not determine its actual duration other than to say we must not dogmatically hold that it will be exactly a thousand years. Possibly its actual duration will be determined by the free will responses of those entering into the Era of Peace after the Great Chastisement, and those born during the Era of Peace. During the era of peace Satan and all his fallen angels and demons will be bound in hell and not able to influence us to sin, how- ever, we will still have our fallen nature and in which we can be tempted to sin.

We have been able by our free will response in accepting the remedies given by Heaven in these last days of the End of the Times to mitigate, i.e., decrease and/or shorten the duration of the chastisements or lessen or eliminate some of them during the purification. Fr. Gobbi in his recent video (1999 - released in 2000) tells us that the prophesied events had all been moved for- ward in time from earlier dates.

Chapter 14

About The Second Coming Of Christ In Glory

Excerpts from the speech by Don Stefano Gobbi On June 24, 1996 in San Marino during that year's International Meeting of Priests in which about 300 priests and 25 bishops took part, as well as Cardinal Echeverria from Ecuador. [Emphasis in these excerpts is by the author of this book]

In this speech Fr. Gobbi clarified for us the Church's position and his opinion about the meaning of the Second Coming of Christ in Glory.

Fr. Gobbi states: "...the triumph of the Immaculate Heart of Mary comes through the Second Coming of Christ in Glory."

On December 24, 1975 Mary said: "... The triumph of my Immaculate Heart will be fulfilled in the <u>rebirth of Jesus in the hearts</u> and the souls of my poor children, who have gone astray.

293

Fire From Heaven

In the message of December 24, 1978 entitled "His Second Coming" **Our Lady stated**: "My beloved sons, His Second Coming will be like His first. As His birth occurred in this night, so the Second Coming of Jesus in Glory will be - prior to His last coming for the Last Judgement. However, this hour is still hidden in the mysteries of the Father.

The world will be totally enwrapped in the darkness of atheism, the rejection of God and the rebellion against the divine laws of His love. The ice of hatred will make the streets of the world barren. So almost no one will be ready to accept Him.

The mighty will not even remember Him, the rich will close their doors to Him, while His disciples will be busy looking for themselves and praising their own deeds...

"When the Son of Man comes: Will He still find faith on earth?" He will come without warning and the world will not be prepared for His coming. He will come for a judgement, for which men will not be prepared. After He has subdued and destroyed His enemies, He will come in order to build His Kingdom in this world.

Also, in this Second Coming, the Son will come to you through His mother. Just as the Word of the Father made use of my virginal womb to come to you, so Jesus will make use of my Immaculate Heart to reign among you."

In his speech Fr. Gobbi asked and answered: "How are we to interpret this Coming of Christ in Glory?"

"I will first read a few words form the Introduction to our book (S.47) and here we can rely on Mons. Don Cabrejos Vidarte Miguel (doctorate in exegesis and Suffragan Bishop of Lima, Peru), who is present today and is an expert on the Holy Scriptures and who endorses this introduction.

"A further example are the sentences, which are frequently repeated and at first glance may seem confusing, which state that the triumph of the Immaculate Heart of Mary coincides with the Glorious Coming of the Kingdom of Christ.

"These sentences are, of course, being interpreted in light of the Holy Scriptures (RV.20, 1-7) and in conformity with the authentic teachings of the Church. Please note how often **Pope John Paul II refers to this subject. He does so in his first encyclical "Redemptor hominis" and in other important documents, in which he speaks of the second advent of the Church, which awaits the Second Coming of Jesus.**"

"Based on our usual mode of thinking, we have always thought the Second Coming of Christ was identical with His Coming for the Last Judgement. There exists no in-depth theological study about this topic. This is also true for other truths, which one believes, without their ever having been made an in-depth study on the subject.

Fire From Heaven

"Lately, after some of these messages mentioned that Christ will return in glory into this world, an in-depth theological study has been made on this subject.

What Do The Holy Scriptures Say About The Second Coming Of Christ?

"Several years ago in Spain, a theologian gave me a book, in order for me to have it translated into Italian - unfortunately, I lost the book somewhere along the way. In this book, he explains that from the Holy Scriptures and the early Fathers of the Church it is clearly evident that Christ will return in glory into this world in order to build His kingdom and that in the end He will return as Judge.

"Some of the passages of the Holy Scripture are clearly of an eschatological nature -these are passages, which speak of the Last Judgement, When, for example, Our Lord says; "For I was hungry and you gave me food .... , this you have done unto me" ('Mt. 25), you, who are at my right side. And you, who are at my left side, have not done this unto me -"Depart from me, you accursed, into the eternal fire" (Mt. 25,41). Time exists no more. The world exists no more.

"But some passages of the Holy Scriptures specifically mention the Second Coming of Christ into this world.

"I want to point out the following:

First, I refer back to the locution of December 24, 1978 I mentioned above: "But when the Son of Man comes, will He find faith on earth?" (Lk, 18,8). If He wants to find faith on earth, then He must return to this earth, my dear brothers! Since, when the Last Judgement occurs, earth will not exist anymore. There will be the Last Judgement, Paradise or Hell, but the earth will have disappeared. When the Son of God returns to find faith on earth, then He must return to this earth. Further, the passage where Jesus stands before the High Priest: "From now on you will see the Son of Man seated at the right hand of the Power' and 'coming on the clouds of heaven'" (Mt. 26,64), here I also quote the passage, which speaks of the Ascension of Jesus into heaven: "Men of Galilee, why are you standing there looking at the sky? This Jesus who has been taken up from you into heaven will return in the same way as you have seen him going into heaven" (Acts. 1,11). But they did see Him "he was lifted up, and a cloud took him from their sight" (compare Acts. 1,9). Just as He will also return with a cloud. Therefore, as long as there are clouds, the Last Judgement has not come. - So Christ is returning with the clouds on this earth.

"And then, dear brothers, it is important that the passage mentioned above in the Book of Revelation (Rv. 20) mentions an immense persecution. During this persecution many will be killed. But at the end the power of Satan will be destroyed, because Satan will be chained and

thrown down an abyss. Then the Holy Scriptures say:
'The angel sealed it, so that it could no longer lead nations astray... (comp. Book of Rv. 20,3) So the power of
Satan will be destroyed. Those, who have not worshiped
the Animal and his image and who have been killed, will
rise from the dead to reign with Christ.

"This is not 'fabricated' theology, but from the Holy
Scriptures! - And this will be the <u>first resurrection</u>. Why
the first? <u>Because the second refers to all humans. The
first resurrection only concerns some humans, those
who have died as martyrs and they will rise from the
dead in order to partake in the reign.</u> The second concerns all humans, for <u>some so they can partake in the
reign, for the others to be damned after the Last Judgement.</u>

"Of course, the number 1000 could have been used as a
symbol. However, aside from this chronology, there remains the reality, which is clearly described: **Christ will
reign after Satan's power has been destroyed, after he
has been rendered powerless. This are the Holy
Scriptures!**"

(Remark by the translator: In the footnote Rv. 13,11-18
we read: "The second beast is described in terms of the
false prophets (cf. Rv 16,13;19,20;20,10) who accompany
the false messiahs (the first beast); cf. Mt. 24,24; Mk
13,22;2 Thes,2,9; cf. also Dt. 13,2-4. Christians had either
to worship the emperor and his image or to suffer martyrdom. Hence it follows that the 'false prophet' will
not be thrown into the sea of burning sulfur only at

the end of the world. His power will be taken from him before and not <u>at the end of the world</u> by a coming of the Lord. Because we read in 2 Thes. 2,8: ... whom the Lord (Jesus) will kill through the breath of this mouth and render powerless by the manifestation of His coming."

(Therefore, the Lord will appear and return before the end of the world.)

How are the Teachings of the Church?

"Dear Brothers, l want to read you some passages o£ what our present Pope says, We shall then see that we not only concur with the Holy Scriptures, but also with the teachings of the church:

From a speech of the Pope in Edmonton, Canada, on Sept. 17, 1984: "The God of Peace be with us, here in Canada and everywhere! May justice and peace embrace each other once more (comp. Ps. 84 (85), 10) at the end of the second millennium, which is preparing us for the glorious Second Coming of Christ."

At large Youth-Meeting in Denver, USA, in 1993, the Holy Father said during the Vigil of Our Lady's Ascension into heaven: "Lord Jesus Christ, we thank You for Your word; 'I came so that they might have life and have it more abundantly' (Jn. 10,10). The young people attending the 8th Youth Festival of the world thank You from their hearts. Maranatha!"

"From this gathering of youth from all over the world here in Cherry Creek State Park in Denver, we cry: "Maranatha!"' "Come, O Lord!" (Rv. 22,20)

"The following day the Pope said to the 500,000 youths: "This pilgrimage must continue! ... It must continue in the life of the church, while she is awaiting the third christian millennium. She must continue as a "new advent", as a moment of hope and expectation until the Second Coming of our Lord in glory..."

"If' we had to wait another 10,000 years for the Second Coming of our Lord, then we would be stupid already now with preparations for this coming. This invitation of the Pope only makes sense if the Lord comes soon." ...

"We are thus in accordance with the Holy Scriptures and the teachings of the church when we believe the Lord will return in glory on this earth. Surely, we must open ourselves to this new perspective. "

[Question Addressed To the Congregation of the Faith]

"The following question was addressed to the Congregation of the Faith some time ago. How are we to understand the Second Coming of Christ in Glory? The Second Coming for the Last Judgement or still on this earth?

"The answer was as follows: "The church has never taken an official stand on this. So one can interpret it one way or the other..."

"I have shown you the reasons why we, according to the Holy Scriptures and the teachings of the church, believe in the second interpretation. The Second Coming of Christ in glory will take place still on this earth."...

"So, what does the Second Coming of Christ mean: Christ is in paradise. He returns because He has already been here in the human nature. He comes again in a relative way because Jesus -- in His divinity and, of course, also in His human nature -- is already present in the Eucharist. He comes again, as far as He wants to reveal Himself in glory to this world and bring His kingdom upon this world.

"In His Second Coming, Christ brings the following elements, which inspire hope, with Him:

"And now Christ will come again in unison with elements, some of which are listed below:

"Finally, the prayer will be entirely fulfilled, which Jesus taught us to pray in the Our Father: 'Your will be done on earth as it is in heaven.'

"All creatures will do God's will in a complete way. That is why the kingdom of Divine Will will come on this earth.

Fire From Heaven

"It will coincide with the Second Pentecost.

"It will be greatest miracle of divine mercy or, to say it differently, the triumph of the merciful love of Jesus, who will open up a new era for this world, a new civilization in order to finally get to know the civilization of love.

"Especially, however, the triumph of the Immaculate Heart of Mary, through the Second glorious Coming of Christ, will coincide with the coming of the Eucharistic kingdom of Jesus." ..."

"But I must still add the following: The final victory of Christ over Satan occurred through His resurrection, the final victory of Christ over Satan at his Second Coming in glory will consist in the complete destruction of the power of Satan over this world, so that this world is able to accept the Kingdom of Christ and will be able to again glorify the Father in a complete way, as it was at the beginning of creation.

"Therefore, the Second Coming of Christ will coincide with the greatest possible glorification of the Heavenly Father.

"Should the Kingdom of Christ, for which has been prayed for since 2000 years, not come? It will come - for the complete glorification of the Father. When this Kingdom of Christ will come, it will help all creatures to fulfill the Will of God in a complete manner." ...

"The creatures will say yes to the Divine Will of God.

"In this complete fulfillment of the Divine Will the creation will be almost transposed into an original state, in a state of a new earthly paradise, in which all creatures say yes to the Divine Will of the heavenly Father." ...

"This is what I think, that <u>the Second Coming of Christ in glory will bring this kingdom of Divine Will.</u>

"Every creature will fulfill the will of the Father completely and the heavenly Father will be glorified by his children, who will say yes to His Divine Will. Christ will bring His kingdom, the kingdom of holiness and of humble obedience to the Will of the heavenly Father.

"<u>The power of Satan will be destroyed, although the weakness of the fallen human nature will remain.</u>" ...

"It is clear that we will retain our weakened nature even after the Second Coming of Christ in glory: <u>It is not the weakness of human nature, which is being destroyed, but the power of Satan.</u> Until now, he has a strong influence on the weakness of our fallen nature. <u>It is by nature that we are being tempted to sin.</u> But today everything is forcing us to sin: the atheistic and pagan environment in which we live, the influence of the mass media, which are almost all centers of evil. Today the world is the center of evil. The evil has an extremely strong influence, and this is where you have

Fire From Heaven

the temptations, seductions and the bad examples, they all want to bring you to fall.

"Today the evil enemy is all-powerful. But tomorrow, when his power will be destroyed, everything will lead you to do good deeds.

"So the weakness of human nature remains, but it will be supported to do good; this will be the exact opposite of what is happening today, the opposite of every temptation to do evil."

The Second Pentecost

Father Gobbi said: "The Second Pentecost will take place on a worldwide scale. It will descend upon the entire world, not only in the room of the Last Supper in Jerusalem and it will transform the hearts and souls of all mankind. All will praise the Lord, so that the angels in heaven might ask themselves: Are all these drunk already at 9 o'clock in the morning?

"Dear brothers, the Second Coming of Christ will, therefore, coincide with the Second Pentecost. I am quoting here from my locution of June 4, 1995 (Pentecost; p. 1270/71): "Tongues of divine fire will bring, warmth and life to mankind, which has become icy through egoism, hate, violence and war.

"So the dried-out earth will open itself to the breath of God's Spirit, who will transform it into a new beauti-

ful garden where the Holy Trinity will then perma-
nently reside.

"Tongues of fire will descend to illuminate and consecrate the church, which is going through the dark
hour of Calvary, with its shepherds beaten, its flock
wounded, abandoned and betrayed by their own, exposed to the storms of false teachings, permeated with
the loss of faith and apostasy.

"The divine fire of the Holy Spirit will heal all their ill-
nesses, cleanse them of all blemishes of unfaithfulness,
clad them in beauty and shine over them so that they
will revert to their oneness and holiness; and then it
will - for the whole world to hear - give complete testimony for Jesus.

"Tongues of fire will descend on all of you, my poor
children, who have been so deceived and led astray by
Satan and all evil spirits, who have achieved their great
victory during these years. So you will be illuminated
by this divine light and recognize yourselves in the
mirror of God's truth and holiness. It will be like a
small judgement, which will open the doors of your
hearts in order to be able to receive the gift of divine
mercy."

The Greatest Miracle of Divine Mercy

"This is why the Second Pentecost will also coincide

with the Triumph of Jesus' Merciful Love, the divine mercy, which will descend upon us.

"Then the Holy Spirit will bring about the new miracle of changing all hearts and lives of mankind: the sinners will convert, the weak will become pillars of strength, the sick will be healed, those who have distanced themselves will return to the house of the Father and those separated and alienated will unite.

"This is how the miracle of the Second Pentecost will come about. It will come with the Triumph of my Immaculate Heart on earth.

"Only then will you see how the tongues of fire of the Spirit of Love will renew the entire world, which will be completely changed through the greatest outpouring of divine mercy.

"And now you will understand that - when all will have been redeemed- we will all breathe in the air of God's kingdom. It will be a kingdom of holiness and justice, of purity, love, joy and peace.

"And since the one will be excluded, who was a murderer from the outset- the one, who does not accept God, who brings into the world hatred, egoism, separation, violence and war - and God will be among us again, then we will finally have a new civilization of the Children of God, who will live in His kingdom of new civilization of love.

The Eucharistic Kingdom of Jesus

"And in this renewed world, in which the Father will be glorified and in which Christ reveals His kingdom, where the wills of all creatures reflect the Will of the Father, where the Holy Spirit has renewed mankind, where the mercy of God has been consummated, where do you think the center of God's influence will be? Christ is in the Eucharist. He can now pour forth all His divine power.

"Dear brothers, we believe that Christ is present in the Eucharist with His glorified body, with His divinity. As in paradise, so also on this earth, with the difference that we, on earth, are impeded to see Him - we see Him only through a veil of the host. But the presence is the same.

"But how is Jesus present in paradise? He is the happiness and joy of all saints. And here on earth in the Eucharist? Why can't He pour out His might and be our joy and become our greatest happiness? Why not?" ...

"I am saying that Christ's power in the Eucharist cannot pour forth as long as we put obstacles in the way. And this is the sin, the sin of each person, the sin of society, the sin, which becomes the standard of our actions. All these sins are a rejection and barriers, which we erect, because of which Christ cannot pour forth His might in the Eucharist.

"However, when Satan is pushed into hell and the

307

door is closed behind him and his power is destroyed, then the obstacles will have been removed
and Jesus will be able to show all His might in the
Eucharist. Behind the veil of the host we will see Him,
we will feel Him, then we will very strongly feel His divine influence within us because in the Eucharist Jesus
is among us in the fullness of His divinity. And so He
will change our hearts, our souls, our families, our nations - a universal act of peace.

"Finally, after so many years of dissension, unity
among Christians will finally be achieved. After so
many unsuccessful attempts, unity will finally come
and we will have the Eucharistic kingdom of Christ
within us. So I almost would like to say: Jesus, who will
return and reveal Himself in glory, united Himself with
"the Jesus", who is present in the Eucharist and it will be
as though He will open the doors of these hosts, who are
still concealing Him, so that He can show Himself with
all His might in order to renew everything and to finally create a new heaven on earth. That is why the
Second Coming of Christ will also coincide with the
greatest triumph of the Eucharist Kingdom of Jesus."

In his summary Fr. Gobbi in this speech said: "At the
end the most [Holy] Eucharist will unfold its complete divine power and we will get to know the joy of
experiencing all the effects of paradise, which the triumph of the eucharistic kingdom of Jesus will bring
about. We will be on the earth and we will be beyond
it. We will not yet be in paradise but it will be a paradise on earth which Our Lady is preparing for us

through the triumph of Her Immaculate Heart in this world. Laudetur Jesus Christus."

Fire From Heaven

Fire From Heaven

Fire From Heaven

Bibliography

Bibliography:

1. Our Lady Of All Nations, Queenship Publishing Company, P.O. Box 42028 Santa Barbara CA 93140-2028.

2. *To The Priests Our Lady's Beloved Sons*, The Marian Movement of Priests, Rev. Albert G. Roux, P.O. Box 8, St. Francis, Maine 04774-0008. Tel. 207-398-3375 / Fax: 207-398-3352.

3. The Great Sign Volume II. Messages to Sadie Jaramillo. St. Dominic's Media, P.O. Box 345, Herndon, VA 20172-0345.

4. Two Hearts As One Messages for the Purification and The Era of Peace. The MaxKol Institute, 1301 Moran Road, Suite 303, Sterling, VA 20166. Tel. (703) 421-1300, Fax: 703-421-1133. Messages To Denise Curtin and Joseph DellaPuca

5. From Jesus Calls Us, Volume 1, pages 218-227

6. The Great Sign [Volume I]. Messages to Sadie Jaramillo. St. Dominic's Media, P.O. Box 345, Herndon, VA 20172-0345.

7. Sister Mary of the Cross Shepherdess of La Salette, by Fr. Paul Gouin. The 101 Foundation, P.O. Box 151, Asbury, New Jersey 08804.

8. Heaven's Messages For The Family, Vol. 2, 1999. Messages to Janie Garza. St. Dominic's Media, P.O. Box 345, Herndon, VA 20172-0345.

9. Tribulations and Triumph, Revelations On the Coming of The Glory of God, Vol. 2, 1998. St. Dominic's Media, P.O. Box 345, Herndon, VA 20172-0345. Messages to Joanne Kriva.

10. Tribulations and Triumph, Revelations On the Coming of The Glory of God Vol. 1. St. Dominic's Media, P.O. Box 345, Herndon, VA 20172-0345. [Out of Print]
11. The Mystery of Freemasonry Unveiled, by the Cardinal of Chile. Christian Book Club of America, P.O. Box 900566, CA 93590, First Printing Circa 1928, Fifth Printing 1992..
12. En Route to Global Occupation, by Gary H. Kah, Huntington House Publishers, P.O. Box 53788, Lafayette, Louisiana 70505, 1992.
13. New World Order: The Ancient Plan of Secret Societies, by William T. Still, Huntington House Publishers, P.O. Box 53788, Lafayette, Louisiana 70505, 1990.
14. Towards World Government, New World Order, by Deirdre Manifold.
15. Grand Orient Freemasonry Unmasked as the Secret Power behind Communism, by Mgr. George E. Dillon, D.D. Lectures Delivered in Edinburg in October, 1884. Republished 1950. Christian Book Club, P.O. Box 900566, Palmdale, CA 93590.
16. Mary's Triumph, Years of Revelation, Via dei Gracchi, 29 B. Roma, Italia.
17. Eucharistic Experiences, Messages to Ida Peerdeman, July 17, 1958 to March 25, 1984. Queenship Publishers.
18. Catholic Prophecy, The Coming Chastisement, by Yves Dupont, 1973. TAN Books and Publishers, Inc., P.O. BOX 424, Rockford, IL 61105.
19. She Went In Haste To The Mountain, Books One, Two, Three. Eusebio Garcia De Pesquera O.F.M. Translated from the Spanish by Gerard Suel & Otto

Miller. 1981 by St. Joseph Publications, 17700 Lorain Avenue, Cleveland, Ohio 44111

20. Divine Mercy In My Soul. Diary. Saint Sister M. Faustina Kowalska. Marian Helpers, Stockbridge, MA 01263.

21. Akita: Mother of God as CoRedemptrix. Modern Miracles of the Holy Eucharist, by Francis Matsuo Fukushima. Visions and Messages to Sr. Agnes Sasagawa, Akita, Japan. Queenship Publishing, P.O. Box 42028 Santa Barbara, CA 93140-2028

22. I Am the Guardian Of The Faith, Reported Apparitions of the Mother of God in Ecuador, by Sr. Isabel Bettwy, 1991. Franciscan University Press, Steubenville, OH 43952.

23. The Keys of This Blood, 1990, by Fr. Malachi Martin, Simon & Shuster, Inc. [Touchstone].

24. The Victorious Queen of the World, 1992, Two Hearts Books and Publishers, P.O. Box 844, Mountain View, CA 94042.

25. Nelly Hurtado, from Internet - e-mail

26. Heaven's Messages For The Family, Vol. 1, 1998. Messages to Janie Garza. St. Dominic's Media, P.O. Box 345, Herndon, VA 20172-0345.

27. Use My Gifts. Jim Z. Singer. Ave Maria Center of Peace, P.O. Box 489, Station U, Toronto, Canada M8Z 5Y8.

28. In The Kingdom of the Spirit. Abba House

29. Conversations in Heaven. Eileen George. Meet The Father Ministry, Millbury, Massachusetts..

30. Please Come Back To Me And My Son, by R. Vincent. Ireland's Eye Publications, Lynn Industrial Estate,

Mullinger, Co, Westmeath, Ireland.
31. Apparitions In Betania, Venezuela, Sister Margaret
Catherine Sims, CSJ, 1992, Marian Messengers, P.O.
Box 647, Framingham, MA 01704-0647
32. The Thunder of Justice, by Ted and Maureen Flynn.
MaxKol, 1993. The MaxKol Institute, 1301 Moran
Road, Suite 303, Sterling, VA 20166. Tel. (703) 421-
1300, Fax: 703-421-1133.
33. Jesus Calls Us, Vol. 1, 2, 3: Vol. 2, 1983. Haupt Cristi -
Verlag, Munchen-Oberschleissheim Vol. 3, 1988, Vol. 1,
1990 In Wahrheit Und Treue, Postfach 279, 8401
Winterthur (Switzerland). All 3 Volumes distributed
by Center of Mary Queen of Light, Route 1, Box 904,
Turner, ME 04282 USA.
34. The Encyclical Quanta Cura and the Syllabus of Errors
issued by Pope Pius IX in 1864 and the Syllabus
concerning the errors of the Modernists (Lamentabili
Sane) and Divini Redemptoris reprinted by the
Remnant.
35. A Catechism of Modernism, The Rev. J.B. Lemius, O.M.
I, TAN Books and Publishers, Rockford, Illinois, 1981
36. The Sorrow, The Sacrifice and The Triumph by
Thomas W. Petrisco. Visions and Messages—
Christina Gallagher. A Touchstone Book, Published by
Simon & Schuster, New York.
37. Interview With Father Stefano Gobbi, Rubbio, Italy,
August 4-5, 1999. The Marian Movement of Priests
National Headquarters, P.O. Box 8, Saint Francis,
Maine 04774-0008.
38. Heaven's Last Call To Humanity, Marantha
Enterprises, 37137 Butternut Ridge Road, Elyria, Ohio
44035, 1996.

B5

39. Secret Societies and Subversive Movements, by Nesta H. Webster, Christian Book Club, 1924.

40. AA-1025, The Memoirs of an Anti-Apostle, Marie Carre, TAN Books and Publishers, Inc., P.O. Box 424, Rockford, Illinois, 61105, 1991.

41. Humanum Genus, Encyclical Letter of His Holiness Pope Leo XIII on Freemasonry, April 20, 1884. TAN Books and Publishers, Inc., P.O. Box 424, Rockford, Illinois, 61105, 1978

42. Marie-Julie Jahenny, The Breton Stigmatist, Marquis de la Franguerie MMR Publishing, P.O. Box 45348, Omaha, Nebraska 68145.

43. Fatima in Lucia's Own Words, Sister Lucia's Memoirs, Edited by Fr. Louis Kondor, SVD. Translated by Dominican Nuns of Perpetual Rosary. Distributed by The Ravengate Press, Box 49, Still Water, Massachusetts 01467.

44. The Reign of Antichrist. Rev. R. Gerald Culleton. TAN Books and Publishers, Rockford, Il 61105.

45. Beyond the Millennium, by John Bird, 1998, Queenship Publishing Company, P.O. Box 42028 Santa Barbara CA 93140-2028.

FIRE FROM HEAVEN

FIRE FROM HEAVEN

FIRE FROM HEAVEN

By Maureen Flynn *Co-author of Best Seller The Thunder of Justice*

This book by Maureen Flynn, the Co-author of *The Thunder of Justice*, describes the path the Church and humanity must travel over the next several years, according to recent prophecies, in order to enter into the promised Era of Peace.

Many are calling this book a great sequel to the bestseller, *The Thunder of Justice. Fire From Heaven – Path To The Era of Peace* is a book you must read if you want to know about updated messages and prophecies on:

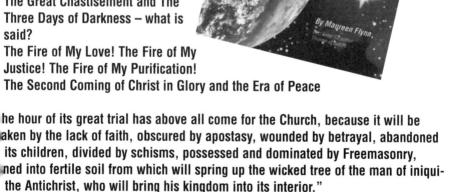

- The Secret of Fatima – was it fully revealed?
- The Warning – The Illumination of Conscience - is it soon to occur?
- The Great Trial for the Church - has it arrived?
- The Co-Rulers of Evil: The False Prophet and the Antichrist - soon to appear?
- The Great Chastisement and The Three Days of Darkness – what is said?
- The Fire of My Love! The Fire of My Justice! The Fire of My Purification!
- The Second Coming of Christ in Glory and the Era of Peace

The hour of its great trial has above all come for the Church, because it will be shaken by the lack of faith, obscured by apostasy, wounded by betrayal, abandoned by its children, divided by schisms, possessed and dominated by Freemasonry, turned into fertile soil from which will spring up the wicked tree of the man of iniquity, the Antichrist, who will bring his kingdom into its interior."

Message # 486 –To The Priests Our Lady's Beloved Sons

"...In The End, My Immaculate Heart Will Triumph"–Our Lady of Fatima

$14.95 plus $4.95 shipping and handling

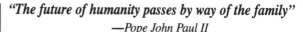

Warnings, Visions & Messages

Father Hebert has written another
BLOCKBUSTER!

A comprehensive overview of the visions, messages and warnings given to various Irish visionaries today about the times we are in; warnings, visions, and messages for the entire world.

Our Lord and his Blessed Mother are warning Mankind before Chastisement disasters strike.

The famous "Our Lady of Knock" silent apparitions of 1879 that opened the Apocalyptic Times blend today with new apparitions, urgent messages and merciful warnings of a Great Chastisement, if the warnings are not heeded.

READ AND LEARN ABOUT:

- *Miraculous phenomena and movements of statues documented on video.*
- *Irish children witnessing biblical visions and warnings of impending judgment if Mankind does not repent.*
- *Christine Gallagher, one of the greatest mystics, stigmatists and visionaries of our times; visionaries Beulah Lynch and Mark Trainer from Bessbrook, Ireland receive Apocalyptic visions and messages of great disasters.*
- *Visions of the Great Era of Peace*

Book Order Form

☐ Yes, I would like to receive ***Warnings, Visions & Messages***. Please send me _____ copies for **$9.95**, plus **$2.95** shipping and handling within the **United States**. Please call for exact **foreign** shipping rates. **Canada - Add $5.00** additional for each book- shipping and handling.

☐ Check or Money Order enclosed. U.S. funds only

☐ MasterCard   ☐ VISA   ☐ Discover   Expiration Date _____

Card # ☐☐☐☐☐☐☐☐☐☐☐☐☐☐☐☐   (Include all 13 or 16 digits)

Signature *(required for credit card orders)* _____

Name/Recipient _____

Address _____

City _____ State _____ Zip _____

Work (____) _____Home (____) _____

Please make checks to SIGNS AND WONDERS for Our Times • P.O. Box 345, Herndon, VA 20172-0345. For immediate attention, call our Order Department at (703) 327-2277 or FAX (703) 327-2888

Tribulations and Triumph

The End of An Evil Era and the Dawn of a New Glorious Time...

Now, a new voice from the American Midwest is added to the Chorus. The Lord is giving an American housewife, Joanne Kriva, words of warning and pleas for peace—and imparting details of events that will soon overtake the world. Joanne's new volume focuses on the messages she received from Our Lord and Lady between February 1995 to August 1996.

Read and Learn:

- why the apparitions of Our Lady are about to close;
- the dangers that threaten Pope John Paul II—and his placewithin the Divine Providence;
- how the Antichrist is alive and plotting to fully exert his power in the world;
- how destruction will be unleashed on a scale never before witnessed in human history;
- what glorious era awaits those who remain faithful during these troubled times.

Book Order Form

☐ Yes, I would like to receive *Tribulations and Triumph!* Volume 2 for $6.95, plus $2.95 shipping and handling for the first copy and $1.00 for each additional copy sent within the US. Canada add $5.00 additional for each book shipping and handling. Please call for exact foreign shipping rates..

☐ Check or Money Order enclosed. U.S. funds only

☐ MasterCard   ☐ VISA   ☐ Discover   Expiration Date _____

Card # ☐☐☐☐☐☐☐☐☐☐☐☐☐☐☐☐   (Include all 13 or 16 digits)

Signature *(required for credit card orders)* _____

My Name/Recipient_____

Address _____

City _____ State _____ Zip _____

Work ( ) _____Home ( ) _____

Please make checks to SIGNS AND WONDERS for Our Times • P.O. Box 345, Herndon, VA 20172-0345. For immediate attention, call our Order Department at (703) 327-2277 or FAX (703) 327-2888

Earthquakes. Abortion. Crime. Family Breakdown. Corruption. War.

Signs and Wonders
for our Times

We, at *Signs and Wonders for Our Times* Catholic magazine, know that heaven is intervening in a powerful way. In these end times, our Blessed Mother has come from Heaven with messages for the whole world—revealing secrets of the future and calling for peace.

With the dramatic increase in apparitions occurring on all continents like never before, *Signs and Wonders for Our Times* exists to provide access to some of the most important information of our age. With the latest messages and visits from heaven, timely features interpreting the *signs of our times, miraculous healing and conversion stories, church history and devotions,* the all-new children's corner—each issue promises to enrich you spiritually and prepare you for what lies ahead. Be part of Our Lady's army and equip yourself

---

Subscription Request Form

☐ Yes, sign me up now for a 1 year subscription (four quarterly issues) to *Signs and Wonders for Our Times*. I understand the price is $24 per year for U.S. subscriptions; $36 to Canada; $60 to all other foreign countries.
U.S. Funds Only.

☐ Check or Money Order enclosed. U.S. funds only

☐ MasterCard ☐ VISA ☐ Discover   Expiration Date _____

Card # ☐☐☐☐☐☐☐☐☐☐☐☐☐☐☐☐ (Include all 13 or 16 digits)

Signature *(required for credit card orders)*_____

My Name/Recipient _____

Address _____

City _____ State _____ Zip _____

Work ( ) _____Home ( ) _____

Phone number is required to process order.

Please make checks to SIGNS AND WONDERS for Our Times • P.O. Box 345, Herndon, VA 20172-0345. For immediate attention, call our Order Department at (703) 327-2277 or FAX (703) 327-2888 Thank you for your love and support.

Read Tomorrow's News TODAY!

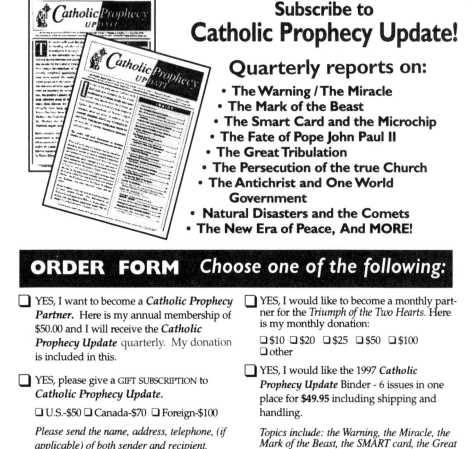

Subscribe to
Catholic Prophecy Update!

Quarterly reports on:

- **The Warning / The Miracle**
- **The Mark of the Beast**
- **The Smart Card and the Microchip**
- **The Fate of Pope John Paul II**
- **The Great Tribulation**
- **The Persecution of the true Church**
- **The Antichrist and One World Government**
- **Natural Disasters and the Comets**
- **The New Era of Peace, And MORE!**